PRAISE FOR
THE BUDDHA SAT RIGHT HERE

"*The Buddha Sat Right Here* is a memoir of illuminated adventure. Dena Moes spins a story of a family finding their place in the world and finding each other as they travel through India and Nepal. . . .This is a memoir of plural voices and plural epiphanies. With tenderness and wit, Moes weaves into her narrative the diaries of her daughter Bella, the paintings and poems of her younger daughter Sophia, the conversations and good advice of newly formed acquaintances and guides in India and Nepal, and the difficult truth of confronting the state of her marriage. By the end of the journey, each character appears awakened and transformed. And the cultures, cities, histories, and individuals who walk across each page become important stories and vivid characters of their own. With each step, Moes takes the reader on a journey into the beauty and idiosyncrasies of South Asian and American life, redefines what family can mean, and builds a breathtaking intimacy between the reader and the page."
—**RITA BANERJEE**, Director, MFA in Writing & Publishing, Vermont College of Fine Arts, and author of *Echo in Four Beats* and *CREDO*

". . . her descriptions of teeming city streets, vibrant landscapes, open country, and the delightful variety of many types of Indians and Nepalese enliven her locations and her spiritual searching."
—*KIRKUS REVIEWS*

"Like all the best travelogues, *The Buddha Sat Right Here* is equal parts far-flung experience—the vivid colors and flavors of India—and internal pilgrimage, and I felt lucky to be along for both. Dena Moes is a writer of great intelligence, humility, and sparkle, plus she made me laugh. I loved reading about her family's wild and beautiful transformation."
—**CATHERINE NEWMAN**, author of *Waiting for Birdy* and *Catastrophic Happiness*

THE BUDDHA SAT
RIGHT HERE

A FAMILY ODYSSEY THROUGH
INDIA AND NEPAL

DENA MOES

WITH DIARY EXCERPTS BY CLARABEL MOES

SHE WRITES PRESS

Published 2019
Printed in the United States of America
ISBN: 978-1-63152-561-2
ISBN:. 978-1-63152-562-9
Library of Congress Control Number: 2018956762

For information, address:
She Writes Press
1569 Solano Ave #546
Berkeley, CA 94707

Interior design by Tabitha Lahr

She Writes Press is a division of SparkPoint Studio, LLC.

Photos courtesy of Dena, Adam, and Bella Moes.

This book is for my teachers, whose guidance keeps me on the path.
For Adam, whose focus on what matters is unwavering.
For Clarabel and Sophia, pure beauty of Life's longing for itself.

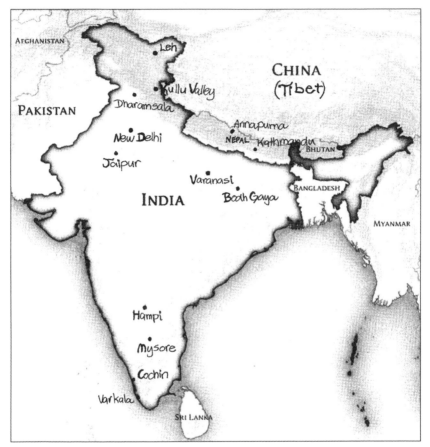

INTRODUCTION

THE ANNAPURNA RANGE, NEPAL
APRIL 2014

I limp behind Adam and the kids as the first drops fall.

"Girls!" I call out. "Put on your rain ponchos!"

We are on the third day of a trek, hiking a ridge at 10,000 feet in view of the Annapurna peaks. The Himalayan sun beat down on us a moment ago, but now the daylight turns dim yellow. I am groggy with exhaustion, so at first I think I am imagining the eerie twilight as it falls. It's only noon, I think, why is it getting dark? I look up to see the granite mountains vanish behind a wall of black clouds. Thunder booms, and streaks of lightning lick the foothills behind us.

Our guide, Isur, leads the way in plastic sandals and skinny jeans, as if this were a stroll in the mall. He drops his rucksack fat with trail bars, our extra clothes, and Adam's ukulele and waits for us to catch up.

"There is a tea house an hour's walk ahead and I will sprint there with your pack," he says.

"Okay, good to know," I say, gasping for breath.

"Just stay on the trail," he calls back as he takes off running.

"I'm going with him!" announces fourteen-year-old Bella, breaking into a run before I can respond. Ten-year-old Sophia is at her heels, a flash of skinny legs and blond ponytail that disappear around a bend. Forget about running, I think, grimacing as I rub my seizing quads, I'm not even sure I can walk another hour. I take off my day pack to fish out my rain poncho, thinking Adam is beside me. When I look up, he is gone too.

"Wait," I say, to no one. "I think we should stay together."

Rain drips into my eyes and soaks through my sneakers. The distance between me and my family grows with every moment I dither, so I stumble on. Twenty minutes pass before the rain turns to thick snow. The snow lays a blanket of silence over the landscape, broken only by an occasional rumble of thunder. Rhododendron blooms sag on the trees, heavy with snowflakes. My wet feet are cold, but the rest of me sweats from exertion. My legs revolt, each step an excruciating override of fatigue. The world blurs into thick white flurries and I can only see a few feet in front of me. I wonder what would happen if I wandered off the trail by mistake. I think about my daughters, running on the slippery path to an unknown destination with Isur, a man we only met two days ago.

How could I have let the girls run ahead? What if they get lost or fall on the ice? A herd of fearful thoughts stamp at the gate, ready to throw me into a panic. I can see the headlines now: *Terrible Fate of California Family Caught in Himalayan Blizzard.* If only we had . . .

"Stop that," I tell myself firmly. "Don't go there. Walk."

I pant with a mix of trepidation and the strain of not quite enough oxygen at 10,000 feet. While I catch my breath, I look this way and that, willing someone to appear and escort me to shelter. A handsome Nepali youth in a colorful wool cap would be my first choice, but a sturdy grandmother in a sari, a shepherd with his goats, anyone would do. No one comes.

I walk on. Part of me wants to feel sorry for myself. I teeter on the edge of self-pity and then get over it. Californians have little tolerance for dramatic weather, we consider sunshine our birthright. This storm came on so quickly though, blotting out mountains, sun, and sky. It is beautiful to be out in this, I decide. The clarity of my single goal—to stay on the trail—is like a meditation. My worries drop away with every step forward. Nothing matters but each footstep pushing into the snow. Everything else is out of my hands now. The children are with Adam and Isur, and they will be safely inside a tea house long before I will. There is no one for me to take care of now but myself.

What a difference from the life I left behind, I think as I trudge along. Our American life was a juggling act, and I was constantly dropping balls. I jumped out of bed every morning, already running late, already tired, to cook breakfast, make lunches, and hustle children off to school. While the girls were in school I ran a home-birth midwifery service. I drove the county roads checking on mothers and their newborn babies, or else conducted prenatal exams in my office. I was often sleep-deprived after being with a laboring mother all night. If I wasn't at a birth, I took kids to violin lessons and play rehearsals after school. Arriving home to "Mom! What's for dinner?" I rushed to get something passable on the table. I fell into bed each night worrying about tomorrow, vowing to catch up on laundry and yard work, and to make a healthy crockpot dinner, too. Unless I was called to a birth. Adam complained that I never had time for him.

Here I have one task—walk. No schedule to keep. No to-do lists. Nobody paging me or pulling at my attention. Just walk. One foot in front of the other, wiping the snow from my eyes, I revel in the simplicity, the focus. My fear of being alone dissipates, the ache in my legs melts away, and my limp becomes a jog. Soon I am galloping along the trail, feeling childlike and free. I laugh at myself. "Ha! I am more alive than I have been for years, not just going through the motions. I may be alone in a mountain blizzard but— "

"I am not driving the carpool today!" I sing into the storm.

"I am not at my computer paying bills!" I yell to the trees.

"I am not wandering the grocery aisles, wondering what's for dinner!" I shout into the snowy void below.

"I am off-call!" I sob. "And out of range!"

I jog faster. The trail descends into a valley, into a forest of towering pines. I run, run, run, stumble, run, run, run, stumble. My feet have their own momentum as I pound down the mountain. I see a level clearing where a house stands tucked into the trees and I make a final dash for it, throwing open the door. *I am a fully-realized heroine! I am powerful, like the storm! I can take these sopping wet sneakers off!*

"I MADE IT!" I shout as I burst through the door.

The room is full of people: my family, European trekkers, and an extended family of Nepalis. A fire blazes in a woodstove, wet clothes hang to dry, and bowls of soup steam on the tables. The mood is calm and quiet, and everyone turns to stare at me, the person who just came through the doorway yelling, dripping with snow, face covered in tears. Sophia grins at me, her spoon poised above a bowl of Maggi noodles. Bella narrows her eyes and glares her warning, *Mom, don't be embarrassing.* Adam stands by the fire warming his hands.

"Namaste," I greet the Nepali woman beside me, clearing my throat and wiping the tears from my face. She seems concerned.

"I am not upset," I say. "These are actually tears of joy." She stares at me, silently.

"Namaste," she finally replies.

CHAPTER 1

[The] first stage of the mythological journey—which we have designated "the call to adventure"—signifies that destiny has summoned the hero and transferred her spiritual center of gravity from within the pale of her society to a zone unknown.

—Joseph Campbell

CHICO, CALIFORNIA
JUNE 2011

Some midwives review emergency scenarios on the way to births. Not me. After training at North Central Bronx Hospital, followed by ten years of attending home births, I trusted my emergency skills would be there if I needed them. No one ever says that resuscitating a newborn baby is like riding a bike, but it kind of *is*. Once you have resuscitated a baby at 3:00 a.m. on the bathroom floor, you won't forget how to do it. Besides, most births are not emergencies. I used the drive to shake off whatever I was doing prior to getting called, so I would arrive at my clients' homes clear-headed and calm. On this drive I was letting go of abandoning my family in the middle of a weekend music festival. They were used to my disappearing like this.

"Om Tare Tam Soha," I mumbled to myself as I drove the tree-lined streets. *Om Tare Tam Soha* was a Tibetan mantra given to me years ago by a Buddhist monk named Chokyi Nyima Rinpoche.

I stood in line to speak to him after a teaching in San Francisco. When my turn came I explained that I was a midwife and asked for a prayer to say on my way to births. "Repeat *Om Tare Tam Soha!*" he advised me in a thick Tibetan accent. "Om Tare Tam Soha—this is the mantra of Tara. But don't be confused. She is not outside yourself. She is not somewhere else. She is your own wisdom and compassion shining through. Tara is in here," he said, thumping his chest. He smiled shards of sunshine into my eyes and turned to the next student.

I pulled my car into Sam and Elena's driveway. The trunk was loaded with bags of IV fluids, two oxygen tanks, an Amish-made birthing stool, a bag of herbal tinctures with names like "Centered Mama" and "Placenta Release," Pitocin, sutures, syringes, and Lidocaine. On the seat next to me sat a bag with Elena's chart, the Doppler, and a blood-pressure cuff. I let myself in through the front door and an old German Shepherd eyed me mournfully. The toddler whose birth I attended two years ago had been picked up by Grandma. In the back bedroom Elena leaned against a dresser with her legs apart, swaying her hips and sipping coconut water. Sam puttered, his face a nervous grin. He hooked up the iPhone and found the right Pandora station, turned on the AC and closed windows against the heat.

"I am here, I'm going to bring my gear in," I whispered to Elena, one hand on her shoulder. She nodded but didn't open her eyes.

My skin tingled with the excitement of a baby's imminent arrival, and all else slipped away. I pulled out the cookie sheet, laid a clean chux pad on it, and began my favorite ritual of opening the sterile packs. First, I opened the blue pack of instruments. Then, without touching anything but the wrappers, I dropped sterile gauze, cord clamp, bulb syringe, and gloves on top of the steel instruments before wrapping them all back up (as if there was anything sterile about birth). I placed an amnihook, a DeLee Mucus Trap, and extra gauze and gloves on the cookie sheet beside the birth pack I had made. My assistant Amber arrived and checked my oxygen tank set-up. When Elena moaned with a strong contraction I told her she was making progress, and that her baby was coming soon. Amber used my hand-held Doppler to listen to the baby's heart every thirty minutes. We kept Elena's glass of water full, but we did not disrupt her inward focus with chatter or fussing. We were there if she needed us, but she never even glanced our way as she swayed through contractions, leaning on the dresser.

An hour later Elena's moans became low, deep grunts. Those grunts are the sound a woman makes when the baby's forehead is pushing on her rectum from the inside. Women in this phase of labor look surprised as they tell me they need to poop, and I know it means the baby is almost here.

"Why don't you get on your hands and knees now," I said.

Elena still didn't look at me but let me guide her to the floor, where I placed towels and chux pads under her. Then her bag of waters broke with a splash, filling the room with the unmistakable, sharp scent of impending birth. The pale top of the baby's head was visible in the folds of her crimson vagina. Amber put my Doppler against Elena's belly and we all heard the "swish, swish, swish" of the baby's heartbeat.

"Your baby's heartbeat sounds perfect," I whispered.

I placed the cookie sheet of instruments beside me. My heart raced from the rush of adrenaline I always get right before a birth, the adrenaline that would help me respond in the event of a complication. I breathed consciously, slowly, to bring my heart rate down while I put a warm wet washcloth against Elena's bulging bottom.

"I see your baby's hair. You can push if you want to," I said softly.

"I don't need to. The baby is already pushing," Elena answered.

The strongest contraction yet rocked through her body. "Muahhhhh," she moaned. My gloved hand pushed against her perineum to protect it from tearing. The baby slid out as far as her forehead, and after a two-second pause the scrunched-up face emerged. Now the baby's head was out, and I watched for the final rotation, the signal that the shoulders had descended into the outlet. The baby's head turned to the side, the shoulders came under my hands' gentle traction, and the baby was out with another gush of waters. Babies are slippery fish, born with their amniotic fluids draining around them, but I have yet to drop one. The baby turned from purple to pink with a gurgly, determined, "Waa!"

I held the seconds-old baby, still tethered to her mother by a spiraling umbilical cord, while Amber helped Elena sit against the bed. Then I passed Elena her baby and watched her bring the newborn to her chest and cover the damp little head with kisses. "It's a girl!" Sam said, because, although I am the first to see, I never tell. Grins, tears, and gasps of delight welcomed the brand-new human. The hour after birth, mothers and babies have the highest levels of oxytocin possible in a human body. Their bloodstreams are literally brimming with love.

Amber took pictures and dried the baby with a receiving blanket. I placed my stethoscope against the baby's back to listen to her lungs, still wet with amniotic fluid but clearing. Heart rate, normal. The placenta glopped into my bowl, after which I rubbed Elena's belly until her uterus contracted into a grapefruit-sized rock.

Over the next two hours the baby nursed, Elena showered, and the family was tucked into a clean bed. We kept the curtains closed, and in the dim light the newborn baby opened her eyes wide and looked around. In gentle tones, I told the baby I would examine her now. First, I checked the features of the baby's face: eyes, ears, nose—all symmetrical. I slid my finger into her mouth to feel her palate and latch reflex. Next came weight and length measurements, and a close listen to her heart and lungs. Her soft belly was palpated for masses, and her neck and hips for normal rotation. I placed a drop of Vitamin K in her mouth and made a set of keepsake footprints. I could have held her for hours, reveling in her soft, alert newness. Remembering to be professional, I placed her back into her mother's arms.

Amber and I cleaned up, started a load of laundry, and made sandwiches for everyone. I reviewed baby care instructions with Sam and Elena, including the danger signs of something wrong. I would come back to assess mother and baby tomorrow and check in later this evening by phone.

After my gear was loaded into my car I glanced into the room one more time. Elena cooed at her newborn while Sam cuddled her. The room was cool and tidy, and a fresh fruit smoothie had been placed on the nightstand. Elena had uncountable nights of not enough sleep ahead of her. So many decisions, so much uncertainty. There would be endless rounds of diaper changes and wiping up spills and uneaten plates of broccoli. Infinite interruptions, days spent driving to children's dentists and lessons, a veritable march of Back to School nights and violin recitals that run way too long. Eventually would come the times when doors would slam and the screamed words "I hate you, Mom!" would ring through the house. My job was to help women start the whole motherhood thing with an empowering, love-filled birth.

Adam and the girls were back, mud-stained and ravenous. I threw their laundry in and put a semblance of dinner together out of remainders from the fridge. At the dinner table Bella took the floor as usual, telling us the details of her friends' social drama, with lengthy commentary and analysis. Over plates of rice, tofu, and sautéed vegetables, Adam, Sophia, and I knew better than to try to change the subject.

While she talked, my mind wandered to the festival I had missed. It was a local event where dozens of families camped out for the weekend, and bands played music on a lakeside stage. In years past our family had been in the lineup as the Moes Family Band, performing our original songs in a sort of three-part harmony while relying heavily on the cute-factor. This summer Bella was too "middle school" to be seen onstage singing with her parents and playing violin solos for their folksy songs. The band was on a break, but the weekend had been a blast anyway.

"Mom, are you listening to me?" Bella demanded, shocking me back to our dinner table.

"Yes. No . . . sorry, I'm just tired from being at a birth."

Adam and Bella finished and started cleaning up while I stayed at the table with Sophia to make sure she ate her vegetables. Sophia was always the last one eating; the girl was mainly a breatharian and looked it. At eight years old she weighed fifty pounds and the scale hadn't budged in two years. Her story of the weekend was that she swam in the creek ten hours a day, and with only Dad in charge ate nothing but candy and Cup O'Noodles. Her personal version of heaven.

If I dug a hole straight down through the center of the earth from Chico, California, I would eventually surface in India. My sister Amy was a foreign correspondent in New Delhi who dreamed of becoming an international journalist while in high school and then went ahead and did it. She had not been interested in having children until, in her mid-thirties, she suddenly was. The Bengali academic she dated for a decade was game to help her start a family, but after two second-trimester miscarriages their relationship cooled. On the eve of their break up, a baby was conceived. Amy was forty-four years old when she found herself pregnant with a healthy baby at last.

As Amy's late November due date approached, I informed her that babies in our family come two weeks late. Mine did, Mom's did, and Grandma's too. I probably over-emphasized that message, because when she called me with stomach pains two weeks *before* her due date she assumed it was a case of Delhi Belly.

"Oh no, Dena, what bad timing. It must be something from the restaurant I went to this evening. I never get sick—why *now*?"

I sat on the street outside a cafe in downtown Chico. It was 3 p.m., and high school kids filled the sidewalks on their way to the pizzerias and Jamba Juice. I closed my eyes to visualize my sister alone in her flat at 3 a.m. on the opposite side of the world.

"Don't worry Amy, it will be all right. Mild food poisoning won't hurt the baby. Do you have peppermint tea? Drink some and call me back in an hour."

About forty-five minutes later, she called back. "Now I am shaking all over. And I just vomited. Do you think that is normal?"

"Umm, Amy?"

"Yeah?"

"Do your stomach pains come and go every few minutes?"

"Yes, now that you mention it, they do."

"Are they kind of like . . . waves of pain?"

"Yes. They are. But now I also can't stop shaking."

"Amy, I think you are in labor. You need to call your doula."

"Nah, I don't want to bother her in the middle of the night. I'll wait until morning. It's only a few more hours."

"*Amy*, call her *now*. As soon as we hang up. I am on the other side of the planet. You need someone who can see you, be with you. You shouldn't be alone. Okay?"

"Okay, fine."

Amy told me later that she took my advice and called the doula. While they were on the phone, her water broke. The doula came right over and could see that Amy was in advanced labor. The doula helped Amy quickly pack a suitcase and drove her to the hospital where the baby arrived, pink and screaming, before the doctor. Two days later, Amy left the hospital in disbelief that she was now the mother of a baby girl. After the heartbreak of the second-trimester miscarriages, and then passing into her mid-forties, she had given up on the idea of motherhood. Yet they were going to let her take this beautiful, perfect baby and *leave*. It happened so fast, she couldn't quite believe it was real.

My sister has a baby, I thought. She is a single mom and no one in our family is with her. *And no one from our family is going*. I hung up the phone and burst into tears. The pull of our sisterhood, that intense need women have for each other, overwhelmed me. I wished I could go to India right now. Adam walked over and I started babbling at him.

"I have to go. Someone should be there with Amy, and that someone should be me."

He considered for a moment, before saying, "All right then, go."

"Go? To India?"

"Isn't that what you said you needed to do?"

"Well, yes. But I didn't think you would say 'Go ahead.' That would mean leaving you here with the kids . . . for Christmas."

I wanted to go but was afraid to be that far away from Bella and Sophia. And for so long. You don't *hop* over to India for a weekend. It takes two days to fly there and then four days to recover from jet lag. A wave of guilt washed over me for even considering this idea. Could I skip out on the holidays? Who would attend the school winter concerts and help with the Secret Santas? Who would bake cookies for the teachers? The answer was always, me.

In truth, we both dreaded the Christmas season. Adam and I were raised Jewish and now were practicing Buddhists. I grew up celebrating Christmas by ditching my own family and spending the day with our Christian neighbors. Adam's family observed the holiday with Chinese takeout and a Charlie Chaplin movie. Adam and I tried to put on some sort of Christmas for our kids but it always felt half-hearted. Bella made sure we knew that our efforts never measured up to what *other kids* got.

"Go ahead. We will be fine," Adam said.

He waited while I waffled back and forth a hundred times. Can I book a flight and take off for India, leaving my children here? Would we all *die* from something like that? No, Adam is giving me this chance without hesitation, I should let him take over for me. I have shouldered the Christmas duties for years. I know it won't be the same here without me, but no one ever suffered permanent psychological damage from a lack of Secret Santa gifts or Christmas cookies.

CHAPTER 2

NEW DELHI TO VARANASI
TO BODH GAYA, INDIA

Three weeks later, I saw my girls off to school with extra hugs and snuggles. Adam tenderly kissed me goodbye and placed my backpack onto my shoulders. He snapped photos of me by the car and then I headed to San Francisco to catch my flight across the world. It was ridiculously easy to pack for one person instead of four, to carry only what *I* needed instead of supplies for what often felt like an entire Girl Scout troop. With an Indian tourist visa stamped into my passport, Hepatitis A and typhoid fever vaccinations taken, and a cheap flight booked, I was off to India, the place I had always wanted to go.

I dated a Bengali American in college, and nearly went with him for a semester abroad in Calcutta. Then Adam inspired me to visit India when I met him in 1996. I found Adam on the outskirts of a Rainbow Gathering, a yearly counter-cultural gathering of hippies, peace activists, musicians, and nature-lovers. The gathering was in a forest in northern California. I had come out from New York with a friend to celebrate finishing my master of science program in nursing. One morning I opened my tent and there he was, under a tree. Adam was sitting in meditation like the Buddha, but with a pile of books at his side. For a Yale girl, any man who has hauled a stack of books into the wilderness is worth a look. As he sat there in meditation he radiated such peacefulness that my first thought was, *whatever it is he is doing, I should probably be doing that too.*

Adam was tall and lean, with slender, graceful hands. His skin was tanned the golden hue of an outdoorsy California boy. He wore a rainbow scarf tied around his waist like a skirt and sandalwood prayer beads around his neck. He was blessed with a classical sort of beauty, high cheekbones, big blue eyes, and a full, expressive mouth that widened into a sweet smile. His long hair was pulled into a topknot but strands of sun-bleached locks fell around his face like a lion's mane, glowing in the morning sun. I thought about the pasty, cigarette-smoking, leather-clad artists I had recently been dating. One does not find sun-kissed, yogi-boys in New York City.

I was twenty-seven years old the summer I finished grad school. While my fellow students applied for jobs and planned their next moves, I had waited. I considered a couple of different options but had been paralyzed by indecision. I sat down beside Adam and we stared into each other's eyes silently for a few minutes. The two words *beautiful* and *children* popped into my mind. I shook my head and asked him about his meditation.

Adam had recently returned from a year in northern India. He sat Zen meditation for years while earning his psychology degree, and then found Tibetan Buddhist teachers in India. Under their guidance he had done meditation retreats in Himalayan caves and studied in Buddhist monasteries. Adam returned to California a devoted practitioner of Tibetan, or *Vajrayana*, Buddhism. His explanation of meditation practice was a jumble of Tibetan, Sanskrit, and odd esoteric English words. What he said was not fully comprehensible, which I found intriguing. I had my career as a nurse-midwife set, but I had been longing for spiritual dimension in my life. I wanted to learn more about the Buddhist path that Adam was on.

We talked about going to India together that summer as we fell in love. Adam wanted to take me to the sacred places he had been and introduce me to his teachers. Some were elderly, he warned, and might not be around much longer. But I needed to get my first job as a nurse-midwife and start paying off my student loans. Then the wedding, his graduate studies in Chinese Medicine, babies, houses, and businesses followed one after the other. The vision of going to India was tabled for some future time. That future moment, I realized as I heard the boarding call for my flight, was right now.

Ananya was a fresh rosebud of a human, with long black lashes that curled against pink cheeks. She slept swaddled in my sister's arms, dreaming of milk and suckling her bottom lip. After two twelve-hour flights, a layover in London, and a cacophonous drive through swarmy Delhi traffic, I kneeled on the floor beside my sister's couch peeking at my niece's tiny face. Dark fuzz covered her temples and forehead. *My sister has a baby!* Amy had flown to the US every couple of years for the last decade to visit our parents, me, and my children. Her childlessness had grown into a subtle wedge between us, an unmentionable sorrow that increased with each miscarriage she suffered. Now that sadness had been washed away in the river of this late-in-life pregnancy and birth.

Amy welcomed me and said, "I can't believe I have a baby. I just walked out of the hospital with Ananya in my arms," in the tremulous, lovesick tone of a postpartum mother.

I listened to her recount her nearly painless birth and told her that most women don't mistake labor for indigestion. Her maid-cook Vandana served us a meal of rice, *sabzi* (vegetable-based sauces), and *roti* (wheels of homemade flat bread). Then my exhaustion fell like a curtain after the first act.

The days with my sister rocked gently by. Jet lag made me like a newborn baby too—my eyes would close and I would drift off right in the middle of the day. Amy was happy to have my company. We chatted on her couch for hours while she nursed. I imparted my expert wisdom on such topics as burping, co-sleeping, and post-partum exercises. When Ananya awakened to scrutinize the world, we held her close and babbled at her in high, excited tones, cameras in hand. I brought Amy my favorite sling, the one I used to carry Sophia everywhere. When Ananya got her evening fussies, bleating inconsolably like a newborn goat, I slipped her into the sling.

I pulled the cloth so it held her tightly against my chest, turned on music, and danced around the room. In minutes she was asleep.

"And voila," I told Amy. "That is the trick. Well, one of them."

When a woman gives birth in the United States, family members may come help afterwards if she is lucky. They might manage household chores and cook for a week or two so the new mother can recover from birth and care for her newborn. I assumed I would be providing that kind of support to Amy, but it was not needed. Vandana took care of both household and food, and she would continue to do so long after I left.

There are no convenience foods in India, no frozen entrees or pre-made meals from deli cases. There is no Trader Joe's selling gourmet organic canned soups and sauces. Vandana went to the market every other day and brought home fresh fruits and veggies, with which she prepared fragrant Indian dishes in the kitchen. She also made and served us tea, did the wash and the dishes, and cleaned the house. She put the laundry *away*, folded, where it belonged. She was there five days a week, and left the fridge stocked with curries, rice, and *rotis* for the weekend. Amy had her help, as well as a driver, and would add a full-time nanny when she returned to work. This was typical for middle, professional, and upper classes in India, as well as in Asia. Families who cannot afford servants live in extended-family households, with in-laws, aunties, and sisters sharing women's work.

Vandana's presence in the house made me uncomfortable at first, as if it were simply wrong to have hired help. But my initial judgment came from my American point of view and did not take into account the realities of India. If you took the United States, quadrupled the population, and then reduced the land mass by two-thirds, you would have the situation in India. India has 1.25 billion people, making people power its greatest natural resource. What a person does for herself in America a whole crew accomplishes in India, thereby creating a complex economy of livelihoods. Amy had her maid and her driver, but there was also someone who delivered the milk, someone else who came to sweep the front walk, someone to take away the trash to sort and sell, and a person waiting outside to polish shoes or mend clothes. Amy treated her staff well with fair salaries and benefits. In return, she could enjoy her eight-month (!) maternity leave without a thought about cooking or keeping house.

In America, we strive for a standard of independence that is impossible for mothers to achieve anyway. I tried not to compare my postpartum experience because, after all, I was *privileged* to live in America, married. But no relatives came to help after either baby and Adam went back to work a couple days after each one was born. I never felt so alone as I did in my house with my little ones. I would sit in my rocker nursing and trying not to glance around the room at toys, blankets, and clothes scattered everywhere. My arms were full of baby; I could not catch up. Here in Amy's pristine flat, the smells of *baingan bharta* (eggplant curry) wafting through the hallway, I was happy for my sister. If she was going to be a single mother, this was certainly the set-up for it.

One afternoon I flipped through the North India section of the *Lonely Planet* guidebook. I had one week left in India and discovered I could visit two sacred sites by taking an overnight train. The first would be the holy city Varanasi on the Ganges river, birthplace of the Hindu god Shiva. From there, a four-hour train could take me to Bodh Gaya, which literally means "Place of Awakening." A young Hindu prince sat under a tree there 2600 years ago until he awakened and became the Buddha. My postpartum-doula gig could shift into a short pilgrimage journey. Amy encouraged me to do it.

My night train left from Old Delhi Railway Station. I took the Delhi Metro from Amy's neighborhood and found the "ladies only" car to ride. With no men in the car, we ladies could look around and make brazen eye contact with each other. We all stared, faint smiles twitching across our mouths: women in saris with baskets of produce; women in skinny jeans with briefcases, tapping on Blackberries; and me, a green-eyed foreigner.

Emerging from the Metro, I found the Old Delhi station beautiful and atmospheric. The space had soaring arches and domes mirroring ancient Mughal style, all done in red and white. I was ahead of schedule, so I sat in a cafe drinking chai and watching the world go by. In the crowds I saw Muslim school boys in caps and long white shirts, women balancing copper trays of spices on their head, and red-uniformed porters carrying luggage straight out of the nineteenth century. I was so absorbed I almost missed my train. It was suddenly time to go, and I had no idea how to find my platform. I peeked into an office where men in khaki uniforms sat around a long table drinking tea. I looked from face to face as I asked about my train.

"Madam, your train has left!" said one officer and my heart sunk.

Arguing in Hindi ensued, until I was directed to a platform where my train stood. A thrill ran down my spine as I climbed aboard. Since giving birth to Bella twelve years ago, I rarely went anywhere alone. When we traveled at home we camped, which meant stuffing sleeping bags and tents, food and a cookstove, pots and pans, and toys and games into our car. Now I only carried a school backpack with an extra *salwar*, my journal, toothbrush, and a camera. I felt light, like a college student again. In Chico, I ran into friends and former clients whenever I left the house. I was pegged. I was Bella and Sophia's *mom*, Adam's *wife*, so many people's *midwife*. Here on this train, my identity fell away like layers of an onion. I was an anonymous stranger—I could be anybody. I lay in my tiny assigned berth with my arms wrapped around my backpack and let the hypnotic motion lull me into slumber. In the morning, villages of mud and thatch huts tucked into rice fields woke up to the day as we rolled by. I saw bullock carts loaded with school children plodding down the dirt road, women at wells and water pumps, Hindu temples, and flocks of goats in blooming mustard fields.

The auto-rickshaw I picked up at the railway station dropped me on a noisy corner in front of an alleyway.

"Go into that alley," the driver told me, "and keep walking. Signs will guide you to the Ganges."

I stepped into the dimness, rounded a corner, and the sounds of cars, trucks, and horns dropped away, blocked by ancient stone buildings. With each step I took, I walked backwards in time. Cows stood like sentries and monkeys clucked at me from balconies high above. Corner temples contained statues of brightly-painted gods. Hand-painted signs with arrows guided me to "River View Hotels" and "Bathing Ghats." I passed very few people, just an ancient Hindu holy man, barefoot and in orange robes, and an old woman leading a donkey laden with copper pots and sacks of rice.

I lunched on my hotel's rooftop terrace, drinking in the silence and the Ganges view. Hindus believe that bathing in the Ganges is a blessing that clears away lifetimes of sin. Pilgrims have been bathing in the river along these *ghats,* or stone embankments, since at least 1200 BC. Boatloads of pilgrims plied the waters, surrounded by haloes of birds. Priests in orange robes sat along the river banks with altars, flowers, and their vermilion powders for third-eye blessings. Goats chewed on old flowers that washed ashore, children played cricket on the wide stone banks, and cows roamed. Colorful fabrics laundered in the river flapped on their lines. The temples and hotels that lined the ghats in both directions were ornate and in varying states of distress and disrepair.

After lunch I wandered the ghats, observing shrines, flower *wallas*, laundry women, monkeys, and cows. I gazed up at the colors and ancient temples, and then down to avoid stepping in litter and cow dung. A procession of mustachioed faces offered various services.

"Guide, madam?"

"Boat ride?"

"Best price tour of the ghats?"

"Come, I'll take you to the best jewelry shop. Or is it silk you wish to buy?"

Dreadlocked, ash-smeared *Shiva babas* gestured at me to sit and join them for a puff. Shiva is one of the three main Hindu gods, along with Vishnu and Brahma. The river Ganges is said to spring from his hair, and the trident he carries represents the unity of the three worlds that a human will face—the inner world, the immediate world, and the broader outer world. Shiva babas renounce their former lives to become homeless devotees. As part of their *puja,* they smoke marijuana-filled chillums which they share with passers-by. Just being here felt like an altered state of consciousness, so I dropped coins into their begging bowls and kept walking.

A temple on the far end of town drew me in. The roof was decorated with a pantheon of carved gods staring with googly eyes. Monkeys played on these statues, leaping from one to another. A baby monkey sat in the palm of one of the god's open hands. I walked up the steps, took off my shoes, and entered. A priest handed me flowers, and I passed him a ten rupee note back.

In the windowless backside of the temple, a four-armed marble statue of Vishnu caught my eye. No one was around so I sat down in the deserted darkness. I observed my breath for a few minutes and felt my excitement ease into calm. My breathing grew slow and even. I thought of the swirl of experiences I was having: traveling *alone* after so many years of motherhood, my fascination with the spiritual devotion here, the contrast of desperation and decay amidst beautiful temples and pilgrims.

A bell began to sound. It rang and rang, and the echoing sounds banged around the marble walls, straight into my skull.

"Wake up!" the bell seemed to call.

I stood and approached the Vishnu statue, gazing into its face. The dim light of the butter lamps flickered, and the worn marble face of the statue appeared to move. I stared and stared, unable to blink before the dancing Vishnu.

"Wake Up!" the voice rang with the bell inside my head. "Wake up!"

Wake up to what? I wondered.

And I seemed to hear this, in the ringing of the bell, "The truth of things is way beyond your thoughts."

The bell fell silent. My mind felt hollow, clear in the sudden absence of sound. The silence caressed me with shivery fingers as I thrilled to the idea that *I just had a spiritual experience!* I placed my flowers at the feet of the statue and stepped out of the temple and into the sunlight.

Further down the river, sweating half-naked men carried massive logs to the river's edge. I hung back and watched as wood was stacked higher and higher until a holy man gave a signal. A long bundle, wrapped in white cloth and covered with flowers, was brought over and placed on the logs. The pyre was lit, the fire was fierce. The cloth burned off and I realized the bundle was a corpse;

the fire, a funeral. As the cloth burned away I glimpsed a foot, an arm. Here in this public, wide-open walkway along the river, the funeral took place. People came and went, crowded around, made and sold chai in a makeshift newsstand, and threw flower offerings into the fire while the body burned. Cows wandered through. Somehow, it made sense—chaos, life, death, fire, water, all happening on a patch of stone embankment where such activities have occurred daily for five thousand years. *The truth of things is way beyond your thoughts.* Through acrid smoke, a blood red sun slipped behind the hills.

On the ghat below my hotel the evening *Aarti* was underway. For this nightly ritual, Hindu priests danced with flaming candelabras to the sound of chanting and drums. Hundreds of people watched from the ghats or in a flotilla of boats. Palm-sized leaf boats with candles shimmered in the water. I stood in the midst of the fray, suddenly dizzy and overstimulated, until two arms pulled at me. I looked up and a plump priestess on a platform bobbled her head. I climbed up and she blessed me and painted my third eye with vermilion powder. I felt like I was in the arms of the Divine Mother, and together we had the best seats in the house.

The train to Gaya was ten hours late so I waited in the Varanasi railway station all night. The station was full of families camped out on blankets, filling the floorspace. Women in colorful saris squatted to serve meals out of steel tiffin boxes, fathers helped children and babies go to the toilet on the tracks, groups of bent and withered elders and Hindu *sadhus* or holy men sat silently with no baggage but copper begging bowls. Monkeys, dogs, rats, and an occasional cow added to the throng. As the night wore on the hours passed more slowly. I could not find a single bench with room for me, so I stood as long as I could, nodding with fatigue. Then I lay on the filthy station floor, using a discarded film of plastic as my blanket.

I questioned what on earth I was doing here.

Adam introduced me to Buddhism the summer we fell in love. Between hikes to desert hot springs we visited Tibetan Buddhist retreat centers in Flagstaff, Arizona; Santa Fe, New Mexico; and Crestone, Colorado. We read Sogyal Rinpoche's *The Tibetan Book of Living and Dying* and Trungpa's *Cutting Through Spiritual Materialism* to each other as we drove. Buddhism's philosophy of caring for all beings resonated with me. There was even a vow, the Bodhisattva vow, to dedicate one's life to freeing beings from suffering. It fit perfectly with my intention to serve mothers and babies as my life's work. How could I have missed this until now? I wondered. I received blessings, initiations, and teachings from Adam's Tibetan friends and teachers, and by the end of the summer had become a student of Buddhism in my own right. And, we decided to get married.

Adam taught me to meditate and I could not believe the roar of random thoughts that crashed through my head when I sat and "meditated." Then I realized that this was how my mind was always operating, but I hadn't ever noticed it before. Adam and I meditated beside clear mountain streams, while steaming ourselves in hot springs, and in Tibetan-style Buddhist temples. Slowly I learned to calm my mind and taste the stillness and serenity that Adam seemed to abide in. Over the sixteen years since that summer, Adam and I kept up our meditation practices to varying degrees. It was harder for me than Adam: babies and nursing, packing school lunches, and recovering from all-night births filled those edges of my day when one might sit. While I found Buddhism meaningful, I also had a nagging feeling that I was borrowing it from someone else. It could never be wholly mine because it belonged to a foreign culture, far away.

At dawn the train pulled in and I stumbled on. I had a bed reserved but still couldn't sleep. If I missed the Gaya stop I had no idea where I could end up. I lay on the greasy vinyl bed watching villages flash by my window. I arrived in Bodh Gaya without sleep or a friend, as far from home as I had ever been.

Bodh Gaya's streets were dusty and lined with India's ubiquitous chai stalls, cows, and bazaars. Motorcycles and rickshaws honked their horns. Beggars squatted and stared. But there was another element that I hadn't seen in Delhi or Varanasi. Tibetans, living in India as refugees from Chinese occupation, walked the roads wearing long wool dresses, hair in thick black braids, babies strapped on the women's backs. They carried hand-held prayer wheels which they spun as they walked. Tibetan monks formed a sea of maroon robes that flowed through the streets and packed into pedicabs, rickshaws, and shops. I saw monks and nuns in orange, mustard, and sky-blue robes too. They were pilgrims from every Buddhist country in the world: Bhutan, Nepal, Burma, Thailand, Sri Lanka, Japan, Korea, and Taiwan.

But the majority were Tibetans, the Dalai Lama's own people. I had admired and studied Tibetan Buddhism for sixteen years yet had only met a few Tibetans in person. I stepped into a chai stall crowded with monks and grinned as I sipped my tea. I couldn't help it—I didn't know there could be so many Buddhists in one place. The monks were friendly and smiled back.

At the gateway of the *Maha Bodhi* (great awakening) park I gazed up at the stone tower, a monument to the awakened heart. One hundred and eighty feet tall, every inch of it was carved with intricate designs. This was the world's living, breathing center of Buddhist pilgrimage. People of all colors, genders, castes, and creeds circled the tower. In every nook and cranny, someone was praying. People offered incense, made bows and prostrations, recited the *sutras* (the teachings of the Buddha), or meditated. The *stupa* was a colossal beehive, humming with the prayers and chants of thousands of Buddhists in dozens of languages. Flat surfaces held Dixie cups of water by the dozen with yellow and orange blossoms floating in them. Flower garlands were draped on upright stones. A veil of peacefulness hung over everything. *This is the Burning Man of Buddhism! This is the Disneyland of Dharma! I have to come back here with the whole family!*

Around the back of the tower the arching branches of a tree shaded a marble-floored area used for prayer. The granddaughter of the original tree stands today where the Buddha's tree was. When the Muslims cut down that tree several hundred years ago, Sri Lankan monks took a cutting of it back home. They cultivated it and cared for it until it was big enough to replant on the original spot.

I read the brass plaque in front of the tree: "Prince Siddhartha attained Buddhahood (full enlightenment) in the year 523 BC on the Vaisakha full moon sitting under this Peepal (Bodhi) Tree." I read the sign four or five times, until tears blurred my vision. *The Buddha is real. It happened here.* The Buddha no longer felt foreign and far away. I sat beneath the branches of the Bodhi tree and felt a swell of love for everybody: Adam, the pilgrims, my guesthouse hosts, the stray dogs, Ananya. My chest puffed up as I took slow, deep breaths. I didn't want this moment to stop, to pop like a balloon and make everything regular again. So, I prayed. For peace in the world, for an end to the poverty I had seen on the streets, for a healthy future for our children and our planet. For my daughters far away in California, being so generous and brave in giving Mommy this break. The energy of the place seemed to carry me into reverence, perhaps because people had been praying daily on this very spot for two thousand years.

The Buddha sat right here, by this descendant of the Bodhi Tree at the Mahabodhi Temple in Bodh Gaya, Bihar, India. The energy is transcendent, and despite zero hours of sleep in thirty-six hours, the author is feeling blazing, amazing.

CHAPTER 3

Bella. Sophia. Bella. Sophia. Adam. Visions of my family flashed through my head as the plane taxied to the runway. Now that I was headed home I let myself feel the distance between us, the time that had passed. Sleep escaped me, so when I couldn't watch one more in-flight movie I day-dreamed about coming back to India, this time with Adam and the girls.

Amy told me she would be in India for a few more years, and that she would happily host us. Her airy Delhi flat could be a landing pad for a family far from home. "If life gives you a sister in India," I mused, "that probably means you should take the family." I had been intimidated by the idea of visiting India until I actually got there. After walking the streets of Delhi, riding an overnight train by myself, and using a railway bathroom, my fears had diminished. The overarching feeling in India is of *life,* not death. The country is teeming with children, thriving even though no one hovers over them with hand sanitizer and baby wipes in case they touch anything.

The drive home from the airport was interminable. After twenty hours on a plane staring at an entertainment console it took all my willpower to keep my eyes open on the highway for three hours. I was caught in a circle of hell consisting of endless blacktop miles and the longing to close my eyes. *I have to get there so I can see my children again.* Finally, I saw the landmarks of home: my freeway exit, my street, my house with its peeling picket fence and unruly front garden. I bounced up the porch steps, opened the door, and threw down my pack. Adam was seeing patients in his clinic, but my daughters waited for me on the sofa. They stared at me blankly as if stunned by my sudden presence in the house. *Where is my mother and who is this stranger in a salwar?* The girls were both lankier and older than I remembered. How can children change that much in three weeks? I wondered. Then, screams of *"Mommy!!!!!"* began.

After the requisite dogpile, both girls wanted to tell me what happened while I was gone. Bella had broken up with her sixthgrade boyfriend and I wasn't even *there* to bring her chocolate. She had suffered her disappointment alone, *motherless.* The gifts I had purchased for Sophia's Secret Santa before I left were lost. Her teacher ended up covering for us, providing gifts for Sophia to give. Both Bella and Sophia had volumes to say about how tough it was to be alone with Dad for three whole weeks.

"He actually put a roasted beet and a boiled potato on my plate one night and said, 'There is dinner!'" whined Bella.

I tried not to smile but couldn't help it. I would be appreciated on a whole new level now.

"Why are you smiling?" Bella demanded. "It's not funny."

"You're right. It's not." I answered, a laugh escaping. I cleared my throat. "I think I am laughing because I am . . . so happy to see you," I finished lamely.

After the girls were tucked into bed Adam closed our bedroom door, drew a bath, and held my hand as I climbed into the warm water beside him. My mouth found its way to his warm, sweet lips. When I pulled away I said, "There is so much to tell you—I don't know where to start!" But words fell away as he picked up my feet one by one and rubbed them with his massage therapist hands.

We stepped out of the bath and lay down, pink and sweaty, on our bed. Adam threw the comforter over us to keep out the winter chill and pulled me to him. I inhaled the woodsy, masculine smell I have always loved. I felt his delicious lips on all the right places and slipped into the sweet closeness that belongs just to us. Afterwards, Adam fell asleep while I spooned him from behind, stroking his thick hair. In this moment I felt fuzzy with gratitude for him, my enigmatic life partner. I didn't always feel like that. I didn't even understand him at times, but India had given me some new insights into who my husband was. There was something about the men in India that reminded me of Adam. They moved at a slower pace, rarely rushing, as if the gene for hurry was missing. Also, Indians have a deep respect for those devoted to spiritual pursuits, be they sadhus, teachers, or monks.

Adam had lived primarily at Rainbow Gatherings and Buddhist retreat centers for the three years prior to our meeting. He was doing spiritual retreat based on instructions he received from his Buddhist masters in India. He practiced his *pujas* and studied philosophical treatises with the same discipline someone else might apply towards, say, medical school. When we were getting to know each other, I asked him what he did for a living, and he answered that he was a professional yogi. He had a way of speaking that was whimsical and tongue-in-cheek, while also truthful. His manner of speech often left people puzzled. Was that a joke, or was he serious? The answer, often, was both.

Adam's lifestyle had made him something of a wilderness expert and the first thing we did together was travel through the American Southwest. I had been a city girl and was entranced by his ability to turn a patch of forest into home. I watched him wrangle a tarp and bungee cords to make a shelter and build a fire in a rainstorm with nothing but matches, wet wood, and fistfuls of pine duff. Then he would put a kettle of tea over the fire and serenade me while I strummed my guitar.

Our road trip ended because I had student loans to pay off. Through a medical recruiter I got a job delivering babies in a small town in Kansas, and we moved into our first apartment together. Our bedroom had two closets, one for me and one for him. Within two weeks the clothes in his closet were in a pile on the floor, and the hangers I had bought hung empty. When I said something, Adam eased my concerns. "I want my clothes like this," he said. "It is called the Random Access Method."

My scholar yogi husband woke up daily at 5 a.m. to meditate, could fix anything from computers to my car's blown air conditioning system, and had a regal bearing despite the fact that he procured his wardrobe from thrift shops. Yet he left pots of rice to burn on the stove, frequently lost his keys or wallet, and had a very loose definition of "on time." When it was only the two of us, I found his quirks amusing. With children in the picture they would add to my sense of being overwhelmed by family responsibilities.

I never considered reincarnation before I met Adam. Buddhists believe that the karma you make in this life affects the conditions of your future lives. Your actions and emotions are like seeds planted now that will flower later. This is why meditation is beneficial—becoming more peaceful will help you be more virtuous, which benefits both this life and the next. In many ways Adam more closely resembled a Himalayan yogi than a typical American male. He did not touch beer, despised pizza, and took no interest in sports, but he could chant in Tibetan and explain esoteric tantra to anyone who cared to listen.

Over the years Adam took me to meet Tibetan lamas when they visited the United States. Some of them, whom Adam had never met in *this lifetime*, bowed back at him, a spark of recognition in their eyes. I watched an eighty-something, frail, elderly lama call him by his Tibetan spiritual name, *Kadag,* or "pure." "Ah, Lama *Kadag,*" he said to my young husband before placing his withered hand on Adam's chest, "you must begin teaching meditation now." Another time a young Tibetan yogi, recently arrived in America, hugged Adam over and over, saying, "I know you, I know you. My spiritual brother!"

"But wait," I wanted to interject. "This guy is no reincarnated Lama—you should see how he leaves his clothes everywhere."

I returned from India incapable of sleep. First there was the jet lag. And then there was my mind, cycling through images and sense memories like a slideshow on repeat. No matter how tired I was I would close my eyes and be back in India with honking horns, crowds and colors, and the sense of history and devotion keeping me awake. In those three short weeks I had seen an unexpected new niece, walked the ghats of Lord Shiva, and sat at the tree where the Buddha had become enlightened. Yet now I was back to making macaroni and cheese, doing laundry, and driving kids to school. I was back on-call, checking my cell phone around the clock to make sure I hadn't missed anything.

"India is a fire in my blood!" I said to Adam, to friends, to anyone who asked me how my trip was. The longing to go back pumped through my veins.

Sweet, clean Chico was gray and bland. Amy told me that after India, wherever else you go feels as if you have cotton gauze over your eyes and ears and nose. My Chico life was draped in gauze. There was only one thing to do—start planning the next trip, a *family* trip. Adam and I began to dream, and then our ideas evolved into plans. We wanted to spend at least six months there, anything less wouldn't be worth the expense of the plane fares. We needed to save money and organize ourselves, but we intended to go before Bella started high school or Amy moved away. I suggested leaving in two years. Sophia would be in fourth grade and Bella would be in eighth. That seemed about right. I started telling friends and family that in less than two years we would leave for an extended trip. I figured it was like quitting smoking; the more people you tell, the more likely you are to do it. It would be embarrassing if we *didn't* go, after telling everyone.

A rough itinerary formed in my mind. We could leave America right before Christmas (*ha!*). We could see South India and Bodh Gaya in the winter and then head up to the Himalayas during spring and summer, when the plains of India heated up. We would return before the monsoons, in time for fall semester. We could be gone for eight months, and have the kids only miss one semester. And we would home-school them while we were away.

Now that I knew we were going to walk away from the routines of our frenetic lives, my ability to bear them dwindled. It was as if something deep within me switched, and I could at last admit that our home life was taking a toll on me. The veil of the cheerful Supermom had been torn away.

"Sixty-three!" I shouted at my husband and kids when they came into the kitchen expecting me to serve a meal one Saturday afternoon. "Do you know what that number is? That is the number of times I feed you each week. Can you even believe it? *Sixty-frig-gin-three.* That is three meals a day for three people, seven days a week. And it is not even counted as a *job*. It is extra, taken for granted, on top of running a midwife service, attending births in the middle of the night, doing laundry, paying the bills, keeping up the house, and arranging and chauffeuring all your damn activities!"

The more I thought about it, the more untenable my home life seemed. *Sixty-three meals a week for thirteen years of parenting and I don't even like cooking.*

I heard Bella ask, "What's with her?" as I stormed out of the kitchen and into my office where I opened my laptop to scroll TripAdvisor.

"This whole American approach to parenting is whack," I thought, remembering my sister's set-up in Delhi. "Shouldn't we live among extended family to help us raise the children? Like in a village compound or something? Or maybe hire a live-in cook?"

Years later, writers would publish essays and articles about the exhaustion and depression of mothers in modern Western society. The term "emotional labor" would be used to describe the way the woman of a household cooks; shops; cleans; knows where everything is, where everyone should be and how they will get there and back; keeps track of all the dental and doctor appointments, teachers conferences; and on and on, often while working full-time. I didn't know that the problem was systemic, a product of patriarchy and materialism and the expectation of a carefully curated childhood for our kids that included GMO-free, organic meals, charter schools that required parent participation, a beautiful de-cluttered home, and a constellation of enriching activities for which mothers were the organizers and chauffeurs. Our life looked so good and I adored my children, so I couldn't understand the anxiety and rage that simmered within me at times. I pegged these problems on the obvious cause—my free-spirited yogi husband who was not plagued by the same worries about paying the bills, preoccupation with myriad complex schedules, and the constant feeling of never being quite enough.

Adam was a loving, present father who always said that his first job was to "back up the midwife." He built his acupuncture clinic behind our house so he could both work and be with the children when I was off at births. But his creative, loosely-scheduled approach to his days left me handling all the details. Tired of feeling like a nag, I thought it was "easier" to do things myself than ask him for help. We fell into a pattern where I would wait until I was so frantic by the time I got around to asking him for anything that I would come at him desperate and incapable of asking nicely. He would be put off by my anxious tone and answer with a "Yes, Dear" that I loathed. At these times I would look at myself in the mirror, dark circles of exhaustion around my eyes, and worry that our marriage was crumbling. My heart would float through my body cavity into my bowel, where it would lie pulsing with sadness and fear.

I wondered if it was just me or if other mothers felt this way. I started asking the moms at school pick-up, violin recitals, and the health food co-op, "How are you? Is your life working for you?"

I got blank stares and shrugs in reply, or heard a litany of complaints about over-extended, lonely lives. This feeling I had, that I was reluctantly running the entire show, was not uncommon. I fantasized about fomenting a rebellion of moms. It would be based on the collective cultural memory we mothers shared of a time when children helped their parents, or at least ran loose on the streets, and mothers had camaraderie with other women integrated into their daily work. It would reshape our society so it would no longer take all of a mother's free time and energy to cater to her children's complicated activities, shuttling them around. It would revisit the dream our mothers had for us in the 1970s, that we would be the first generation to have it all: career and family, but without requiring the third and fourth shifts needed to make it so.

In the meantime, I acknowledged this truth—I wanted to walk away from all of it and live out of a backpack.

When Adam and I first opened our private practices, mine in midwifery and his in acupuncture and herbal medicine, a financial adviser scared us into saving a chunk of money.

"Self-employed people aren't eligible for disability benefits or paid time off," she told us, "so you should always have four months of family expenses saved for an emergency."

While she talked I bounced an infant on my hip and watched my precocious toddler out of the corner of my eye. We had recently moved to Chico, had no family nearby to help, and had a brand-new mortgage to keep up with. *What if one of us broke something and was bedridden for months? Of course we need a safety net!* Bit by bit, from tax-earned income credit, family gifts, and sheer thrift, we scrounged up four months' worth of living expenses and tucked it into a savings account where it sat for years. Now I considered cracking that egg open.

The family travel blogs I read estimated that fifty dollars a day can cover a family of four traveling in Southeast Asia in mid-range budget style. Most of those blogging families traveled with babies and toddlers, so with my bigger children I estimated seventy dollars per day. That was about $500 a week, or $2000 a month, including food, lodging, and travel. Later we found that it took only twenty to thirty dollars a day to visit many parts of India. The bottom line was that it would be much more affordable to travel in India than it would ever be to live our normal lives in California.

Guilt occasionally stabbed at me for using our nest egg. But the injuries we had saved for never happened, and the girls were older now. Our lives no longer felt quite so precarious. *Shouldn't we hold onto it for the kids' college expenses or something?* At those moments of doubt my Jewish fairy guilt-mother whispered in my ear, "You are using this money for something *you* want to do, and not spending it on the children—for shame!" This trip was my dream, but I also trusted that it would be good for the kids; good in a different way than school, violin, and GMO-free mac and cheese.

Underneath the ebb and flow of our busy lives, a dark undercurrent of uncertainty simmered. My difficulties with the local doctors started when I opened my home-birth service, and then led to trouble with the Board of Nursing. In 2005, women in Chico begged me to start attending home births. There had only been one midwife in the area for years and another was needed. I was taking maternity leave from a hospital job, Sophia had been born the year before, and Bella was a toddler. Deep down, I knew I didn't want to return to a hectic hospital job and be that absent, overworked mom who barely knew her kids because she practically lived at the hospital.

In my circle of friends, women were getting ready to have a second or third child, and they asked me to assist them at home. I did, and then families found me by word of mouth and my home-birth practice filled. Eighty percent of the births went as planned, the miracle of the baby's entrance into the world honored in the peaceful home setting. I would become a lifelong friend to the family and soar home at dawn with an oxytocin high, grateful to have the best job in the world despite the sleep deprivation.

Then, there was the twenty percent that needed hospitalization. The most common reason was that after a long labor, a first-time mother would grow tired and need either pain medication or Pitocin to finish the birth. My clients were not unusual in this—across the United States most home births transport for this very reason. These were not emergencies, yet the doctors at my local hospital would receive me and my clients with varying degrees of hostility. We never knew until we got there. Some doctors would pull me into the hallway and yell at me for attending home births. Some would deride my clients to their faces before providing medical care. Some assisted us and kept their opinions to themselves.

The bullying I received stunned me. I was normally so articulate and could easily discuss my clinical decision-making as well as the safety statistics of home birth in my own practice and nationally. But when the doctors dressed me down my mouth went dry, my intestines turned to stone, and I was incapable of responding. My Yale-trained brain froze. Later, on the drive home, it would thaw out and I would think of everything I should have said.

One doctor was the worst. Women cringed at the sight of the knobby ham-hands on this three-hundred-pound man. Dr. Stern would enter the labor room like a storm, his brusque speaking voice sounding like a shout. "Oh, that's how Dr. Stern is," the nurses would say after he left the room, as if that were a valid defense for his terrible bedside manner. Buddhism teaches that when problems arise in your life it is karma returning from your actions in this and previous lives. Dr. Stern and I seemed to be karmically linked. The only explanation I have is that we must have had past-life dealings with each other. Although there were twelve OB doctors on hospital rotation, Dr. Stern was almost always the one on-call when I arrived with a patient. Including the one time disaster struck.

In 2009 I took on a client named Meredith who wanted a VBAC, a vaginal birth after a cesarean. When I was trained at Yale in the mid-nineties VBACs were considered normal deliveries. Then, in the early 2000s, VBACs were banned by most hospitals. Overnight, it was decided by a coalition of doctors and insurance companies that women who had had previous cesareans must continue to have them; they were no longer to be given the option of a vaginal birth. I found it unethical to force mothers to have major abdominal surgery when there was no medical indication. So, when hospitals stopped providing VBACs, I, along with most other midwives, continued to attend them. There was nothing in my nurse-midwife regulations preventing me from doing so. The ban on VBACs was "hospital policy," not law.

Pregnant in Chico, Meredith had three options. She could have a repeat cesarean against her will, she could drive three hours in labor with a toddler in tow to San Francisco where a hospital still offered VBACs, or she could have a home birth. Meredith chose home birth, and she was a few days past her due date when her labor began. I went to the house to check on her and found her in early, but not yet active, labor. Her cervix had dilated to two centimeters, her baby was in a good position, and the fetal heart tones were normal.

I went home, knowing that I would be called back to the labor in a few hours. In the middle of the night my phone rang, and I heard Meredith's husband, John, say, "Meredith has had a seizure."

"What do you mean she had a seizure?"

"Well, her whole body contorted, like every muscle was contracting, and her tongue lolled out and she foamed at the mouth. She was unconscious for a few minutes."

Oh. My. God. "Have you called 911?" I asked.

"No." John said.

"Hang up and call 911 right now. I am on my way."

A seizure. A seizure! Fear gripped my heart as I sped to Meredith's house. Years of my life were skimmed off the top during that drive. I arrived as the paramedics were wheeling Meredith to the ambulance on a gurney. She was woozy but conscious. I pulled my Doppler out of my purse and the paramedics waited while I checked for fetal heart tones. I searched around and then found the normal "swish, swish, swish" of 120 beats a minute. The baby was alive. I met John's petrified eyes.

"Your baby is okay," I said.

I repeated myself so Meredith could hear. "Your baby is okay." I stepped aside, and Meredith was rolled into the maw of the ambulance.

Who was on call at the hospital to start IV anti-seizure medications and deliver the baby? Dr. Stern, of course. Meredith's seizure had been triggered by the sudden onset of a rare but serious complication called pre-eclampsia. It would have happened if she had been under a doctor's care. It would have happened if she had been in a car on her way to San Francisco. It had nothing to do with her previous cesarean. But Dr. Stern was livid that I had planned to assist with a VBAC and wrote a letter of complaint to the Board of Nursing, sparking an investigation of my practice that would grind along for six years.

The question was whether I had followed the scope of practice regulations in California's Nursing Practice Act. The board's regulations were vague, and there were no rules specifically about

VBACs in them. But I was in a legal and bureaucratic mess and hired an attorney who was an expert in medical licensing law. It cost me $250 an hour to speak to him, and this was a fifty percent discount from his usual fee. He gave me the discount because I was a rural midwife, and he knew I often bartered my services for such things as fence repair or a handmade chicken coop.

My lawyer, Peter, told me that it could take years for the investigation to finish. In the meantime, I would remain in limbo while waiting for a verdict. The complaint could be dismissed without merit, or formal charges against me could be filed. Those charges could then be fought in court, but that would easily cost a hundred thousand dollars in legal fees. In the months before we left, my heart leapt into my throat each day when the mail came. *Would the verdict come today?* I was certain that the adrenaline surge I got with the daily mail was shaving years of healthy kidney function off my life. This investigation I was facing was confidential, a secret from everyone but a few of my closest friends. I hadn't even told my parents. My livelihood, my calling, was in jeopardy of being lost and I did not want to admit it, not even to myself.

CHAPTER 4

CHICO CALIFORNIA
SEPTEMBER 2013

While we planned the trip, Bella blossomed into a teenager. I assumed the journey would be a welcome respite from the cruelty of middle school. Those years were tortuous for me. I was voted "Ugliest Girl in the Class" by the sixth-grade boys, and that news was broken to me by my mad crush, freckle-faced Todd Marshall. But Bella enjoyed middle school and had worked hard to overcome her hippie upbringing and become a "Popular." After transferring to a "normal" junior high from her alternative Waldorf grade school, she had everything she wanted: a smart phone, a bell schedule, and access to both Starbucks and the mall. She was even crowned the Junior High Winter Queen before we left. The only cruel thing about middle school was that her parents were pulling her out of school and taking her to India—totally *abnormal*.

The fall before we left, she was hardly around. She had sleepovers on the weekends and spent her free time with friends at the mall or a coffee shop instead of playing at home with her sister. My red-cheeked, precocious ragamuffin who wore a tattered Cinderella ball gown *everywhere* had been replaced by a young woman who stood 5'6". Her long thick hair was tucked in a neat braid and she wore skinny jeans, a burgundy cardigan, and tasteful make-up. Her childhood was ending; when we returned she would be almost fifteen. I was snatching her back, away from her peers, constant social media contact, and the persistent march towards independence for one final, epic childhood adventure.

I stopped taking new midwifery clients. On my website I posted the dates I would be gone, as well as contact information for other midwives. I was down to my final births before our departure. Cathy's labor started during an autumn storm. Her sister-in-law, Beth, who had her two babies with me, made the call. "Cathy is in really strong labor. I think she will be ready to push soon." Cathy lived nearly an hour away, at the end of a three-mile dirt road full of potholes and rocks.

"Why didn't you call me sooner?" I whispered into the phone, as I hustled out of bed trying not to wake Adam.

I gave my pregnant families detailed instructions, including an easy-to-read flowchart, about when to call me in labor. I liked to arrive at the birth neither too early nor too late. It was obvious my instructions had not been followed

"You know Cathy. She didn't want to make a fuss and call people out on such a stormy night. She hoped it was a false alarm."

I did know Cathy. I was her midwife two years before when she had birthed her first son in a quiet, no-nonsense manner.

"Okay. Well. I am on my way but I will be at least an hour. If you think she will have the baby before I arrive you are welcome to call 911 and have an ambulance come to assist."

"No, I know she doesn't want to do that."

"Well, then you can wait for me but have her take short, panting breaths if she feels like pushing. And call me back if that happens, too. Hopefully my phone will have service all the way."

"Thanks, Dena."

Amber met me at my house. We loaded my gear in the pounding

rain and I raced onto the highway, windshield wipers fighting the deluge. The wind howled, and my car listed into the other lane. I could not drive quickly in that squall. I didn't hear back from Cathy's family until we were fifteen minutes away. *We are going to make it!* I coached her on the phone to breathe through the contractions while bumping maniacally down the dirt road. I could hardly see through the windshield. We pulled in, leapt out of the car, and went through the front door. The house was eerily quiet. Beth waved me into the back bedroom where Cathy lay on a large bed surrounded by her relatives.

She rolled over and faced me. "I have to push really bad."

"Okay. Try not to push while I set up my tray."

I grabbed the cookie sheet, threw sterile instruments on it, tore open the packs containing the cord clamp and bulb syringe, and tossed sterile gloves on top. Amber hastily tested and turned on the oxygen, just in case. I placed my tray on the bed and climbed up next to Cathy, figuring the baby was about to emerge.

Cathy screwed up her face and pushed. She pushed again, and then she said quizzically, "Something doesn't feel right."

Amber placed the Doppler on her belly and we listened to the fetal heart tones, 130 beats per minute, normal.

Another contraction came. Cathy pushed hard, again.

"Let me check your cervix. Maybe it needs to dilate a little more."

I gloved up, dipped my fingers in sterile KY jelly and slid them inside Cathy's vagina to feel the cervix. I felt all around the baby's head.

"Nope, the cervix is completely out of the way. But what the . . . ?"

My fingers passed gently over what should have been the top of the baby's head and penetrated into an orifice. *There is no orifice on a baby's head. Is that the anus?* I felt again. The presenting part was hard and round like a head, not a butt, but again, my fingers slipped into something. *Is that the baby's eye I am poking? His mouth?*

"Cathy, I want you to turn to your left side and DON'T PUSH." I gave Amber my "Seriously Do It" face and she helped Cathy onto her side. I tried to keep my voice calm while I talked to her and her family. "So, what's happening is that I am not really sure what part of the baby I am feeling. Possibly the baby is breech, or perhaps a face presentation. This is the first time that I have ever been so unsure of my exam. What I do know is that you shouldn't push, and we need to go to the hospital."

Cathy's mother-in-law, sisters-in-law, sisters, and husband Josh stood around me. They had all been at Beth's two home births, and Cathy's previous birth, and were baffled by my pronouncement.

"Come on," I said to Josh. I thought about the ferocious storm outside, the interminable rocky dirt road, and the fact that the closest hospital was a small rural one that I had never been to located thirty minutes away. "We need Cathy's insurance card and the newborn car seat. I usually drive in a hospital transport but in this weather, on this road, you better drive us in your truck."

I spent the ride to the hospital in the back seat with Cathy, listening to the baby's heart tones and coaching her not to push as we careened along winding country roads. Cathy labored on, with strong contractions three minutes apart. I sat beside her, listening to her groan as she heroically fought against the urge to push.

A decade seemed to pass before we arrived. Cathy was placed in a wheelchair and rushed to labor and delivery with Josh and me at the nurse's heels. I had called the hospital so they knew we were coming in.

Dr. Johanssen, who I had never met, was there to see us.

"Hey kiddo." The tall, gray-haired doctor boomed in a bass-toned voice. "Let's get you on the bed so I can check and see what's going on."

Cathy climbed onto the bed so the doctor could examine her. He gloved up, checked, and announced, "Your baby is breech!"

He paused and felt again. "No, your baby is presenting with his face. But how . . . ?" He felt and felt, evidently as confused as I had been. "Ah, the little guy just bit my finger."

The baby's neck was bent backwards, and the little one was attempting to be born mouth first. With every push the baby's neck would get further cranked back, eventually resulting in neck and brain damage. The only safe delivery was a cesarean section.

After the surgery, Dr Johanssen came in to see Cathy once more before leaving. I stood up to shake his hand and he did the most unexpected thing. He put his arm around me in a friendly hug and said to Cathy, "You have an exceptional midwife. Her documentation is meticulous, and she did everything correctly, so that you now have a healthy baby in your arms."

I thought I must have heard him wrong. I had finally run into a local doctor who could see past his profession's biases about home birth to recognize who I was and what I did.

In September I booked our flight for the Winter Solstice and made lists of *Things to Do So We Survive and Even Have a Life to Come Home To*. But first, I attended Back to School night. While the teachers discussed the coming year, I realized my girls would only be there for half of it. These teachers didn't know it yet, but we were pulling my daughters out of school midway through and disrupting something that was organized, planned, and set, to make space for something that was uncharted and unknown. None of the other parents were contemplating the ramifications of pulling their kids out of school to travel in India, and I panicked. *Why do I always do hard, crazy things? Is this really right for them? Why can't I be a normal mom?*

I mentioned these thoughts to my mother, a retired school teacher who is travel-averse. Big mistake. She glommed onto this as the perfect reason for us not to go after all.

"Aren't you afraid that they will forget how to learn and you will *ruin school forever for them*?" she asked.

"Um, no. That actually hadn't crossed my mind," I answered. "I think that they will learn far more traveling in India for eight months than they would ever learn in a classroom for that period of time."

"Hmph. I am not sure," she said.

My kids' teachers and school administrators had the opposite reactions. "What lucky kids!" they said when I informed them of our plan. "They will learn so much—I wish I could go with you." We would withdraw our children from their schools at the end of the term and declare ourselves a private home school. Our teachers gave us math workbooks so the girls could keep up while we traveled, we would bring some books and journals, and that was that.

Tall, green-eyed Bella was our child who began reading at age four. The strange thing was, no one taught her. She did not even attend preschool. Sure, we read to her a lot, starting with *Good Night Moon* and *Pat the Bunny*, and then moving on to Dr. Seuss and Beatrix Potter. But when she turned four, Bella started reading the books to us instead. And that was that. By sixth grade she was a top student in math and English, an accomplished violinist, and had played the lead role in musicals from *Alice in Wonderland* to *The Aristocats*. She tested out of pre-algebra without having done much math. Teachers asked us if Bella could please join their orchestra, this program, that play. Bella was far enough ahead of her peers that I had no concern about her missing a term.

But I did worry about Sophia. Lithe and petite, with a grace she got from her dad's side, Sophia resembled a child of the fairy race. A fairy with a streak of mischief, that is. Sophia was a climber, a spinner, a dance-around-the-houser, and only stopped moving when she sat down to draw. Sophia built a fort in every closet and under every table in the house. When important items were missing, we could always find them in her latest hidcout. "I didn't think they belonged to anybody," she would explain. Several times she hid from me until I was in a panicked frenzy. When I finally found her, she batted the curled black lashes around her emerald eyes and my determination to punish her turned to mush like a chocolate bar left in the sun.

Unlike her sister, Sophia took little interest in academics. She was easily distracted from her lessons by other kids' shenanigans and had a hard time sitting still. We home-schooled her for second and third grade to take the pressure off, and our home-school teacher suspected she had dyslexia. She could read, but very slowly, and never for pleasure. At ten years old she felt discouraged, especially when Bella reminded us how *she* taught herself to read at age *four*.

"Look at you," whispered my inner Jewish fairy guilt-mother. "Going gallivanting off to India and raising an illiterate daughter!" Not *illiterate*, I whispered back. *Dyslexic.*

How do you prepare children who have never been outside the US for something like this? I wondered. I figured that taking them camping at Rainbow Gatherings, which we had done throughout their childhoods, had been a good start. I knew they could adapt to simple conditions, living on beans and rice, and using trenches dug into the ground as toilets. Adam and I warned them about crowded trains, cold showers, and a complete lack of macaroni and cheese.

"I am both frightened and excited," Sophia said. Bella nodded in agreement. Then Bella added, "I am glad we are going, but I am worried about missing my friends and missing out on important social stuff."

When the kids were off to bed, Adam admitted, "I guess I am a little scared, too." In eighteen years of knowing him, I had never heard him say that. Not when my pregnancy had run two weeks overdue, not when Bella had a fever of 105°, not even when Sophia was lost at a music festival in the dark. I actually liked hearing him sound so vulnerable, so *human*, and not having the answer. I climbed under the covers and cuddled him. As we drifted off to sleep I considered my secret worry. The truth was, we were embarking on this adventure despite the fact that our relationship had its issues. Deep down, I worried that this trip would either make, or break, our marriage.

We were each fitted with a backpack and would carry our own things. I gave everyone a copy of my packing list: underwear, socks, swimsuit, shoes, and a pair of jeans. Books. The silk sleeping sacks we ordered from Vietnam. A flashlight. A tee shirt and a jacket. That's it. "We will buy clothes when we get there," I explained. "Everything else stays behind."

Adam volunteered to be Safety Officer. He would make sure we all had working headlamps and always carried multiple methods to purify water: a SteriPEN, iodine tablets, and even a tiny camping stove to boil water. When he told the girls that they could not just scamper off and disappear like they do in Chico, but would need to have an adult by their side, they listened, eyes wide. At dinner one night he explained about consensus process.

"When I was in college," he said, "I took a wilderness psychology class. The final was to live in the woods for two weeks as a group. Before we left, everyone made the commitment to keep themselves safe and consider the group. Decisions that affect the whole group involve consensus—if everyone agrees, we do it. When everyone feels included there are no emotional struggles, which is when injuries or accidents happen."

"Cool, Dad," Sophia said.

Adam and I summed up our approach to this journey with a "Moes Family Travel Creed." Bella and Sophia both agreed that the principles were solid and captured our family's values. It went something like this:

> As guests in India, we will try to fit in. We will wear local clothing, learn some of the languages, eat what the locals eat, travel on local transport, and follow the norms and rules of the culture as best we can.
>
> We consider our family Ambassadors of Peace from the United States, here to promote harmony and understanding between the nations. We are not tourists!
>
> We will avoid thinking "Oh, at home it is like this, and at home we get that."
>
> We will withhold judgment and criticism, knowing that Indian culture is ancient and complex and that we will not even begin to understand much of what we see. We are pilgrims, not critics.
>
> We are strong, we will have everything we need, and we are ready for adventure!

One night I dreamed that we arrived in Varanasi, India—my family, my sister and her baby, and . . . one of our backyard chickens in Sophia's arms? *Gosh, how did I ever let Sophia talk me into bringing one of our chickens? That was NOT on the packing list. I spoil that girl!* As we walked the narrow, busy streets looking for our hotel, the chicken got away. Now we were searching for the chicken among gazillions of people, dogs, cows, under motorcycles and rickshaws. I woke up laughing. Yes, India. No, bringing chickens!

What had been the distant future was now a week away. My ambition to clean out the house for our renters became all-consuming. Seven years' worth of old mail, kids' drawings, clothes and shoes that didn't fit anyone, broken skates and crayons and pet toys, and random unused items filled our cupboards, corners, and drawers. I forgot we were leaving for India in my cleaning frenzy. I was determined to get through every last bit of it so I would not have to come home to it.

Finally, our closets and drawers were cleaned out and packed away. Our passports stood ready in money belts, stamped with Indian tourist visas, and our packs were loaded. The kids' "bare minimum" school supplies had somehow expanded to a stack of books, sheaves of paper, and a mountain of art supplies. We pulled out a big suitcase to take empty and bring back filled with Indian treasures. However, that night, in a sudden compulsion, Adam packed into it everything he would need to run a small acupuncture and herbal medicine clinic, just in case. A second old suitcase was dug out to take empty, but that was filled with the load of school supplies. These heavy, full suitcases, lugged across the world, would spend a peaceful eight months sitting in my sister's Delhi apartment while we traveled.

On the morning of December 20th, Adam and I woke at 4 a.m. I felt half-mad, and half-sedated. *Today we are leaving for India. All of us. For eight months.* We had time to go through the house one more time, a peaceful couple of hours together before the kids got up. We checked the instructions for our renters, said goodbye to our pets, and checked my lists one more time. We must be forgetting something . . . but there was only one thing left to check off—get on the plane.

The kids woke up, and I made them the last breakfast I would make for eight months. The last dishes were washed. The last crumbs were sponged off the counter. In a reverie of slow, deliberate, final clean-up, Amber arrived to take us to the bus station. Suddenly after months, no, years, of dreaming and planning, it was time to go or we would miss the train to San Francisco! The kids said mournful goodbyes to our dog Bodie and the cat, and we scrambled to hoist on our heavy packs. I asked, "Bella, did you pack the cord to your iPod?" for the 611th time and I counted the passports, one, two, three, four. It was time to go. Our neighbors stood on the sidewalk, waving and blowing kisses at us as we piled into Amber's van and departed for the family adventure of our lives.

CHAPTER 5

CALIFORNIA TO NORTH INDIA
DECEMBER 20, 2013

The train hummed through rice fields and oak trees. Flocks of geese in *V* formations cruised south across the pale sky. For months I had been packing, planning, scheming, running. Now I sat in suspended animation, riding the immaculate and mostly-empty Amtrak train to San Francisco, dazed by the sudden lack of anything *to do*. Adam listened to Buddhist podcasts through earbuds and Sophia played games on an old phone. Bella furiously texted. She wanted constant contact with John, her new boyfriend, while she still had connection. At the winter dance a week ago, she and John held hands and then had one brief but promising kiss. Sure, they were eighth graders, and sure, their relationship had lasted only a single week, but Bella had committed herself to him. She promised to miss John, to FaceTime often, and to stay faithful to their love for our eight months of international travel. "Please Bella," I begged her, "don't do this. Don't spend your trip missing someone you kissed once. Long distance relationships are heartache, take my word for it."

My friend Hae Min met us in her SUV to take us to the airport. She bought a box of French pastries for the ride, which would have been the perfect gesture except there was only one chocolate crois-sant. The girls got into a loud, vehement debate over who should get it so I grabbed it and popped half of it in my mouth.

The girls were still yelling about the "Unfair Pastry Debacle" when we arrived at the airport. Hae Min did not have children of her own and was impressed by the volume and passion of the din. She helped unload our bags and then asked me, "You guys are really going for eight months?" She looked at my kids, one eyebrow raised, as if to say "You actually think you can survive eight months of travel with *them*?"

"Yup, we are. My kids are great travelers. Usually." I told her, hearing my words ring hollow. "We're just . . . excited."

With that, we put on our cumbersome packs and walked, well, staggered into the glass and steel terminal. Indeed, the argument dissipated into silence as the kids realized that we were going to *fly to the other side of the world* now. We found the Cathay Pacific counter where a woman nodded and asked me in lilting Hong Kong English, "How ah you today?"

I burst into tears.

"Sorry." I sniffled. "It is just that we are leaving today for an eight-month trip. I am very well today . . . feeling so blessed that—"

"Mom," Bella interrupted. "Pull yourself together! She doesn't care. Give her our tickets."

"Right." My hand fumbled in my purse. "Here are the pass-ports . . . and here are the tickets." I turned and met Adam's cool blue eyes as my heart pounded. *The moment of truth—will they let us on the plane or have I forgotten something essential?*

The woman took her time examining passports, visas, names, faces. Finally, she handed me four boarding passes and our passports and wished us a good trip. Adam's face softened into a half-smile and I thought I might break into a tap dance. We were cleared for take-off. I envisioned my seven-page to-do list left at home and mentally checked off the last item—get on the plane.

The long-hauler plane at the gate looked way too enormous to get off the ground, but I wasn't going to let the kids know I thought so. I could surreptitiously wipe the sweat off my palms and play the part of a calm, confident airline passenger for my children. I had Adam's warm fingers to wrap mine around. He would softly chant Tibetan prayers while we took off, which would settle my nerves. We took our seats, played with our personal entertainment consoles, and then were smoothly taken 36,000 feet in the air. Halfway between home and far away, above who knows which country, we sat in the unlikely flying box of aluminum and carbon-reinforced plastic for twelve hours. The sunset lasted for half the flight, blue-white fields of Arctic tundra sharply contrasting the glowing pink and golden sky. Adam and Bella marveled at the view, faces and cameras pressed to the window. I marveled at them, same wide cheekbones and full lips, same slender but strong builds, Adam's hair an Einstein-like shock of salt and pepper and Bella's a thick blond ponytail.

Sophia's eyes stayed glued to her screen. Movies and soda were her two favorite things and strictly limited at home. But during the long flights she had free rein to watch as many movies and drink as many cups of Sprite as she wanted. "I could actually live like this," she informed me happily as she swigged soda and programmed her sixth movie. "I could get a job when I grow up, where I fly from place to place."

We landed in Hong Kong in a timeless twilight and were ushered in circles through the windowless bowels of the terminal. Petite Chinese ladies in perfect makeup and smart red blazers chanted "Delhi—this way. Delhi—this way," as they rounded yet another bend and led us down another hall. We stumbled through security in a state of sleep-deprived delirium, hair disheveled and breath rank, getting onto our Delhi flight right as they were closing the gates. We were greeted by rows of passengers in turbans and bright saris. When the safety instructions were given in English and then repeated in Hindi, Bella's bright green eyes met mine and I saw her wide-eyed wonder. *Are we doing this?* I grinned at her, feeling gooseflesh on my neck and arms. *Yes, we are.*

Sometimes I dozed, but mostly I didn't. Then I stood with my family in the Delhi terminal at midnight, twenty-two hours after leaving San Francisco, glancing through the crowd of drivers and taxi men until I recognized Amy's driver, Naresh, who was holding a sign.

WELCOME

MOES FAMILY

Naresh led us out to the lot where we piled ourselves and our baggage into Amy's car. The night was dark and thick with winter fog. Bella gazed at the sky and wrinkled her nose.

"Mom, what is that *smell*?"

I breathed in the foggy air, which carried the night smell of sixteen million humans in one city, of cows and diesel and curry and insufficient sewage systems. Of incense and butter-lamps and frying samosas on the roadside. Of the turmeric-infused sweat of migrant construction workers and the perfume of politicians.

"This, my dear, is the smell of India."

I lay in bed with Adam by the big street-facing window, listening to morning in Amy's neighborhood of "Defence Colony," named for retired military officers housed there in the 1960s. Her street was canopied by broad-leafed but dusty trees, and flowering shrubs that grew among two- and three-story apartments. The birds in Delhi sounded different than the ones at home, their songs exotic to my ears. Neighborhood swifts and parakeets and babblers sang what sounded to me like the call to adventure. *We made it! We are on the other side of the world, away from my pager, school schedules, to-do lists. We are so far away from the nursing board now, who cares what they do?* The melodic Hindi songs of the knife-sharpener, the fruit-cart man, and the milk-man calling to their customers rose up from the street below. As the day brightened, the distant cacophony of horns commenced on the thoroughfare a few blocks away. I got up, grabbed a mug of spicy-sweet chai from a teapot in the kitchen, and stood on the balcony to watch the street below. Drivers washed cars, uniformed children walked to school, women in saris swept their porches, and bike-rickshaws hustled people off to work, ringing their bells as they passed. Ananya, now a busy, chattering two-year-old, came out and offered me a wooden bowl filled with toy food.

After breakfast we walked to the clothing bazaar and bought loose cotton salwars for me and the girls. Our tank tops were packed away and we admired ourselves in the mirror, dressed in colorful, but modest, Indian style. When Adam saw me in my long purple salwar with red trim he grabbed my hands and stared in admiration.

"Have I mentioned lately how beautiful you are?" he asked.

"Why no, I don't think you have."

"Well, let me do it now, then. You're beautiful."

"Thank you."

We flagged down a yellow and green auto-rickshaw to take us to the neighborhood market. Sophia's eyes bulged as we climbed onto the bench and she saw there were no seatbelts. She squealed with laughter and delight for the entire ride as the rickshaw careened around bicycle pedicabs and the wind whipped up our hair. "Best forty cents I ever spent," Adam said. Then we discovered that an ice cream also cost only forty cents and bought Sophia two at once.

Dec 23, 2013
Defence Colony, New Delhi

Dear Diary,

I had quite the experience today. I went to the market with Vandana, Amy's cook. When we arrived at the market, it was a huge bustle. People talking fast, bargaining in Hindi. Dogs running through the streets caked with mud and dirt. Young children without shoes playing. Cows draped in bright flowers eating garbage from the gutters. Strange mixtures of smells confuse my senses. Piles of strange fruits and vegetables lie under dusty tarps. The calls of salesmen trying to convince us that theirs is better than the ten others that

sell the same thing. I know this is such a "tourist" thing
to do, but I took some pictures.

Love,
Bella

"This is the little sister I have always wanted but you never
gave me," Sophia said, pausing as she chased Ananya from room
to room. Sophia and Bella spent hours coloring, doing puzzles, and
reading stories with their baby cousin while we stayed at Amy's
for the week. India is the largest democracy in the world, and the
country was preparing for a major election. Amy went to the office
each day to cover the unfolding story, leaving us in the competent
hands of her household staff, Lalli and Vandana. Bespectacled Lalli
had been hired on as Ananya's ayah, or nanny, and also happened to
be Vandana's mother. The mother/daughter team lavished attention
on us, plying us with food and motherly advice. These talkative,
cheerful women made Amy's home bright and warm, full of the
smells of cardamom and curry.

Walking the Defence Colony neighborhood we learned the
rules of the road, completely opposite to those at home. We practiced the art of crossing busy intersections with rickshaws and
motorcycles swarming toward us from the "wrong" direction. In
India, traffic does not stop for pedestrians. Rather, the biggest thing
gets the run of the road; bikes get out of the way for rickshaws,
rickshaws move aside for cars, and when buses roar through everything scuttles to the side. The one exception is the cow. Beloved to
the god Krishna and therefore sacred to Hinduism, cows in India
freely roam the roads, and traffic deferentially goes around them.

Adam and I had always been physically affectionate with each
other. We walked together holding hands or with our arms around
each other. We would sit in a restaurant squeezed tightly together
in a booth. We had been this way since we first fell in love in 1996.
But in India, people of different sexes are not to touch in public, even
married couples. Men walk hand in hand with each other, women
walk together, but not mixed-gender couples. We would respect the

cultural norm here but interacting without touching would take some getting used to.

Ananya spoke Hindi with Lalli and English with Amy. I watched in awe as she sat in her high chair and tore into a mound of rice and dal and vegetables. Then she stared, mystified, as Sophia picked at her plate of plain buttered noodles. It never occurred to her to say "No" to rice and vegetables until her American cousins came to stay. I let Sophia live on noodles and toast at Amy's as a concession to the change and unfamiliarity. Okay, here's the truth: I let Sophia eat noodles and toast because I always let her do that, because I was a sorry, enabling excuse for a mother. Or just a busy and exhausted mother. Either way, Vandana's Indian food was fresh and fragrant, and within a couple of days Sophia couldn't resist it. She tasted the dark, creamed spinach dish called *saag paneer* and then ate an entire bowl of it, sopping up dal on the side with freshly made chapatis. Ananya, to my sister's dismay, now asked for plain noodles with every meal. Her bowl of noodles in front of her, she gazed at her cousin adoringly and announced, "Like Tho-phia!"

Adam and I bought matching Guru 1200s from the Sikh electronics shop in the Defence Colony market. The Guru 1200 was a twenty-dollar cell phone that worked anywhere within India with a three-dollar a month prepaid SIM card. With these phones we could call Amy, book lodging and trains, and connect with each other in case we got separated. Amy could dial me up and put Ananya on, who could then ask for Sophia and sing her Happy Birthday. Every week. For months.

Leaving the market with our twenty-dollar phones in one hand and forty-cent ice creams in the other, I was struck by our Western privilege. I considered the strange inequities of the global economy and our position of advantage within it. The moment we stepped onto Indian soil we had lifted ourselves from struggling-to-stay-in-the-middle-class to wealthy. India was giving us the perfect intersection of enough time and enough money. At home we never ate at restaurants because it cost too much, yet here we would be able to eat out *and* order dessert.

Weeks ago, I had wired Amy our precious travel funds so her bank could change our dollars into rupees. I thought Amy would open an account for us, with an Indian ATM card to access money during the trip. I was wrong, because her bank had strict rules limiting foreigner's accounts. A few days after our arrival Amy called me into her bedroom, closed the door, and handed me three months' worth of rupees in a stack of money the size of a brick.

"I'm sorry. This sucks, but there is no other way. Find someplace in your stuff to hide it."

I put the brick of rupees in the bottom of my backpack hidden in a plastic bag of Maxi Pads. It terrified me to think that I would be carrying around half our travel fund in the bottom of my pack. All I could do was *act* like I wasn't carrying a brick of money. And it worked—no one would run off with such a big pack and no one would think to check for valuables in a bag of pads. Menstruation and its products are taboo in Hindu culture.

Amy took time off and planned a weekend getaway for us. The morning before Christmas we loaded into Amy's car like a gaggle of Bollywood starlets and Naresh drove us out of Delhi.

Of all our wild schemes for traversing the remote corners of the subcontinent, this first weekend jaunt worried me the most. More than terrorists, misogyny, fiery train wrecks, or wild elephants, tense family dynamics gave me the jitters. Amy and Adam were two of my most favorite people on the earth, and they were carefully kind to each other. But between them there was a certain amount of eye-rolling when one looked the other way. Adam could not believe Amy had lived in India for a decade and remained untouched by the wisdom of its spiritual traditions. And Amy found Adam's fascination with Indian spirituality romanticized and naïve in the face of India's socio-economic realities. It was as if they each existed in a separate India, and their discussions on this subject had the potential to get volatile. On top of this, Adam was used to tolerating a household of three Alpha females, but now he would be on a road trip with *five* Alpha females. It would be an overdose of estrogen for any man.

The roads through Delhi lacked discernable lanes, so drivers followed the "school of fish" approach to sharing the road. Bike-rickshaws, auto-rickshaws, trucks, buses, and the occasional car moved in a swarm, passing each other with barely centimeters of space. Most motorcycles had a whole family riding, with a woman in a sari side-saddle behind a man, legs delicately crossed and a child or two on her lap. Colors jumped out as we cruised: bright yellow and green auto-rickshaws, trucks decorated with garish plastic flowers and vivid rainbow paint, and the sparkling fabrics of the sari-clad women. Cows stood calmly in the middle of the chaos chewing on trash while vehicles swerved around them. Everyone blew their horns. Trucks had painted signs on their backsides asking, "Horn Please!" It was like some modern orchestral art piece, a discordant symphony of horns that never stopped from dawn till dusk.

Beside these loud and chaotic roads, men squatted around cookfires, cows roamed, and colorful laundry waved from overpasses and fences. Groups of women in saris strolled with trays and pots balanced on their heads, children played, dogs foraged, and men with wheeled carts sold fruit, cakes, and deep-fried sizzling foods. On the outskirts of Delhi we drove on one of India's only multi-lane highways, passing construction sites for a future high-rise megalopolis. Then we turned off the main roadway and onto a rural lane. The scenery changed as the car wove along a narrow winding street through a village, passing festively decorated camels, thronging bazaars, and donkey carts piled with mountains of goods. A camel pulling a wagon walked beside our car which threw the girls into fits of laughter. The wagon driver sat atop a load of goods and stared into our car at our faces, as curious about us as we were about him.

We pulled into a walled-in farm, set amidst blooming yellow mustard fields. A Rajasthani family ran this farm as a guesthouse. The house had been in their family's possession for generations, with spare rooms recently converted into guest rooms. We discovered that this model of family home turned guesthouse is repeated by the thousands in cities, towns, and villages all over India. This alternative to hotels allows a traveler to stay in a personal, family environment and eat "restaurant meals" that are actually home-cooked.

The farm was renovated and planted with flowers and fruit trees. A baby calf stood by the gate where we entered, and children waited to meet and play with our girls. We ate lunch in the garden under the bright blue sky, relieved to be out from under the dome of Delhi pollution. Our hosts served fried *parathas* stuffed with potatoes, garlic, and curry, with a side of yogurt made with fresh milk from their own cow. Bella and Sophia ate one after another as if they had discovered their new favorite food.

Bella and Sophia played badminton with the kids, and Adam was content to sit in the sunny, flower-filled garden and read, but Amy was anxious to get Ananya to the bird sanctuary. "Ananya loves birds," Amy kept telling us. Adam and I looked at each other. *Birdwatching in India—who knew?* I gathered the family and settled them into the car again.

The Bharatpur Bird Sanctuary was created 250 years ago for the reigning maharaja and is one of the most diverse birding areas in the world. The wetland preserve is home to thousands of birds during the winter, over 300 species of them, and hosts thousands of Indian tourists each day. We arrived at the gate and were regaled by men offering to be our guide.

"We may as well hire one," Amy said, "because otherwise we will be hassled all afternoon by people asking to be our guide."

We rode rickety bikes on a lane crowded with Indian tourists in pedicabs. Amy and Ananya rode in a hired pedicab beside us and we all stopped frequently to admire birds in the marshlands and trees. "Look, Ananya look!" Amy yelled to Ananya, trying to get the two-year-old engaged in bird-watching. Ananya was mainly amused by Sophia, who biked around and around her pedicab, making faces and singing. Our guide spotted birds we would have never seen and told us stories about them while we snapped photos.

Back at the farm, we huddled around a warm fire as the winter night fell. Sophia went to play with the farm children in their room. I was nodding off in my chair so I went back to our room and fell into the soft bed, on the verge of slumber. Then I remembered Sophia. *Where was she?* I got up to find her.

I found her in a room filled by two wide beds where the farm's parents, grandparents, children, uncles, and cousins slept together.

Sophia was asleep in a bed with six other people. In America, if six people were already sharing one bed they would tell a foreign house guest to scram and go get into her own bed. In India, there is always room for one more. I bowed "thank you" to the grandparents as Adam picked her up and carried her to our room.

The next morning Amy attempted to hustle us out early. Her plan was to visit two nearby sites, the Mughal ruin complex of Fatehpur Sikri and then the Taj Mahal. Adam and I wanted to relax in the sunshine while the children played. Sophia could barely be pulled away from the brown calf with giant eyes. She helped prepare the calf's breakfast of grains cooked over an outdoor fire. Bella played badminton with the older kids. So, we dawdled and watched Amy get annoyed with us. Finally, we all got in the car, ready for a day of sight-seeing. Well, maybe not really ready, because it was almost lunch time and we had nothing to eat with us. We assumed Christmas would be a normal, or even slow, day in North India because eighty percent of Indians are Hindu, fourteen percent are Muslim, and only two percent are Christian. We had no idea how crowded these sites would be on Christmas.

Our first stop, Fatehpur Sikri, was a city built by the Mughal Emperor, Akbar, in 1569. Its red sandstone palaces, harems, mosques, and courtyards are considered the apex of Islamic architecture. The city was abandoned in 1720 due to a lack of water and has been a majestic ghost town ever since.

The streets leading to Fatehpur Sikri were lined with vendors offering horse-and-buggy rides, balloons, and trinkets. We drove into a lane that was so packed with cars, taxis, and buses, we couldn't move in any direction. Families with women and children dressed in their finest saris thronged the road. We left Naresh in the car and followed Amy as she picked up Ananya and plunged through the crowds to get into the ruin complex.

By now it was well past lunch, and my family was too hungry to be interested in ancient Mughal architecture. So, we did a sort of jogging tour of the grounds, across elegant colonnades with soaring arches and domes, briskly glancing at the sacred geometry of the inlaid mosaics that were everywhere we turned. Bella pushed Ananya in her stroller, which took her mind off her rumbling belly for about twenty minutes.

"This is great," Bella said. "But now I need *food*."

"We need to feed the bear," Adam told Amy. Amy was disappointed and gave me a withering look as she dialed Naresh to pick us up.

We made a lunch stop at a South Indian restaurant where we ate our first *dosas*. The dosas, broad and very thin crispy lentil-flour pancakes, were torn into pieces and dipped into a spicy/sweet coconut curry sauce. Amy sulked about our lackluster sightseeing, laying it on thick about how rarely she gets out of town with Ananya, until I apologized. Then she admitted she had been starving too. "Sistah!" we sang out in unison while hugging, our childhood reconciliation ritual. We drank sweet mango lassis, used the clean restrooms, and were in good humor again and ready to see the Taj.

We arrived at the Taj Mahal a couple of hours before sunset. In 1631, Mughal Emperor Shah Jahan was bereft when his favorite wife and beloved companion, Mumtaz Mahal, died during the birth of their fourteenth child. He built the white marble Wonder of the World to house her tomb. The crowd in the massive Taj parking lot was extreme. *I have not truly understood the concept of "mob scene" until this moment.* I pictured the headline —*American Family Trampled in Christmas Crush at the Taj.* Naresh dropped us off as close to the gate as he could drive. As he disappeared into a sea of brown and white cars crammed together into infinity, I thought, *we will never see him again.* I clung to Sophia but she was nearly run down by a bus anyway. Then she stepped in (probably human) excrement. *At least she has her shoes on.* People stopped and stared at us, perhaps the first Caucasian family they had ever seen. Then they pulled out smartphones, asking, "Hello, what is your good name? Where you from? One snap, please?" as they ran to stand next to us for a picture.

Amy with Ananya in her arms, Adam with his arm linked through Bella's, and me clutching Sophia, passed through a dark stone gateway and glanced across the broad Mughal gardens to gaze upon the biggest monument to love ever built. The white dome of the Taj Mahal floated against the blue sky and green Yamuna river. It did not appear to be anchored to this earth. The enormous, graceful structure was the most beautiful man-made thing I had ever seen.

We stared in amazement, took photos, and then strolled across the gardens to see it up close. And here was our Christmas miracle: Naresh had lived his whole life three hours away but had never seen the Taj. Amy had given him money to buy a ticket after he parked the car. In the middle of the gardens, amidst thousands of people, Naresh silently and suddenly appeared at our side. How he found us, I will never know. We snapped our family Taj Mahal portrait with Naresh in it and I still smile when I see it, remembering his happiness. We stayed through dusk, when the soaring dome changed from white to gold and then pink with the setting sun. In the dark the crowds thinned, and the Taj Mahal turned a luminous blue-grey as mists rose from the river to blanket it.

CHAPTER 6

VARANSI

A few days later we went through our backpacks and left everything we possibly could behind in the suitcases. *Travel light, travel light, we reminded ourselves, we need to walk easily with our packs.* The thirty pounds of school supplies were not going to go anywhere but the corner of Amy's guest room. "Bring your math workbooks and a book to read," I told the girls as I checked each of their packs.

Indian Railways is the most-used railway system on earth. The billion people of India travel primarily by bus and train, not cars. The British left behind an extensive railway system that connects nearly every place on the subcontinent, one positive legacy of their two-hundred-year occupation. Indian trains are tiered so that everyone can afford to ride. Occasionally trains have a first-class car, which are expensive by Indian standards. Most trains have some 2AC and/or 3AC cars. These are upper-class cars with AC running, and beds either stacked two or three high. There are no separate cabins, but a porter provides clean bedding. The cars are fairly clean, and passengers tend to be middle- to upper-class Indians and foreign travelers. These tickets cost about half the price of first class.

The next level is "Sleeper Class," the lowest reserved seating class. Bunks are reserved, but no bedding is provided. The seats, floors, and bathrooms are grimy. There is no AC, and the windows are open to the air, with wooden slats over them. Costing a couple of dollars' worth of rupees a night, these seats are popular, and the cars tend to be full. Then there is "General Class." No seats, no reservation, and the ride costs only a few cents. When the train pulls in, those traveling General Class run to get on. The faster they dash, the better chance they have of landing a spot on a wooden bench and not having to stand through the night. These cars are always packed, with people literally hanging out of the doors or even climbing up to ride on the roof.

Naresh dropped us at the station and we staggered through pushy crowds and up and down stairs searching for the correct platform. It was obvious that our backpacks were still too heavy. I didn't look directly at the girls, knowing that if I made eye contact an explosion of complaints would fly. Amy's travel agent, Pankaj, had reserved us first-class tickets, a treat because most Indian trains don't even have first-class cars. When the train pulled in, the single first-class car went speeding by, so we hoisted on our packs, grimaced in pain, and sprinted after it.

First class meant our family had its own cozy cabin for the night. A petite man in a khaki uniform and matching hat came in, made up our beds for us, and served cups of chai. We ate French baguettes and peanut butter from Amy's Defence Colony bakery for dinner. After a week at Amy's we were happy to be a four-person unit again.

"Girls," Adam said, "now we are on pilgrimage. What is a pilgrimage, you may ask?"

Bella rolled her eyes and sighed, and Sophia shrugged her shoulders, with a "beats me" face.

"Well, let me tell you," Adam went on. "It is a spiritual journey to holy, sacred places. We get the blessings of these places, and our hearts and minds will be changed and we will not come back the same. And it usually involves some challenges, which can be seen as purification. It is not a vacation, it is a transformation."

Lecture over, his tone softened. "And I am honored to be doing this with you three lovely ladies."

"Awww, Dad!" shouted the girls, and then a howling pillow fight began. We giggled for hours about nothing at all and slept well in our tight quarters.

December 30, 2013

Dear Diary,

I woke up on the train in Varanasi today. When we found our hotel, we took a long walk along the ghats. Beggars with missing limbs asked for food. Cows roamed everywhere. Hindu holy men bathed in the sacred Ganga. Salesmen called out, especially boat rowers. I have been getting attention from young men. Here, people openly stare at me. It is intimidating.

In the evening, we got on a boat and were rowed out to a huge Hindu puja on the holy river. Hundreds of people sang and chanted, then released flowering candles into the river. By day, the Ganges is a sea of gray muck. By night, a shimmering river of light and devotion. This has been my favorite day.

Love, Bella

The staff at the Ganges-view hotel where I stayed two years ago remembered me and welcomed my family. Glasses of chai in our hands, we stood on the roof terrace and gazed at the Ganges below, feeling the pull of five thousand years of continuous prayer. Morning fog still cloaked the river, but the red sun eventually burst through, sending pink sparks across the water. Boats full of singing pilgrims went by. A sadhu sat in meditation, a vision in bright orange robes. A man stood knee-deep and poured copper kettles of water over his head, again and again, washing away his sins. Prayers had been sent into these waters as incense, music, flowers, and the ashes of loved ones, daily since time began. The beauty of so much devotion was palpable, molecules of the sacred Ganges herself evaporated into the brackish air we breathed. Bella and Sophia took it in, California girls who had grown up without consistent religious exposure. I felt like we had arrived at the India we came here for.

We walked the ghats together, exploring ornate, ancient temples and shrines to Lord Shiva that we found every few paces. In each shrine, no matter how small, someone had placed fresh flowers, left a butter-lamp, and lit incense. The ancient statues were freshly painted with splashes of color. We shyly waved at the ash-covered Shiva babas as we dropped coins into their bowls. Local boys invited Bella and Sophia to join their cricket match, but we didn't know the rules so we just watched. Cows gazed at us with giant, gentle eyes. Puppies were constantly underfoot; at every shrine and set of steps, a stray mama-dog with full teats and poking-out ribs watched over another scampering litter.

Along one stone wall, groups of young artists were painting murals. We chatted with them and observed their work. We found the temple with the Vishnu statue from my last visit, and I led us in to meditate in the womb-like, marble interior. We sat down together and the accumulated blessings from the ancient statues seemed to meditate *us*. I couldn't believe I was here with Adam and the girls. It seemed like a dream, and if I pinched myself hard I would be back in Chico. And I knew what Adam would say . . . that this *is* all a dream. At twilight we climbed into a boat and the boatman took us back to the central ghat to view the grand *Aarti* from the water. The river was lit up with hundreds of floating candle lamps and the priests danced with flaming candelabras on the shore.

But Varanasi is a city of extreme contrast. The mythic spiritual power of the river, the mangy dogs. The priests in orange robes with mountains of flowers, the lepers begging for food. Five thousand years of worship, plastic trash left on the ground. Over the next couple of days, as we became more familiar with where we were, awareness of these discrepancies crept in. Exploring the winding, picturesque alley-ways of the Old City, we bumped into filthy children defecating in the open and skinny cows living off the garbage strewn about. When lepers approached us we gingerly dropped money into their bowls. Bella and Sophia became confused; how could a place so sacred be horrible at the same time? I did not know what to say.

We sat on the bed in our hotel room to talk these things over, and the girls turned to Adam for his insight. "In every corner of the world, people suffer." Adam said. "Even back in Chico, there are homeless, there are people who are sick, alone, addicted to drugs, victims of violence. In America the suffering tends to be out of sight, tucked away. We get a sanitized version of things. Here, we are seeing suffering we personally haven't witnessed before. It is more out in the open. At the Burning Ghats they cremate the dead, right in front of everyone. Life and death are not so hidden. So, this is an opportunity to deepen our caring about the world. We want to help, but we cannot 'fix' the problems we see here while on such a short visit. We can 'fix' ourselves, however. We can widen our hearts and change our attitudes about what we had previously taken for granted."

Sophia wanted to tell us something, but she began to cry, and then the crying turned into those inconsolable sobs that grated the cheese of my heart. "What is it Sophia, what is it?" I asked, pulling her to me and squeezing her. All I could make out was something about dogs. Maybe this was about the mangy dogs we saw, the ones with patches of their coats missing to reveal raw pink skin. *Maybe this is too much for us and my crazy dream is actually a nightmare.* When she calmed down enough to talk, Sophia told us that she had seen a man pick up a puppy by the head and toss it out of his way. She thought maybe that had killed the puppy. Now she could not get the image of that abuse out of her head, and on top of that, she couldn't bear the sight of puppy blood splattered all over the ground.

"Where are you seeing puppy blood on the ground?" I asked her.

"Everywhere!" she answered. "Right outside the hotel! The blood of injured puppies is *all over.* Come and see for yourself."

We put on our shoes and followed her down the hotel steps and out onto the ghat. Sophia pointed at what she thought was blood. I sighed with relief.

"That is not blood," I told her. "Those are paan stains. People here chew paan and then spit the red juice on the ground."

"What the heck is paan?"

"It's a betel nut thing that people have used here forever. It is a chew mixed with lime paste and flavors. It gives you sort of a lift when you chew it, like coffee or tobacco or something."

The ghats of Varanasi were covered with red paan stains, which I hadn't noticed until Sophia pointed them out to me, thinking it was blood. Once we cleared that misconception up, Sophia felt better.

"Well, when I grow up, I am going to become a veterinarian and move here to open a clinic for the stray dogs, anyway."

"Do it Sophia," I responded. "I'll back you up a hundred percent."

We returned to our hotel to find that the Varanasi contrast-pendulum had swung wildly again. A lively New Year's Eve party was getting underway for both the hotel guests and the friends and relatives of the staff. The rooftop terrace had been draped with white curtains and was lit up like a Bollywood set. Musicians with sitar, harmonium, and tabla drums sat on a rug in a half-circle with a group of singers, surrounded by mikes and stacks of speakers. As the concert began, we found chairs and plopped down, mesmerized. The expressive scales of the classical *ragas* dipped and soared, carrying us along. The hotel manager came around with candy and helium balloons for the children. Bella, a violinist since she was eight, was enthralled by Indian melodies and the rhythms of the tabla drums.

Kathak dancers stepped onto the stage. Wearing costumes embroidered with jewels that flashed under the lights, the dancers told classical myths with their elegant hand gestures, fantastically made-up faces, and undulating hips. They simultaneously kicked out rhythms with the bells around their ankles. Two of the six dancers were clearly men in drag. One of them was young and adorable, and kept winking at Bella to her utter delight.

Silver trays were brought out, and a dozen of the most fragrant, delicious dishes of Northern India were served. Our plates were loaded, yet the hotel staff kept coming around asking "Why only one plate? Go have another, please, a little more won't you? Where are the children? Here is more candy for them." The music, lights, and feast were dazzling. All this, while a few hours before we had been in despair, examining the dirty ground for signs of injured-puppy blood. The local families were friendly and eager to meet Americans. They asked me, voices full with pride and anticipation, "How are you finding Varanasi?"

I could see from their expressions that they did not feel an existential crisis about the litter or stray dogs. This was their world and they did not know anything different. I did not want to critique their sacred Varanasi by giving them an earful of my delicate Western sensibilities. I thought of something a Buddhist monk once told me—as a thing is viewed, so it appears. I wanted to see India as Indians did.

"So blessed, really beautiful." I answered.

They smiled and agreed. "Yes, yes, it is, isn't it?"

At midnight the owner of the hotel came out and set off fireworks. The air filled with the stench of sulphur, the sparkling colors barely clearing the balcony before they exploded, and it sounded like a war had broken out. The Indians cheered, the Westerners cringed, and Sophia's eyes nearly popped out of her head. This was followed by cake, and more candy and balloons to top the night off. With that, 2014 was ushered in, India-style.

A Sadhu *(Holy Man)*, a calf, and boats full of pilgrims on the Ganges in Varansi, Uttar Pradesh, India.

"Happy New Year!" Adam said, kissing me and waking me up in the morning. "Time for my dip in the Ganges."

I rolled over and pulled him to me. The girls were still asleep. His lean, strong body against mine, I gave him a long kiss. I smoothed his hair from his face and said "Please don't sweetie. I am afraid you'll get sick. Please, please, please!"

But Adam had done it twenty-two years ago, and he was going to do it again. Back at home, I had shown him science papers describing high concentrations of the worst bacteria imaginable in Ganges river water. But for the spiritual pilgrims of India, including Adam, these facts were irrelevant. "The holy water will cleanse my deep India soul," he told me, as I tried various tactics to talk him out of it.

"Fine, well I am not going to watch. Go, and have fun." I turned over and closed my eyes, pretending to go back to sleep.

And so, Adam went and washed away his sins in the filthy, ice-cold Ganges.

I couldn't fall back asleep, so I left a note for the sleeping girls and went to visit the Kashi Vishwanath Temple, the oldest, holiest temple in Indian Hinduism. As I neared the temple, I passed clusters of armed soldiers guarding the temple. This holy site was a frequent target of Islamic terrorist threats, so at a security checkpoint the numbers in my passport were carefully written into a massive ledger. A fellow bobbled his head at me and gestured to a rack of shoes. It was time to take my shoes off.

I hesitated as I looked at the marble floors ahead, sopping wet with Ganges river water and gooey with spots of cow dung. I peeled my socks off, thought of Adam swimming in the Ganges, and decided I would survive holy offal on my feet. I stepped onto the temple's cold, wet floor, and nearly burst into laughter as I beheld the chaotic beauty. Silver, gold, and marble; statues, gods, and altars within and within and within each other filling every inch of space. Thousands of bright orange and magenta flowers were strewn about and piled on the altars, the smoke of incense filled the air, and there was a constant *splash* as worshippers tossed copper kettles of Ganges river water over gods and altars. The sounds of chanting and chattering and constantly ringing bells resounded off the marble walls and floors. It was colorful and wet and loud and crowded, and on top of that the whole place pulsated with movement—monkeys. Monkeys climbed everywhere, making the inanimate alters appear alive.

The center of the temple was an inner sanctum containing a four-foot-tall Shiva *lingham*, or *phallus*, on a pure silver altar. That space was packed full of people, with a high priest on a stool giving blessings. In the Indian spirit of *there is always room for one more,* people gestured at me to "come in, come in." I squeezed in and got my blessing from the priest in exchange for a handful of rupee notes. My ribs were compressed by the push of people leaning in to touch the lingham. There was no easy exit, and more people were entering. It took several minutes of patient doing to worm my way out.

Parvati is the wife of Shiva, and I found her shrine room off to the side, with more breathing room. I placed my flowers at her feet. I thought I was alone with the statues until I noticed the priest in the corner. He was wild-eyed and grinning as he dabbed my third eye with his red paint. I reached into my pocket and discovered I was out of rupees. I sheepishly smiled at him, and then we both watched as a four-foot-long garland of marigold flowers spontaneously fell off of a *Ganesh* (elephant god) statue. I picked it up off the floor and reached to put it back on the statue but the priest said "No, No! It is for you! Ganesh has given it to you!" He placed the garland around my neck and I slipped out of the room with a "Namaste."

Stepping into the courtyard I saw a couple of monkeys out of the corner of my eye. Suddenly, *zoom,* a monkey leapt at me and his perfect fetal hand yanked a flower from off my neck. He popped it in his mouth and gobbled it up. I was stunned and frightened at first, and then a feeling of delight crept through my whole being. I laughed as I tore more flowers off my neck and tossed them to the monkeys to eat. "Here!" I told them, "Ganesh has given these to you!"

When I returned to the hotel, Adam was using a whole bar of soap to scrub himself down in the shower. I gave him the last of Ganesh's marigolds, and thus he was cleansed for the new year, both inside and out.

Adam had visited a nearby Buddhist site called Sarnath twenty years ago and remembered it as a peaceful, holy place. After he attained enlightenment, the Buddha walked to Sarnath from Bodh Gaya and gave his first teaching there. Sarnath wasn't far so we decided to go by rickshaw. We said goodbye to the Ganges and hiked out through the narrow streets of the Old City onto a wide avenue where the sound of honking horns welcomed us back to modern life. I noticed it was already easier to walk with our packs. A rickshaw pulled up and a portly, smiling man offered to drive us.

"*Chalo!*" the driver said to us after we negotiated a price.

"What does '*Chalo*' mean?" Sophia asked him.

"It means 'Here we go, together,'" he answered. We could barely fit in the rickshaw with our four big packs. Our bags and Sophia were piled on top of Adam, Bella, and me. But Indian drivers never consider this—the question is not "Are you comfortable?" but rather "Can you fit?" And the answer, no matter what, is always, *Yes.*

Jan 1, 2014
Dear Diary,

Today my family and I took an auto-rickshaw all the way from Varanasi to Sarnath with all our gear. We packed in a tiny vehicle with our massive backpacks in our laps, and our driver, with a big belly and a merry disposition, took off. As soon as we tore into thick oncoming traffic, this man turned from sweet jolly man to road rage demon driver. We zipped along, jostling between cars, people, and other rickshaws while he blasted the horn. My mom screamed when he suddenly turned onto a tiny rickshaw-wide cobblestone street. From there it was INSANE! We raced along broken pathways, screeching to a halt for other rickshaws, random fruit stands, and pedestrians. I laughed, Sophia buried her head in the back packs, and Mom said "Slow down, slow down." Imagine being on a roller coaster for an hour straight. That is what it was like. Probably one of the highlights of my time here so far.

Love,
Bella

Instead of serenity, Sarnath was bedlam. We had arrived during a *Mela*, a religious fair celebrating one of the hundreds of Hindu goddesses. Thousands of people filled the streets, dressed in their finest, kicking up storm clouds of dust. Oversized plastic souvenirs and noisemakers were sold by vendors lining the roads. Children by the gazillion were blowing into these noisemakers making horrific high-decibel honks.

"This is exactly what India needs." I yelled over the din to Adam, "Really loud noisemakers."

Hindi music blasted from stacks of speakers, and buses packed with people roared by belching diesel smoke in our faces and blaring their horns as we scrambled to get out of the way. The sacred park had been the site of thousands of picnic lunches that day, and all the garbage had been left behind, scattered over the grounds. Dogs and cows were doing their best to clean it up.

"Whatever 'sacred sites' are here, I can't deal with this," I told Adam.

Adam remembered where the Buddhist monasteries were located and led us down a side street. The crowds dropped away, and the decibels dropped. We entered the gates of a Tibetan Buddhist monastery and did not leave the peaceful gardens for the remainder of the day. The monastery rented us rooms for the night, among the quiet, smiling Buddhist monks. We meditated in the ornate temple, turned the prayer wheels in the garden, and wrote in our journals until evening.

We were invited to New Year's dinner at the Ladakh Youth Centre across the street. Ladakh is a Himalayan kingdom on the Northern tip of India, closely related to, and right beside, Tibet. Because the map was drawn so that Ladakh exists within the borders of India, it has remained freely Buddhist. We went over and were served plates of rice with dal and veggies by Ladakhi University students. Although we were the only non-Ladakhis there, we felt welcome and joined everyone where they sat on the floor, eating in a friendly circle.

After dinner our youthful hosts in jeans and sweatshirts, along with wizened elders in long wool dresses, prayer beads, and braids, got up and danced. Tinny music with distorted high-pitched singing played from the speakers. Young and old alike knew every lyric, every hand gesture and step. Around and around in a circle they danced, singing and waving their arms. They gestured to us, *join us, join us*, as they spun. The moves seem simple enough, I thought, shaking off my body-shyness and raising my arms to dance.

CHAPTER 7

Never commit any evil deeds
Accumulate a wealth of merits
Completely tame one's own mind
These are the teachings of the Buddha

BODH GAYA

In 563 BC, Queen Mayadevi of Kapilavastu dreamed that a white elephant appeared in her bedroom and entered her womb. A few weeks later she discovered she was pregnant with her first child. Kapilavastu was located amidst the lush forests of what is now the border of India and Nepal. Following the customs of the time, Mayadevi traveled to her parents' home in Lumbini to give birth to the child. She almost made it, too. Just outside of town she went into labor, wandered over to a tree, and as she stood hanging onto a branch, gave birth to a baby boy. Later, people said that the baby leapt out of her side and then got up and walked, leaving lotus blossoms where his feet fell. (As a midwife, I am not so sure about that part.) Nonetheless, the baby was named Siddhartha, which means "every wish fulfilled."

When Queen Mayadevi returned to the palace with her baby boy, a Brahmin seer was summoned to predict his future. The seer told the king, "He will either become the ruler of the world, expert in military victory, or else a great religious prophet." The king cared mostly about politics and protecting his kingdom, of course, and so wanted option A for his son. He hired the best teachers to tutor Siddhartha, but still worried his son would leave the palace and become a homeless seeker. He decided to protect him from anything that might steer him towards religious inquiry. Specifically, he kept from him any knowledge of suffering or death. Siddhartha grew up inside the palace walls, surrounded by youth and beauty. At sixteen he was married to his gorgeous cousin, Yasodhara. Wouldn't you know it, even with all the pretty things he could possibly desire, Siddhartha grew restless. He convinced his charioteer, Channa, to take him outside the palace walls. On his first venture out, he saw an old, bent man walking along the road.

"What is wrong with that man? Why is his hair white, his skin withered, his back bent so he leans on a stick to walk?" Siddhartha asked Channa.

"Nothing is wrong with him. That is old age," Channa answered. "Everyone gets old, my friend. Someday you will be an old man too."

Siddhartha was astonished. He went out with Channa three more times. Each time he saw another facet of suffering, people who were ill, a corpse in a funeral procession. Finally, he observed an ascetic wanderer.

"What is the ascetic doing?" Siddhartha asked his charioteer.

"He is seeking liberation from suffering by renouncing his worldly life and practicing meditation in the forest," Channa answered.

Even in ancient times, whatever a parent tries to keep his child from, draws that child straight to it. Siddhartha snuck out of the palace one night at age twenty-nine to join the spiritual seekers in the forest and find what frees people from suffering. He shaved his head and took off his jewels, sending his servant back to the palace with these personal items, along with the promise that he would return someday.

Siddhartha spent the next six years doing various practices to release his mind from the demands of his body. The final ascetic practice he undertook was fasting, which he did until he was nothing but skin and bones. He realized that physical austerity was killing him, not bringing him closer to enlightenment. He left his ascetic friends and went down to the river where a young girl named Sujata gave him a bowl of rice and milk, which saved his life. He watched a musician tune a sitar, and realized his mind was like a sitar string, which only works when it is neither too tight nor too slack. The truth lies in the "middle way."

Siddhartha walked to a forest outside of Gaya. He spread his Kusha grass mat under a tree and vowed to sit there until he found enlightenment. He calmly watched his breath and then delved into his unconscious. The demon of illusion and ego, Mara, awakened. First, Mara sent his three sexy daughters to seduce him. They danced around him in lascivious splendor but Siddhartha sat and watched his breath until they dissolved away. Then Mara sent an army of demons at him. The demons shot poisoned arrows, which turned into flower blossoms that rained down instead. Mara then showed up as the Lord of Death. He stood over Siddhartha and bellowed "You can't awaken! You are going to die!"

Siddhartha saw that Mara was actually an aspect of himself. He touched the earth, and said "With the earth as my witness, I will not be led by ego, desire, and fear."

With that, he was truly free of suffering, and awakened into full enlightenment. He was called the Buddha after that, which means "Awakened One."

The Buddha sat in bliss for seven days. He then arose from his seat. He thought that what he had realized was too profound and subtle to teach. He walked toward Sarnath in complete silence for six weeks, until the gods begged him to share what he had learned with others. He found his ascetic friends in Sarnath and gave them his first teaching. These ascetics became his first disciples. As promised, he went home and reunited with his family. He went on to teach for forty years, building communities of monks, nuns, and lay people all over India and Nepal. He taught everyone, regardless of class, caste, or gender, which was in itself radical and new. His aunt became the first nun in India, ever. His teachings were recorded by his students and are known as the *sutras* and *tantras*. Many thousands of them still exist today. The Buddha lived 2600 years ago and there are 500 million Buddhists worldwide today, walking the middle way.

Sophia, with her usual impeccable timing, needed to poop on the train. Of course, she wanted me to come with her. We were booked on the extremely inexpensive Sleeper Class since we were traveling during daylight, and only for four hours, from Varanasi to Gaya. I regretted not spending the extra money for 3AC class the minute we boarded. The car was filthy, and disheveled men crowded near to gape at Bella and Sophia. I took Sophia and left my purse on the seat between Bella and Adam, so it wouldn't get dirty in the toilet.

Locking the toilet door, I assessed the closet's grimy surfaces. Sophia placed her feet on the metal footpads, pulled down her pants, and squatted over the crusty hole. I held her hands tightly to keep her balanced as the train jolted along. "This is a game," I told her. "It's called Squat over a Hole and Poop on a Rocking Train. You are *out* if you touch anything but my hands." Adam drifted off to sleep and Bella became engrossed in her book. While we played the game, the train pulled into a station, and a hand reached in through the wooden slats of the window and snatched my purse, with money, cell phone, sundry items, and my camera full of pictures.

Bella screamed with fright at the disembodied arm reaching across her through the window to grab my purse. When I heard her scream, I abandoned Sophia in the toilet with her pants down, so she screamed, too. Passengers pointed out the window, mumbling, "Gone, gone . . . sorry Madam." I visualized the pictures I had taken in Varanasi, which would never be seen again. Our family on the rooftop above the Ganges, the girls peering into flower-filled shrines, the Shiva baba living beneath our hotel, New Year's Eve.

"I'm sorry, Mommy," Bella said, as we stared out the window. "I feel so bad. I should have saved your purse. But I was scared, and it happened so fast."

"It's not your fault, Bella," I assured her. "It's mine. I should have never taken my purse off and left it next to an open window . . ."

Not much money was lost because I had followed Adam's advice to carry only a tiny bit of cash in my purse at any time, less than $20. *No one can slip my big pack with its hidden brick of money through slats in the window,* I thought. I tried to shake the whole thing off. We were in impoverished Bihar, after all. What was green forest in the Buddha's time was now a dry and dusty state that lagged behind the rest of India in social and economic development. *Pilgrimage. Sacrifice. Letting go.* We had discussed this.

We traveled the eight kilometers from the Gaya station to Bodh Gaya by auto-rickshaw. Oversized buses honked and swerved through the narrow roads, passing bikes, rickshaws, and pedestrians with only inches to spare. My stomach burned and I doubted the wisdom of coming here as a family.

Our rickshaw turned off the main street that runs through Bodh Gaya and bumped down a dirt road. The road noise diminished, and we passed a green field full of children playing cricket. Water buffalo grazed in a meadow beside two mud and thatch huts. Laundry on the line waved a rainbow of saris in the breeze. We turned down an even bumpier road. I thought the overloaded rickshaw would fall to pieces with all the jolting. We slowed down for a herd of goats led by a wizened shepherd. A sign that read Shantidevi Guesthouse hung beside a white home covered in blooming bougainvillea. A young man named Akash, with dazzling white teeth, waited at the gate. He led us into a tile courtyard full of flowers, and up the stairs to our room. The charm of the room, accented with antiques from Pondicherry, the pretty courtyard, and the quiet green road lifted my spirits. I squeezed Bella, who still felt bad. "It's okay Bella. It's been quite a day, but we are going to be all right."

Last time I had been in Bodh Gaya for barely thirty-six hours. This time our family stayed two weeks, so we could settle in. At first, I was worried about how we would do sharing one small room. But with the frenetic pace of India outside the guesthouse walls, we enjoyed the coziness of being together. It was like camping, only in a room instead of a tent. Mornings were intimate; we lay in bed describing our dreams. Bedtimes were full of flinging pillows and the girls making videos of each other jumping on the bed, and me asking them to stop because I was trying to write in my journal, while Adam missed the festivities by meditating out on the balcony.

I replaced my purse and its contents with goods from the local bazaar. Now I wore a *salwar* accessorized by an Indian purse, sunglasses, wallet, and even an Indian digital camera. I suddenly felt glad; now I looked like I really lived here, only my Birkenstocks came from elsewhere. Plus, our travel insurance was going to send us a check for the cost of the new camera. "We are becoming Indian," Bella observed, examining us in the bathroom mirror. She also wore a salwar, with her hair in a ponytail like Indian women, and her face free of makeup. "We need less personal space. I am getting used to sleeping in a bed with two other people and having Sophia sit on my lap when we go anywhere." I felt a surge of mother-pride for my middle schooler adapting to this new environment.

Adam had always been a light sleeper, so the girls and I shared the bouncy bed while he slept on a mat on the floor. This meant a complete hold on our sex life, but I got to watch my daughters sleep instead, like I did when they were little. In the early morning hours their somnolent faces were soft, lashes against plump cheeks, and I could see in them the babies that had slept in my arms for years.

To get to the Maha Bodhi park, we walked our dirt road past thatch-roofed huts and grazing water buffalo. Then we took bicycle rickshaws to the center of town. This stretch of the journey was bedlam: monks, villagers, tourist buses, camels, motorcycles, rickshaws, and pony carts competed for space on the narrow and dusty road. When we entered the park together the first time and viewed the towering stupa, we all felt it. The tangible aura of peace, the pull of devotion, the rainbow of people from around the world here for one reason—a holy connection to the tree where the Buddha sat. We watched pilgrims wrapped in robes and saris circle the stupa. Bella broke our collective silence, saying, "Wow. This is beautiful. There are a lot of Buddhists in the world besides Dad."

In the daytime the park was bright with millions of flower offerings and the colorful robes of monks, and they buzzed with chants and prayers. At the Bodhi tree itself, pilgrims rotated through constantly, either chanting in groups, sitting in silent meditation, or simply bowing with devotion. Teachers of various lineages and traditions gave lectures and read sutras to their students. Tibetan yogis sang their mantras in every nook and under every tree. When night fell, the crowds thinned and pastel-hued lights softly illuminated the monuments. The stones and trees were magical in the misty dark as we walked out. Bella echoed my exact thoughts two years ago: "This is like Buddhist Disneyland."

I ate at the Tibet Om Cafe last time, and I took the family to try it for dinner. We sat down to a meal of *mo-mos*, Tibetan dumplings, and *thentuk*, Tibetan noodle soup, and the girls exclaimed that they could eat this every night. So, we did, for the whole two weeks, with a revolving circle of new friends. The girls liked the eating-out lifestyle; they were as sick of my cooking as I was. Tibetan dinner was a great motivator to get them to the Maha Bodhi park each afternoon. We lingered at the cafe until late at night, developing an international community of friends: an Italian woman who had studied Buddhism in India for years, a handsome British ballet dancer turned monk who lived in Bhutan, a Chinese actor turned Buddhist filmmaker, a French yogi and his Argentinian girlfriend, a giant Swedish lama, and many Tibetans. People winter in Bodh Gaya to complete cycles of prayers or prostrations, to give or receive teachings, and to absorb the blessings from the holy site. Our conversations ranged from Buddhist wisdom to adventures in India travel. During these dinners I scribbled down travel tips in my notebook from these India veterans, which proved useful for months to come.

The seventeenth Karmapa was visiting Bodh Gaya, giving a week of teachings in his monastery. He was the second most revered spiritual leader of Tibet, beside the Dalai Lama. The sixteenth Karmapa passed away in 1983 and now his young reincarnation was in his mid-twenties again. Karmapa Ogyen Trinley Dorje was born in 1985 to a nomadic family in rugged eastern Tibet. At age seven, he was enthroned at Tsurphu Monastery, his traditional seat in Tibet. Ogyen was the first *tulku* (reincarnate) to be officially recognized by the Chinese government. Chinese press called him "Living Buddha"

The Mahabodhi Temple, A UNESCO World Heritage Site, has been a pilgrimage destination for over two thousand years.

and portrayed him as happily ensconced in the Chinese-controlled Tsurphu monastery.

I vaguely remembered hearing rumors that he was a "puppet" lama for the Chinese government who would help keep the Tibetan people obedient to Chinese rule. But that was not the case. In late 1999, fourteen-year-old Ogyen Trinley Dorje decided that the restrictions China placed on him were limiting his spiritual progress. The young teen planned a daring escape over the Himalayas in the middle of winter, telling only two adults about his plan, who then accompanied him. He evaded Chinese authorities at the border and made his way through Nepal and on to India. He arrived, to the astonishment of the Dalai Lama and other Tibetan leaders, in Dharamsala, India, (home of the exiled Dalai Lama) on January 5, 2000. His cold plate of food was still sitting, uneaten, outside his meditation room in Tibet.

We walked out to his monastery one morning, where a crowd of thousands of Tibetans and Chinese gathered in an airy pavilion that resembled an airplane hangar. We found space on a rug shared by extended Tibetan families, just before chanting and bowing began. Monks came by, pouring salty butter tea into cups and handing out doughy wheels of Tibetan bread. Adam handed out earbuds, which he plugged into his FM radio for English translation.

The Karmapa explained the meaning of the word *Buddha*: "The word for Buddha in Tibetan is *sangye. Sang* means 'negative habit patterns dispelled,' and *gye* means 'positive qualities, fully realized.' These positive qualities are already within everyone. The seeds of Buddhahood are already present, in all of us."

This idea that all beings have Buddha-nature, or the potential to awaken to enlightenment, is a foundation of the Buddhist path. You don't have to be special, born in India, from a good family, or a *man*. Everyone possesses the seeds of enlightenment, it just depends on whether a person cultivates them or not. I loved hearing that. It was always a good reminder for me, prone as I was to thinking I was a hopeless case, too busy with my materialistic life to ever make progress on a spiritual path. Our true nature, the Karmapa told us, is beyond the labels and judgments with which we separate each other. We are no different from our gurus. There is no separation between ourselves and other.

Finally, he talked about love and compassion, which are the basis for the Buddhist path. "The worst danger we face is not disaster, epidemic, or whatever. Becoming a society without compassion is the biggest danger of all. We need to help and love one another. We have a natural capacity for compassion, we are not like burned seeds that cannot sprout. Compassion is hardwired in us. Now we need to develop it and enter into a new kind of maturity."

On the walk back to town, Sophia asked, "What is a refugee?"

I took a deep breath and thought about how to approach this topic. I decided to start right here, with the Tibetans.

"Well, in 1959, the Chinese invaded Tibet, which had been Buddhist for a thousand years. The Chinese were Communist, so their party line was that religion is poison. They did not want people to practice Buddhism. Terrible things happened. Monasteries and holy sites in Tibet were destroyed. Lamas and monks were imprisoned for resisting China's rules. Still today, China occupies Tibet. The Tibetans that are here left their home, crossing the Himalayas to India to seek religious freedom. They walked over the Himalayas in winter, so the Chinese would be less likely to come after them. Many didn't survive the journey. Those that did arrived here penniless and with no home. Can you even imagine coming to India without any money for a place to stay or food to eat? They came seeking refuge from violence and persecution, hence the word *refugee*. India, despite all its own problems, has opened its doors to whoever can make it here from Tibet."

Sophia was astounded to learn that such things happen. That the people she greeted each day at the park, as well as the Dalai Lama and the Karmapa, had risked their lives, leaving their homeland for the sake of religious freedom. This was something she had never valued before, or known as a right that could be taken away. Bella expressed anger that America doesn't do anything about it.

We walked in silence. Tibetans were all around us, walking home from their days, selling prayer beads from pushcarts, spinning prayer wheels and mumbling mantras. Their calm, peaceful way was palpable.

"I really thought Buddhism was some weird thing only Dad did," Bella said. "I think I might be Buddhist too."

Jan 6
Dear Diary,

I am feeling very homesick right now. I am in a foul mood, and got in a fight with my mom, my sister, and my dad. Yesterday, school started for everyone. I haven't been getting much sleep because I keep checking the clock, calculating what time it is there, and imagining what everyone is doing. I especially miss John and Zoe. I spend way too much time thinking about them. Every night, I fall asleep and dream about them. It is very hard to feel happy right now, even though I know I should.

Love,
Bella

We were in Bodh Gaya for spiritual transformation, and Adam's clarity about that helped me stay the course and not obsess over how much fun the kids were having. I may have been the trip planner, but Adam was our spiritual guide. Adam's commitment to the Buddha's path was authentic and unwavering and had always been his first priority since I found him meditating under a tree almost twenty years before.

In California, I felt that sometimes Adam's spiritual focus conflicted with my (perhaps, over) concern with the details of being homeowners, business owners, and parents. In my skewed and biased memory, it seemed as if I got the kids ready for school every morning for years, while he meditated in his man-cave. Then, when he would suggest I try to meditate more, I'd feel my stomach burn. Here, with no house to maintain or school schedules to keep, we were on more equal footing. People back home in Chico sometimes confessed to me that they didn't really "get" Adam. Adam consistently saw things through the lens of Dharma, which did not always align with progressive Chico's secular culture. In Bodh Gaya, Adam was seen and understood for exactly who he was. I found myself appreciating him more, too.

I brought a cloth bundle of prayers and meditation instructions to India, guidance that I had been given over the years. At home I rarely tried to meditate. I was too easily distracted by a sink full of dishes, a floor covered with toys, and stacks of bills to pay. I was waiting for my pager to go off, or exhausted from being at a birth all night. My morning puja was making four breakfasts, three lunches, and coffee all at once, while using telepathic powers to remotely locate missing socks and homework. At night, when the girls were finally in bed, I was too sleepy to concentrate. Now, at the Maha Bodhi park, I was free of those responsibilities and I wanted to meditate. I strolled around the park looking for my place to sit. I stopped walking at the tree—the place where the Buddha sat and woke up to the true nature of things; the place where people have been meditating daily for 2600 years without a break.

I sat down and began the simplest of the Buddha's meditation instructions, in-and-out breathing. I watched my breath go in, and then I watched my breath go out. I counted six breaths and then started over at one. After a while, I felt calm, and could loosen my concentration on the breathing while still maintaining focus. *I am doing it, I am meditating! (Ha, ha, that ruined it.)* I started again and grew calm again. I heard the wind in the trees, and the soulful chants of Tibetans, Burmese, and Thai. Those sounds flowed through me without snagging my mind with thoughts, and filled me with rushes of bliss. I sat like that for some time, until thoughts started bouncing around. I became distracted by the people around me and by the discomfort in my legs. I worried about the girls getting bored. I pictured *thentuk* at the Tibet Om Cafe and started salivating. My meditation was finished, for now.

Another day I claimed a slab of stone on a different side of the stupa. I sat down, pulled out my notes, and skimmed them for guidance. I started reading *Four Thoughts that Turn the Mind Toward Dharma*. The first is appreciation for this precious human life. The second is the contemplation of impermanence, the third, the law of cause and effect (karma), and the last, the shortcomings of worldly life.

I thought about the second truth—impermanence. The Buddha taught that our lives are like dreams, fleeting, passing. We think we have forever, but we don't. We worry about the future and let the present pass us by. From the vantage point of this moment, my Chico life seemed completely unreal now. *Everything at home seemed so real and solid, but in only three short weeks it is all a vague memory. And when we return home, Bodh Gaya will be a dream to me. So, what is actually real?*

I sat with that question and had no answer. What the Buddha realized, what we call enlightenment, is real and unchanging, that much I knew. There is something beyond the impermanence of worldly life. There is something about each present moment, which cannot be held onto or grasped. As soon as you start thinking, the planning or remembering begins, and the moment is lost. I wished I could stay in the present, and I remembered the Karmapa's words: *The seeds of Buddhahood are already present, in all of us.* That gave me hope. *The truth of things is way beyond your thoughts.*

Will the girls find Bodh Gaya boring and complain that they have nothing to do? There was nothing here that fit the American idea of family fun—no amusement parks, no places to swim or play. None of our new acquaintances had children with them. But Sophia and Bella found ways to make their own kind of pilgrimage.

For the first few days we were followed around the park by five Indian monks Bella's age. Bella got annoyed, and finally turned, faced them, and asked what was up. This broke the ice and they excitedly introduced themselves. They were local kids from Hindu families, who had taken the orange robes of Theravadin monks to receive an education in the monastery. They were eager to practice their English, which was sweetly melodic and old-fashioned, full of "Madams" and "Good Sirs."

Bella would sit with the preteen monks in a semi-circle on the grass. They meditated together, and then shared stories about the Buddha's life. The boys knew what the stones and monuments in the park signified. "This is where the Buddha slept for two nights when he first arrived. And that stone marks where he sat for the first two weeks, until he changed and went to sit under the Bodhi tree. And that spot is where he stayed after." Even Adam was impressed. Then they spent hours talking about America.

Bella wanted to learn how to meditate. She asked for instructions from our Swedish friend, Lama Nils, and his teacher, a wandering Tibetan yogi named Lama Gelek. Lama Gelek spoke only Tibetan, but his eyes were lit on fire, and he was always grinning. Bella told us that sitting next to him sent waves of joy through her. I wondered if that was what it was like for the disciples of the actual Buddha. When we sat by the Bodhi tree with Nils and Lama Gelek and practiced a meditation, I felt it too.

Every day we stopped at the market to buy snacks for the afternoon: packages of cookies, chocolates, crackers, oranges, and tiny sweet bananas. Sophia took hers and scrambled up to the ledge on top of a small stone tower. She sat up there for hours drawing, snacking, and meditating. Below Sophia's tower Tibetans did their prostrations on wooden boards: muscular young men in tee shirts, monks and nuns in their robes, mothers and old women in woolen dresses, or *chubas*. Sophia became friendly with them and climbed down at intervals to place chocolates and cookies on the personal altars of the people around her.

I asked her one day what she meditated on while sitting on her ledge.

"Well I listen to the birds sing, I feel the tree energy, and I feel this warmth in my heart," she answered.

I brought the first Harry Potter book all the way from home, and surprised Sophia with it one morning. She took one look and was overwhelmed by the small print and number of pages.

"No way can I read that," she told me.

"It's okay. I will read a page, and then you will read a page. We will do it like that," I replied.

And so, it began. At bedtime, I would read one page aloud, and then she would stumble slowly through one page, aloud. Exhausted by the effort, she would pass the book back to me.

"Good job," I would say, encouragingly. And my dyslexic daughter would squint at me, knowing I was being nice. Sometimes Bella would read with her in the mornings, one page on and one page off.

One sunny afternoon, Sophia brought her Harry Potter to the Maha Bodhi park in her day pack, pulled it out, and sat under a tree to read. I could tell she was deep in the story, not just stumbling over the words.

"Look Adam. Sophia is *reading*. By her own choice."

I couldn't help myself. After a few minutes I went over. "Sophia, what are you doing?"

"I was too impatient to wait until bedtime, so I am going to read whenever I want to, from now on."

And so, she did, in restaurants while waiting for the food, on buses, trains, and boats. We traded in Harry Potter book after Harry

Potter book in used bookstores all over India. By the combined bless-ings of the Buddha and the wizards, her dyslexia was cured.

January 8, 2014

Dear Diary,

Today I visited a Tibetan Buddhist leader who is the reincarnation of a very holy man named Dilgo Khenste Rinpoche. When my dad was twenty-four, he visited Dilgo Khenste here in India. Soon after, Dilgo Khen-ste passed away. The young man we had the honor of meeting today is supposedly the reincarnation. As we walked in, I felt a rush of warmth wash over me. We knelt down and bowed to him. He looked at Dad with ancient eyes in a baby face and said "I have met you before." This man remembered him from his past life. I'm shocked.

Love, Bella

CHAPTER 8

STILL IN BODH GAYA

An American veterinarian took me and the girls to meet Rajnee the Elephant one afternoon. We passed through a peeling archway on the edge of town and walked to the back of a Hindu ashram where an elephant stable stood beside the river. I had told the girls that at some point on this trip we might ride one of India's legendary elephants. Elephants are intertwined with Indian culture. Centuries ago, India teemed with wild Asian elephants. Today, fifty percent of the world's wild elephants live in India's diminishing forests. India evolved with domesticated elephants used for transportation, labor, and ceremony. Cave paintings dated as early as 6000 BC depict domesticated elephants. Ancient royals traveled on elephants and rode them into battle. It is said that one Mughal emperor had 100,000 captive elephants. When the god Shiva cut off his son's head by mistake, he fixed things by plopping an elephant head on him. Thus Ganesh, the elephant-headed Hindu god renowned for removing obstacles, was born. In modern India, a few hundred elephants are still used in Hindu festivals and parades.

Rajnee was a temple elephant, kept for parades and religious celebrations. Temple elephants are living symbols of sacredness, loyalty, and status. Rajnee's *mahout*, or caretaker, a slip of a weathered old man, slept in the stable near her on a straw mattress. Elephants prefer to live among elephant companions, and Rajnee had a male companion elephant, who happened to be away visiting another temple. Rajnee's mahout bathed her and walked her in the dry riverbed daily.

The mahout already knew the young veterinarian and welcomed us with hand gestures. He led us to where Rajnee stood chomping on leafy branches. We tentatively held bananas to her, and her dexterous trunk snatched them from our hands. Bella and Sophia squealed. Rajnee was fascinatingly alien: wrinkled leather skin, colossal floppy ears, feet like boulders, and her inquisitive, roving trunk that seemed to have a mind of its own. She had a giant third eye painted on her forehead. Elephants are massive but gentle, and obviously intelligent. Little Sophia drew closer and closer until she was hugging and stroking her, then Bella followed. I snapped away with my new Indian camera. The Hindi-speaking mahout, using a young man as a translator, offered to let us ride her tomorrow for a fee. My stomach flipped and flopped at the idea but Sophia batted her eyes at me and grinned, which settled the matter.

When we arrived at her stables the following day, the mahout was waiting for us. He gave Rajnee a command, and she kneeled down to the ground. He threw some blankets on her back and tied these on with rope that went around her belly. He climbed on so he sat in the crook between her head and neck and gestured to us to get on behind him. We awkwardly climbed on. Bella and Sophia sat squeezed between the mahout in the front, and me at the back. The mahout spoke to Rajnee again in a guttural voice, and she stood up. Her front legs went up first, and we screamed as we were tilted backwards with nothing to hold onto. No reins, no harness, nothing. Then her hind legs straightened and her back evened out. I wanted to voice my concern, to ask about safety, mention my fear of heights, but we had no common language. We were riding the elephant, and that was it.

Rajnee moved, slowly, out onto the river bank. Elephants ambulate with an incredible swaying motion. I felt her rhythm and settled into it. For a time, we felt like queens, riding high, observing life along the river as we passed. Women squatted with copper pots around a water pump. Children played cricket in a barren field. Cows stared with melancholic eyes. An altar to Ganesh was bright with marigold-blossom offerings. Rajnee approached a set of steep stone steps which led to the dry riverbed and turned to descend them. Leaning forward as we went down was fine, but I worried about coming back up, tilting backwards with nothing to hold onto. I shifted around, looking for something besides Bella's shirt to hold. I could almost reach the knot of rope that held the blankets we were sitting on. But it seemed to me that the frayed knot could easily come undone.

Rajnee took her walk across the vast riverbed and I tried not to fixate on the return climb. The people we passed conversed in Hindi with the mahout. I imagined they were saying, "Wow, today is your lucky day, isn't it? Three foreign girls to ride with you, ah? What will you do with the money tonight?" I hoped they are not saying "Gee, look at this. This would never pass American safety standards. I wonder if these girls will manage to stay on? Remember what happened to the last bunch who rode?"

Rajnee turned around and headed back to the ashram. My heart raced as the angle of her back slanted dangerously on the first step. As she swayed and tilted up the stairs, I clung to Bella's sweatshirt to avoid falling off. I would be the first to slide backwards, falling fifteen feet to crack my back on the stone steps below. It seemed inevitable. *I suppose that if I must die, Bodh Gaya is a good place to do it. All I can reasonably hope for is that my daughters won't follow.* But then we were at the top and I was still on, clutching Bella's shirt with pale, clammy fists. On the walk back into town I floated, reborn, mostly the same me but a little fiercer.

Sometimes staying in Bodh Gaya felt like hanging onto that elephant. Bodh Gaya was an international hub of Buddhist activities located in the middle of the poorest part of India. The contrast between the serene beauty of the park and the abject poverty of the surrounding villages was stark. Our Swedish friend, Nils, told me that even a person who loves India will have occasional, intense moments when they want to get out. Plenty of people do that. A sizable portion of travelers cut their India trips short and return home or go elsewhere after a couple weeks. The diarrhea and the poverty were more than they bargained for, and they tell everyone

Sophia and Bella make friends with Rajnee, Bodh Gaya's resident temple elephant, at a river-side Ashram in Bodh Gaya, Bihar, India.

who asks that "INDIA" stands for "I'll Never Do it Again."

We faced a circle of beggars each day outside the Maha Bodhi park. Dirty children with matted hair, elders with hollow cheeks, and women with babies in their arms lined the walkway to the gate. People came from far and wide to beg at the park gates because beggars and pilgrims have a symbiotic relationship. It is believed that the merit of pilgrimage is increased by giving away money at holy sites. Many pilgrims from Taiwan, Japan, China, and Korea come to Bodh Gaya for only a day or two, staying in the couple of luxury hotels, and riding in behemoth, air-conditioned buses. They get off those buses with zip-locked bags of coins, ready to give to the beggars as part of the planned experience. For those of us staying here longer term, we were not organized to give out money daily for weeks, and when we did have spare coins, not having enough to give to every single beggar became a problem.

I carried coins to drop into the bowls of the elderly and disabled, but I tried not to give money to children. Our Tibet Om clan explained that the child beggars usually have either their parents or a pimp lurking nearby to collect their earnings. They don't keep any of the money. Some said that the babies are rented out to women so they can hold them while they beg. I refused to participate in the use of children for begging. But on our last day, I bought bags of fruit, snacks, and candy which Bella and Sophia handed out to the children. There was an impulsive part of me that was tempted to bring out my brick of cash from the bottom of my backpack and take it to the beggars. *I could give it all away in a total act of renunciation and generosity!* Even then, the problem of poverty for the people I gave it to would not be solved. And our trip would be over.

I searched for some way to be of service instead, and found a soup kitchen run by the Karmapa's monastery. Sophia and I spent several afternoons volunteering there. It was a free lunch program for villagers, located across the road from a free medical clinic where Adam donated his time providing acupuncture treatments. The meal was served in a garden, with a colossal statue of a standing Buddha watching over us. Sophia was given the job of greeter and hand washer. When villagers arrived, she said *"Namaste, Hadoo! Hadoo!"* (Hello, wash hands first!) and then pumped washing water for them. People sat in rows in the garden and we handed out plates made from woven banana leaves. Mountains of rice, dal, and vegetables were devoured, and children left with full tummies.

Gina, a beautiful Italian woman, was doing 100,000 prostrations. On the Tibetan Buddhist path there are practices that are known as "foundational." Like tilling the soil before you plant, they prepare the mind for enlightenment. Doing 100,000 prostrations over the course of several months, or years, is one of these foundations. Gina spent five hours at the stupa every day, bowing to the ground on a smooth wooden board, then standing again, while saying a brief prayer. She used a *mala,* or string of prayer beads, in her hand to count, and could do four or five hundred each day. A whole section of the park was filled by these wooden boards, where people, mostly Tibetan, did prostrations. She was preparing to receive the highest teachings of the Tibetan Vajrayana tradition, the *Dzogchen.*

I had been given prostration instructions fifteen years ago in America. I had occasionally attempted a prostration or two but felt so silly doing them I quickly gave up. I mean, *who bows to anything in America?* Here in Bodh Gaya I was surrounded by people doing prostrations. It did not seem so silly. One afternoon I hemmed and hawed and then sheepishly asked Gina, "Um, do you think . . . that . . . maybe I could try a few prostrations on your board?"

"Of course," she replied, with her thick Italian accent. "You know, the Vietnamese nun whose board is next to mine is gone for the week. Why not use hers? I will set you up with sliders and show you how to do it."

We walked over to the boards and she showed me how to use cushions for my knees and oven mitt-like sliders to glide my hands across the board as I lay completely down. "Thank you," I said, as I sipped my water and prepared to prostrate.

"Om Ah Hung," I whispered as I clasped my hands together at my third eye, throat, and heart. These three syllables stand for the three jewels: Buddha (awakened one), Dharma (the way), and Sangha (spiritual community). I bowed to the ground, the sliders allowing my hands to move easily forward. Then I stood. I did that about five more times and stopped, panting. Several Tibetans watched me and tried not to chuckle at my lack of endurance. They nodded at me encouragingly. The girls wandered over.

"Wow, Mom. That is pretty special."

"Okay Bella, that's enough. Go away please. And don't watch me."

My children wandered off and I tried again. "Om Ah Hung." Kneel, bow to the ground, rise. Again. "Om Ah Hung." Kneel, bow to the ground, rise. I fell into a rhythm. I felt like I was surrendering something each time I lay down.

Bow. *I don't know how to be a Buddha.* Rise.
Bow. *I don't know what enlightenment is.* Rise.
Bow. *I don't know how to save the world.* Rise.
Bow. *I don't know how to stop the wars.* Rise.

Each time I lay down, I imagined I was laying down the *trying,* the *attempt* to have all the answers. That felt remarkably *good.*

Bow. *Look Buddha, God, Great Spirit, I know I don't know, and I am asking for guidance.* Rise.

Bow. *Asking for guidance.* Rise.

Bow. *For guidance. please.* Rise.

Bow, *I don't know how to keep my mind peaceful, not get angry and irritated at little stupid things.* Rise.

Bow. *Angry. Little. Things.* Rise.

Bow. *I am cranky and selfish.* Rise

Bow. *Help.* Rise

Bow. *I lay down the illusion of "having it together."* The illusion of perfection that I have made with our lovely house, above-average children, and happy Facebook posts. Rise.

Bow. *Don't even get me started . . . I am laying that shit down.* Rise.

Bow. *Lay that shit down!* Rise.

Bow. *I admit . . . I am totally imperfect.* Rise.

Bow. *I surrender. I'm ready to change.* Rise.

Bow. *Please show me the way.* Rise.

I kept going now. Body and mind were working together. Now, as I bowed down each time I laid down something else: materialism, arrogance, greed—the illusions we invest so much of our precious time into. Each time I rose, I stood for my search for truth. I stood up clear, elated, feeling like I was getting closer to what I was looking for. An old Tibetan yogi waved me over. He blessed me, mumbling mantras and tapping my head with his worn prayer beads. I felt his taps all the way to my toes. Then he handed me a chocolate bar and an orange. Behind me, my girls had found boards to use and started bowing too.

I suddenly imagined the Buddha, staring at his navel, laughing. We try so hard, when the truth is so simple, so free.

Prince, the most chatty and exuberant of Bella's teen monk-friends, handed her a letter written on lined paper in pink marker. The letter said,

> Hello. I am Prince. I love you too much. I want you allot. You are my first girl came into my life. I can not live without you. See you soon my sweet hart. Tell me face to face me alone I love you. When I saw first time in the temple you are likefull for me. See you my sweet hard, my lovely friend. Love is the life.

Bella was delighted by the letter and read it to us over and over again. Then she let him down gently, explaining that we were leaving in a couple days, and he should keep his monk robes and study hard at school. He reluctantly agreed. She folded up the letter and taped it into her journal. Four years later, they would still be Facebook friends.

I snuck out of bed without waking anyone, threw on clothes, and went outside. It was our last morning in Bodh Gaya. The water buffalo eyed me as I crossed the cold, misty field. A woman stood outside the mud and thatch hut, feeding her sweater-clad goats. On the main road I found a stall I had passed by but never seen. Adam had said I would find exceptional chai over here, at No. 1 Tea.

A man with a gold tooth and an enormous belly beckoned me over. A faded sign told me that I had found the No. 1 Tea in Bodh Gaya, "World's Best and Finest." The man cooked over a coal fire on a handmade mud and straw oven. A fragrant potion of tea, cardamom, sugar, and milk simmered in a steel pot. He ground herbs with a stone mortar and pestle and tossed those in, and then gestured to one of the broken plastic chairs in front of his shop. I sat and watched as he poured some of the mixture into a smaller kettle and then poured it back and forth between two kettles, until it was frothy. He placed a warm glass in my cold hand.

I sipped the creamy, fragrant brew, and decided that this was indeed the No. 1 Tea. How had I never seen it, walking by here daily for two weeks? *In India, there is always something new to discover, even on the last day.* Bodh Gaya slowly came to life. Trucks packed with school children sped by. Tibetan families walked together to town, spinning hand-held prayer wheels. Lots and lots of Buddhist monks, piled on motorcycles and crammed into rickshaws, were off to morning prayers. A rickshaw filled to the brim with cauliflower went whistling by. A family of goats strolled past. My belly was warm and my head abuzz from the tea. I felt proud of us, my family, for doing well during our two weeks here. Of all the places we would go in India, Bodh Gaya was one of the most impoverished, and at the same time, the most holy. *India teaches me, again and again, that the categories into which I like to neatly divide things don't hold up.*

CHAPTER 9

BODH GAYA TO DELHI TO KERALA

The Gaya train station teemed with life. People huddled in groups on blankets, covering nearly the entire floor. Stray dogs wandered through. A sad-eyed cow gazed at us. We kept moving, barely avoiding the blankets and the bodies as we navigated through with our bulky packs. People stared at us, the lone Caucasian family amidst the hullabaloo, as though we were apparitions from another world. We certainly were. A sign said "2AC waiting room this way" and we headed for it.

The waiting room had chairs, although most were occupied. We found two seats side by side, and the four of us squeezed in, India-style. Mustachioed men walked through with kettles of steaming chai and Dixie cups, singing out "Chai! Chai! Garam chai!" We drank multiple five-rupee cups while I read aloud from *Lonely Planet* about white sand beaches in green, easy-going Kerala. Excitement bubbled through me as I read about South India. I am a firm believer in balance, where children are concerned. And I am a firm believer in beaches, where I am concerned. After two weeks studying Buddhism in Bihar, it was time for relaxation.

Amy, Ananya, Lalli, and Vandana welcomed us home. Lalli and Vandana had prepared their family's cherished *paratha* recipe: potato pancakes chock-full of vegetables, and fragrant, but not spicy, seasonings. We ate them dipped in homemade yogurt, with grapes and apples that had been cleaned in a multi-step, multi-hour process rendering them edible, skin and all, to tender-tummied Americans. Between bites, we shared stories of our experiences in Bodh Gaya. Adam gave Lalli a gold-embossed prayer card from the Karmapa's monastery. When Adam visited her home months later, it was on her family's altar, in a place of honor beside her family's traditional Hindu deities.

"Lighter, lighter, bring the bare minimum," we reminded ourselves as we emptied out our packs and put back only the essentials. Now we knew that seeing India by train involved not only lots of walking but also running, climbing stairs, and squeezing through crowds. Our destination, the equatorial South, favored packing light. We dug swimsuits, sandals, and sunscreen out of our two suitcases and put shoes and jackets away. Adam's ukulele was tucked into a suitcase. Ananya kneeled beside our suitcases, taking our things out to examine as fast as we packed them in.

We each carried a few items besides clothes. Adam had a foam pad and lightweight sleeping bag that squished down to the size of a bread loaf. When our hotel room only had one bed, three of us could share and someone could sleep on the floor. We saved thousands of rupees over the months because we could manage with one room. Although we found bottled water wherever we went, he brought a SteriPEN and iodine tablets, just in case. Of course, he could not be without his Dharma texts and pujas, and a bag of Chinese herbs. I had the fat cosmetics bag with emergency meds, herbal bug spray, and toothpaste. We each had our silk sleeping sacks, headlamps, cameras, and books. Sophia traveled with a DSi game, several small journals, and colored pens and pencils. In her bag, Bella had an iPod and a mini-laptop, which we all used to check our emails when there was Wi-Fi. The math workbooks had to come. We briefly admired the other home-school supplies we had brought, but, with Ananya's help, we put them back in the suitcases.

Amy took us to an art opening at the India National Gallery of Modern Art in the evening.

"This is going to be quite the event," she told us. "Subodh Gupta is an old friend of mine, and his installation art pieces have become an international phenomenon."

The palatial stone museum was set behind a vast lawn, in a neighborhood of politicians' mansions. A party was already humming on the manicured grounds. Under a white tent, speakers acknowledged and thanked people to vast applause and the flash of the paparazzi's cameras. The other guests wore elegant combinations of Indian and French-inspired couture. Fine jewelry glittered under the lights. I flashed to the image of people huddled on the ground in the Gaya railway station the previous night and shuddered at the startling contrast.

We wandered out of the tent and onto the lawn. I grabbed Adam's arm and said in wonderment, "Look at that! It's a life-sized replica of the Bodhi Tree!"

We walked toward it. The enormous tree appeared to be made of glass or jewels, so beautifully was it lit up in the dark night. But as we got closer, the true materials from which it was made became obvious: welded together stainless-steel pots, pans, kettles, and ladles.

Subodh Gupta grew up in a rural village in Bihar, not far from Bodh Gaya. He used stainless-steel kitchen items central to life in an Indian village as the materials for his sculptures and installation pieces. His art celebrated the centrality of home and hearth and women's work in Indian rural culture, while creating giant works with more universal themes. An entire room inside the museum was full of pots and pans welded together to create an elaborate dripping water feature. Other sculptures were made from cast-off motorcycle and rickshaw parts. The exhibit even contained a hut made entirely of cow dung patties, because cow dung patties are used for cooking fuel in rural India. I watched cosmopolitan art critics in stiletto heels strolling in and out of the cow dung hut and marveled at how this artwork was bridging the two worlds of India

I knew—village life in rural Bihar and the cosmopolitan Delhiites of my sister's circle.

"I am touched," I told Subodh, when Amy introduced us. "I wandered Bodh Gaya, peeking into village neighborhoods where women cooked and did the wash outside their thatched huts. There was something timeless and beautiful about them, as if they were living works of art. And here are pieces of that village life, literally turned into works of art!"

I stood before the tall bespectacled artist, dashingly handsome in his crisp white shirt, black skinny jeans, and shiny black shoes, wishing I could put that gush of words back in. I was sure I sounded presumptuous, colonialist, and offensively white and privileged. *Who am I to comment on his ancestral home, to find rural poverty enchanting to behold?* I thought, embarrassed and appalled. But he thanked me and surrounded me in a warm hug.

"You understand," he said.

"Thank you for going IndiGo, Asia's fastest growing low-cost carrier," said the high-pitched, lilting voice over a crackling intercom. "If you need anything, our SpiceGirls are here for you." Wearing wigs of short-bobbed hair, theatrical makeup, and short (for India) skirts ending at the knee, the young SpiceGirls were obviously the hippest flight crew in India's skies. Sophia spent the flight time with them in the back of the plane where they fawned over her and gave her free soda.

I awoke from a nap to watch as the plane began its descent. Green coconut palm trees covered the land to the horizon. Beside the emerald jungle, the Arabian Sea glittered pale blue. We landed in a minuscule pink airport, on a landing strip carved out of the jungle. The name Thiruvananthapuram seemed bigger than the place. I thought about what I had heard about Kerala from Amy and my guide books.

"Where North India has intense, masculine energy, South India is relaxed and feminine."

"Kerala is cleaner and greener than the rest of India; it is like a different country."

"Kerala has the highest literacy rate in India, a 600-year-old matriarchal culture, and has been run by democratically-elected communists since 1957."

"South India has not had the dramatic, bloody history that North India had. The Muslim invasions of the Mughal empire never made it this far south. Kerala has never been invaded in its thousands of years of history, except recently by tourists."

When we stepped off the plane, no one pushed. There were no crowds. No drivers jostled to get our fare at the airport exit. At a desk labeled PRE-PAID TAXI STAND a woman in a golden sari bobbled her head at us. We told her where we were going, paid her, and were given a pink receipt. We stepped outside and the heat slapped us into its warm wet hug. Trickles of sweat ran from multiple body parts simultaneously.

A single driver sauntered towards us. Keralans move slowly, perhaps as an adaptation to the heat. This was, after all, their winter. The famous Indian head-bobble, which originates in Kerala, is an extension of the swaying, sensuous way South Indians move altogether. Our male driver wore a pink skirt that ended above his knobby knees, a look I found entirely endearing. We soon discovered that Keralan men, young and old, wear these skirts, or *lungis*, instead of pants.

We were headed to the beach resort town of Varkala. A surge of anxiety shot through me, as I hoped this would be the beach holiday I had always dreamed of. Over the years, friends had gone to Thailand, Costa Rica, Bali, and Mexico to return tan and healthy with stories of warm seas, tropical fruit, and affordable accommodations. We camped on the northern California or Oregon coast during summers, but the frigid waters of the North Pacific bite tender feet like ice, and the wind that blows keeps us in our coats, even in July. Our taxi wound through lush jungles and over bridges spanning lazy waterways. Canoes cruised along those waters. The villages were carved out of the jungle. The reds and pinks of the buildings, the green of the trees, and the bright blue sky were outrageously vivid after the muted colors of the dusty North Indian countryside. Hindu temples stood on every corner, decorated with brightly-painted, elaborate statues of gods, elephants, lotuses, swirls and whorls. Altars graced the bases of the larger trees along the road. The road itself, clear of rubbish, traffic, and cows, felt like a runway to heaven.

I had researched Kerala beaches months ago. I picked Varkala because it was not over-developed with large hotels like some other beaches, nor too isolated either. I had found this resort and paid for eight days based on TripAdvisor reviews. At $35 a night it was the most expensive place we would stay in India. Adam had balked at the price, but with a swimming pool it seemed worth it to me.

"Where's the pool?" the girls begged to know, the second we arrived.

I asked a waiter in the hotel café about the pool and he bobbled his head. Following his glance, I took the girls down the path to a blue-tiled swimming pool surrounded by flowering trees and mermaid statues. Children played in the pool while adults sipped tall, fruity drinks in lounge chairs. The place was not crowded, nor deserted either. It was just right. A sunburned Brit pointed to a gate and told us that the beach was a two-minute walk that way.

We jumped in the pool. After our swim we followed a dirt road out the back gate where a few homes were tucked in among banana trees. Several of them advertised AYURVEDIC MASSAGE HERE. Sundresses and hats were sold from stalls along the path. Past the Chill Out Juice Bar we rounded a curve and came to the top of a high cliff that protected the actual beach from development. The beach was down a steep flight of stairs. The sand was white and soft, and the blue sea formed into body-surfing waves.

"I did it—I found paradise!" I said to Adam, feeling like a rock star travel agent and cruise director.

One look at him and I could tell he missed Bodh Gaya. He felt home there among the Buddhists, and now we were here as tourists. He would have been happy to have stayed in Bodh Gaya for another month. Or maybe forever.

"Paradise is a state of mind," he said softly.

Jan 19, 2014

Dear Diary,

Hoe. Lee. Crap. I have died and gone to heaven. We are in be-you-tee-ful Varkala. Sunny, hot weather. Clean air. Cleaner surroundings. More colorful everything. Warm beaches with crystal clear water and coconut trees waving. It is soooo lovely here. The hotel has a massive blue pool and we have fresh seafood every night for dinner. I am not homesick at all.

Love, Bella.

The days rolled in and out. We went from the pool to the beach and back to the pool. Evenings we watched the red sun dip into the sea against a fiery sky. Then we dined in candlelit, seaside cafés. Moments were like postcards sent to me from my tropical vacation dreams. One afternoon the four of us swam together for hours. We flung ourselves into oncoming waves and rode them far into the shore, getting sand-burns on our bellies. Some days I read by the pool while the girls choreographed water ballets like I did with Amy as a child. When we were thirsty on the beach a woman would come by with a basket of coconuts for coconut-water drinks.

We befriended another family staying at our hotel. Reggie was an Indian dentist, raised in Mumbai. His wife Gemma was British, and they were raising their three boys, close to our girls' ages, in London. We made easy connections with each other and the girls were glad to have other kids to play with. We took outings to remote beaches with them and went to dinners together. In Bodh Gaya, Bella would wake up in the night to wonder what her friends were doing *right now* at Chico Junior High—what was she missing out on? But in Varkala, she felt that her friends back home were missing out. She posted photos on Instagram each day and the envious responses from friends boosted her spirits.

But Adam was right of course, paradise *is* a state of mind. The tourist vibe began to wear on us after the initial dazzle wore off. Wealthy foreigners played and natives worked; this is the reality of any developing-world resort destination. A ten-minute walk down the beach took us away from the tourists in bikinis and speedos to where an ancient Hindu temple stood beside a sacred spring, holy water gurgling out of the cliff. Local families, dressed in bright saris and pastel lungis, came down to that beach for blessings from the springs and a fully-clothed splash in the sea. Swimsuits reveal too much of one's body for the modest culture here. Adam and I also found we could walk twenty minutes inland to the actual Varkala village. We explored the narrow streets, shopping for fruit at the fruit stands and lunching at hole-in-the wall *dhabas,* mostly frequented by rickshaw drivers. Adam came home with a pink lunghi one day, and then wore it for the rest of our Kerala stay.

Sophia never got homesick, but then she got *sick* sick. The first day she was mildly sick, jumping out of the pool to run to the toilet. She nibbled on something here and there, and I made sure she stayed hydrated. The following day the vomiting started. Now it was coming out both ends, and I began to worry. This kid weighed barely fifty pounds, so she didn't have anything to spare. But I figured that, like with most stomach bugs, we were still on a "this will quickly run its course" trajectory. She ate nothing that day but Adam's herbs and Sprite. The third day the vomiting stopped, so I thought she was getting better, but then she was feverish through the night. Adam and I decided we would take her to a doctor if she was not better in the morning. Fevers fight off illnesses, I thought, during that mostly sleepless night. This should definitely be the end of it. I lay in our bed beside her burning body, listening to her rapid breathing and talking myself out of the dread that tried to force its way into my mind.

The following morning, she listlessly lay beside the pool. When I looked in the toilet to examine the strange gray sludge coming out of my daughter, that was it. "Time to seek medical attention!" I thought, shaking, thinking I might throw up, myself. I was about to go arrange that when Reggie, our friend from Mumbai, came by. He thought she had dysentery and gave me pediatric antibiotics to treat it. "If it is bacterial, it will clear up quickly," he told me. "If it is amoebas, that is another story." I looked up dysentery on Bella's laptop and agreed with the diagnosis. I skipped the parts about amoebas, not wanting to even consider that possibility unless we had to. I fed her a bubble-gum flavored dose of antibiotics, and within a couple of hours she sat up and said she would like to take a swim. The diarrhea stopped and she guzzled down two bottles of Sprite. A second dose that afternoon, and she regained her appetite.

"I am so ravenous, I could eat an entire roast chicken!" she told us that evening.

We had been vegetarian since our arrival in India. With unreliable electricity in most places, keeping meats properly refrigerated was not assured. Additionally, more than forty percent of Indians are strictly vegetarian, and others living on the coasts are pescatarian, meaning they eat fish. In many places only "pure veg" food was available. Nonetheless, Adam said, "Okay, let's go get you one."

We strolled down the promenade, found the finest restaurant there was, and ordered a roast chicken. Chickens in India are scrawny, bony things, but good for her word, Sophia ate all of it. She took her time, and between bouts of eating she chirped to us about this and that in her happy, high-pitched voice. I sat there watching her and listening to that cheerful chatter, wanting to cry from both exhaustion and relief. If there has ever been an appropriate use of an antibiotic, this is it, I thought. I was glad that this antibiotic had come from India itself, and I wanted to think that all mothers in India had access to medicine like this, if their children needed it. I wasn't sure about that, but I hoped and then fervently prayed so.

One evening we went to a temple festival in a neighboring village, on the advice of our hotel manager. A hired rickshaw whistled us through the twilit jungle. The driver killed the engine beside a bridge, where the sound of faint drumming lured us across the darkness and onto the main road of a village. People lined the village street, strings of lights and torches glowed warm and colorful, and massive stacks of speakers pumped out music at decibel levels unknown to the Western world. In front of one house an altar was lit up by a person-sized candelabra. Someone in the doorway of the house pointed us to a narrow staircase up to the roof, "Come up, come up!"

From the roof, we watched the parade arrive. First came a drum troupe dressed in white, stepping in unison and pounding their drums in a frenetic rhythm. They stopped at the altar below us and played an impressive set. The girls and I bounced ecstatically to the music, while the family whose roof we were standing on filmed us with their cell phones. An odd group of women danced sensually before the all-male drummers. The dancers wore heavy make-up and had strangely masculine bodies cloaked in saris.

I realized what they were and leaned into Adam to say "Those are eunuchs!"

Adam: "Eunuchs?"

Me: "Eunuchs. I read about them. In a culture where gender roles are so clearly defined, their presence at rites and festivals is auspicious."

Sophia, screaming in her squeaky voice: "What is a EUNUCH?"

Me, avoiding the topic of castration for now: "A man dressed as a woman."

Bella, with eye-roll: "*MOM!*"

The drumming reached a fever pitch, and then abruptly stopped. The troupe marched away. Behind them came a series of two-story tall animatronic Hindu gods. Each god was pulled by a truck, and had strobe lights, music, and robotic moving parts. I recognized Rama and Sita, hero and heroine of the Ramayana, plus Ganesh, the elephant-headed god; Lord Shiva; and Hanuman, the Monkey God. Each one stopped in front of the blazing altar below us and enacted its piece of a story. The Hanuman god stood twenty feet tall before us and then tore his chest open with a roaring "JAI SHRI RAM!" and a puff of smoke, to reveal Rama and Sita sitting inside his heart. Sophia screamed and buried her face in my salwar.

After the gods came male spinners and dancers wearing elaborate costumes and headdresses of peacocks and deities. More drummers followed, and another group of dancing eunuchs. Behind them, as the grand finale, came elephants. Twenty of them walked single file, adorned with golden head-ornaments, garlands of flowers, and bright pastel body paint from head to wrinkled toe. We thanked the family whose roof we shared and ran downstairs to stroll alongside an elephant to where our driver was waiting.

By American standards, this village was impoverished. Tiny, simple houses, dusty dirt roads, unreliable electricity, barely a storefront or two. Yet the villagers must have pooled their resources for this religious festival, and probably others as well. They had transformed their village into a place of magic and beauty, which they enjoyed collectively, in the common space. How different this is from American Christmas, I thought, where each family celebrates behind its own walls, according to its own means.

CHAPTER 10

KERALA BACKWATERS TO AMRITAPURI

Jan 26

Dear Diary,

Unless you have been on an India local train, you have never felt claustrophobia. People take up every square inch. They pack themselves in like it is nothing. I was standing, sandwiched between four people. The heat and the smell were overwhelming. Imagine being on a city bus at full capacity. Now pack in forty more people and turn up the temperature to 95 degrees. Have fun! I actually did.

Love, Bella

I felt a wave of regret as we left our hotel, the one and only resort we would indulge in during our trip. The heat, as we stood melting on the train platform, did not lighten my mood. My back was drenched with sweat under my pack. Sophia complained that it wasn't fair she had been sick for the best part of the trip. I told her that there would be even better parts, but she didn't believe me. A European traveler touched my belly and asked when my baby was due. I answered that the baby was a money belt containing three passports. And too many lemon pancakes.

We wanted to see the Keralan backwaters, which *Lonely Planet* lists as one of the "Seven Places to Visit Before you Die." But I was beginning to sense how it goes with *Lonely Planet*. They find beautiful places and write them up in their book. People come in increasing numbers to see them, and then follows the whole tourist infrastructure of hotels, guides, shops, etc. Then the place is no longer the same as it was when it was written about. A good friend sent me a note before we left Chico:

> "*My advice—use that book as your last resort.*
> *Let India's magic and Bhagwan guide you*
> *The planet is not lonely . . .*
> *The inner guide book is triumphant.*"

I had studied the map of Kerala and discovered that there were hundreds of kilometers of backwaters, not only in the couple of places *Lonely Planet* mentions. I found a homestay listed online, located in a village far from the tourist hub. Our hosts were an older couple named Bapu and Visala, who had three grown sons but no grandchildren yet. We were their fifth guests, ever, and when they saw that we came with two children, Visala was beyond delighted. It was as if she had opened her home for guests for the off chance that a Sophia Moes might happen to come and stay.

The room was spare and the beds hard, but the meals Visala cooked for us more than compensated. From a dark kitchen smaller than an American closet, Visala produced three meals a day for us that were fit for a maharaja. Sophia kept her company while she cooked, making mud-patties in the kitchen garden just outside the open door. Visala served us river oysters (gathered by Bapu that morning) in coconut curry sauce, spicy fish curry, coconut beet yogurt salad, fragrant coconut rice, coconut chutney, and veggies in red hot curry. Coconut, the abundant, ubiquitous weed-tree of plenty, was a theme. At mealtime we were each presented a plate with a mountain of large-grain Keralan rice, with sauces and curries to pour on top. The dining room had a sink for handwashing beside the table because Keralans eat with their hands. I struggled to pick up bite-sized clumps of saucy rice with my fingers, but Adam and the girls dove in like they had eaten without silverware their entire lives.

"Food tastes better when you eat it with your hands," Sophia informed us.

Sophia was looking a tad gaunt after her bout of dysentery, so Bapu sat beside her at dinner, gesturing at her to *keep eating, keep eating*, any time she started to slow down. Visala hovered over us, adding sauces to our plates as our rice-mountains dwindled. I unbuttoned my khaki pants to fit it all in.

Across the road from the house a wide river shone like a blue pearl. The sun set over the coconut fringe on the far bank, pouring pink paint across the sky, and canoes silently skimmed the water. Men came home from work, fishers brought in their catch, and women delivered coconuts, all by canoe. A canoe also ferried school children and their bikes home. This was not a resort, but we were glimpsing a way of life, precious, ancient, and endangered, like all things beautiful and wild.

A tranquil afternoon on the backwaters near Kollum, Kerala.

A couple of days later, we said our goodbyes. Visala cried and invited Sophia to stay and live with them while we traveled, which we politely declined. A taxi drove us off the island and took us an hour away to a colossal enclosed compound. A sign next to the gate read *AMRITAPURI* in curly script. We pushed open the creaky metal gate and stepped into the home of Amma the Divine Mother, the Hugging Saint, the global guru whose face graces altars at Rainbow Gatherings, Burning Man, and music festivals around the world. Amma, who makes a yearly trip to San Francisco where 20,000 people stand in line all night for a holy hug, grew up right here in this Kerala backwater. Amma, who has hugged thirty-four million people thus far and is seen as an embodiment of God herself, was home, and we had arrived for lunch.

The enormous cotton-candy colored ashram consisted of temples, multi-story dorms, and pavilions, built on a thin strip of jungle between a river and the sea. The clankety-clank of hammers building ever more dorms, the chanting of prayers, the chattering of three thousand devotees, assailed our ears. "If you go right now to the main pavilion," the German greeter at the international office told us, "Amma will personally hand you your lunch. She does this every Tuesday at 1 p.m. You are just in time." My watch said 12:55, so we threw down our packs and went.

In the pavilion, a dark-skinned middle-aged woman in a white salwar sat on a platform, deep in meditation. A couple of thousand people, mostly also dressed in white, sat in hushed reverence around her. More than half the devotees were Indians of various ages and backgrounds and the rest were Westerners. It was the most racially mixed scene we had encountered in India. I found it fascinating that here, in male-dominated India, a woman with a fourth-grade education was revered as a living god and was a leader of education and social justice. I had read that Amma built hospitals, orphanages, and schools throughout India. She led the disaster relief for South India after the 2004 tsunami and has created environmental and humanitarian programs throughout the world. I did not know much else; we came for the experience of staying in a Hindu ashram and hoped to get one of her famous hugs during our stay.

Amma finished meditating. She said prayers, and everyone got out of their seats and pushed towards her. I stepped up and Amma handed me my plate of *thali*: rice with curry, curd, crispy papadums and sauces. Our eyes met briefly, and I was startled by her happy, relaxed demeanor. Somehow, I imagined that being the focus of so much attention from thousands of devotees would make one . . . stressed and uptight, I guess.

After lunch I bought Sophia a children's book about Amma's life. We read that the ashram stands on the land of her original family home. The book told how Amma was special, even as a child. She would go missing, and her parents would find her under trees, merging with the Divine through prayers and meditations. Amma stopped going to school after fourth grade because her mother became ill and Amma took over caring for her siblings. When Amma was a teen her family demanded she stop dancing with the Divine in the yard because the neighbors were starting to talk. She would not stop her communion with the gods, but to spare her family embarrassment, she ran away. She lived in the forest alone for a time, although one of her uncle's cows came to her and wouldn't leave her side, providing milk for her sustenance until her family took her back.

When Amma gathered food scraps from neighbors for her family's cows and goats, she was confronted with the poverty and suffering of others. She would bring people food and clothing from her own home. Her family, which was not wealthy, scolded and punished her. She also began to spontaneously embrace people, to comfort them in their sorrow. By the time she was twenty, Amma's hugs were known throughout South India for having miraculous healing power. She held *darshan*, or blessing gatherings, in the cow-shed that still stands in the center of the ashram. People traveled to receive the blessing of her hugs, considered straight from God. Her followers grew, and a decade later someone from the West discovered her and that was it. Within a few more years she became a major spiritual leader with hundreds of thousands of devotees all over the world who donate to her charitable organization, "Embracing the World." "My religion is love. An unbroken stream of love flows from Amma to all beings in the universe," she has said. "This is Amma's inborn nature . . . to lovingly caress people, to console and wipe their tears until the end of this mortal frame—this is Amma's wish."

Our room was in a sixteen-story tall dormitory with an elevator, the only elevator in Kerala. The room itself was worn and dingy, but clean, with four small beds and a cold-water-only bathroom. We could see the jungle backwaters from our window. Pictures of Amma had been taped to the walls, otherwise there was no décor. For 250 rupees ($4) a night per person, which included free vegetarian Indian meals, I was certainly not complaining.

The ashram was a town unto itself. There was a Western Canteen where international visitors could buy mochas, cakes, pizza, and French fries. There was an Ayurvedic healing center, a store, a thrift shop, an ice cream stand, a children's library, spiritual and yoga classes, and a medical clinic. People were friendly, dedicated to a life of love and service like their guru, Amma. Sophia befriended a group of girls and ran off to play. We decided Bella could walk around the ashram by herself, getting some of the independence she craved. She signed up to work in the canteen, baking bread and helping with food prep.

"Do you want one of us to do that with you, Bella?" I asked.

"No way! That is the whole point."

Amma gave her hugging darshan the following day. At 11 a.m. she came up to the stage and began. She did not stop until everyone who wanted a hug received one. She did not take a bathroom break, or stop to eat, for over twelve hours. The music that accompanied her changed throughout the day as a parade of musicians rotated through, and included both Western and Indian styles. Her devotees kept the darshan running smoothly with numerous rules and protocols. As new arrivals, we received tokens for a hug. Our tokens had high numbers which meant the hug would be late in the day.

Adam went across the river to a robotics fair at Amma's engineering university. The fact that her formal education ended early did not deter her from founding institutions of higher learning.

Amma invested heavily in the development of science, education, and health care in her home state.

Sophia went off with a gaggle of girls her age and Bella chopped vegetables in the canteen kitchen. I sat on the stage and watched Amma for a couple hours. Sitting behind her, I could see the faces of the people before and after their hugs lit up with love and devotion, sometimes wet with tears. Sadhus and Hindu priests, tribal families from the jungle, whole schools of children in matching uniforms, and men dressed in smart business suits who appeared to be politicians or high-level bureaucrats, got hugs. There were also police officers, army officers, rich couples from urban areas, and untouchables. The barriers of caste, gender, social standing, and skin-tone that run so deep in Indian culture were absent. Everyone was equal in the arms of the Divine Mother.

How does she do it? I wondered. How does she give unconditional love, continually, all day long? I remembered that when I was nearly nine months pregnant with Bella, Adam took me to San Francisco to meet a holy Tibetan master. The beautiful old yogi blessed me, and I asked him how I could practice the Dharma while busy being a mama. He answered that my spiritual path was simple. I should love *all beings* as if they were my precious baby. I always kept that noble goal in mind but was far from achieving it. But that was exactly what Amma was doing.

At 5:30 my family met up in the canteen for cappuccino and cake. It was time to get in line. The music changed over from *Kirtan* to Western. Someone began singing "You are So Beautiful to Me" in a breathy, sweet voice, a song Adam sang to me often during the summer we fell in love. After forty-five minutes we were brought onto the stage for the final hug line, which took another hour or so. There, we could see the hugs as we moved closer one seat at a time. I was surprised by how long each hug took. I had heard each hug lasts between two and eight seconds but today some were lasting a minute or more. We got closer to her and my palms dripped with sweat.

Finally, we were in the last seats before the hug. "Kids first," we were told, and we scrambled around to comply. A man brought Sophia to her knees and then pushed her into the sitting Amma's arms; her hug was over in seconds. Hands brought Sophia up, and then Bella was next. Bella was hugged for a long time, while Amma talked to someone over her head. I could see that Sophia was disappointed by how short her hug had been. Then it was my turn. I noticed the makeup smeared on her sari from the day's faces, the strong smell of her flowery perfume, and then I was mashed into her and I closed my eyes and everything went black. I imagined for a brief second that I was swirling in the ocean of the universe.

I was lifted up and back by the attendants and Adam got his hug. Amma began to laugh while she hugged him. She kept holding him and laughing. In an impulsive moment of maternal love, I disregarded the protocols and the burly men who enforced them, grabbed my disappointed Sophia, and shoved her towards Amma again so she could join Adam's super-long hug. Instead of pulling her away, the attendants said "Family. Family." Then they pushed me back to Amma and Bella was pushed in as well, and we made a clumpy group hug. Amma's laugh was deep and gorgeous and contagious. Her whole voluptuous body rolled and shook, our faces pressed against it. Sophia laughed and then I laughed and soon everyone on stage was laughing and saying "Family. Family!"

Then it was done. I couldn't really tell how the hug affected me. I wasn't a different person, I didn't feel like I had been in the arms of God. I felt happy; the people around me were beautiful, and kind, and reverent. It seemed like we were in a bubble—seaside jungle, cotton-candy temples, abundance of food and treats and goodness. But it had been that way before the hug, too. What I did feel was awe and respect for Amma, and gratitude that my daughters could experience this.

Jan 29

Dear Diary,

I got to hug Amma! Amma is a living saint, and the embodiment of the Divine Mother. Wow. It was as though the stars in the sky were singing. She pressed me to her and my heart fluttered. She started laughing and her whole body shook. I heard a voice in my head saying, "Bella, you have accomplished so much, and are so ambitious, and yet you cannot overcome simple things like losing your temper and biting your nails." Then she handed me a small candy and pulled me away, saying something in Malayalam.

Love, Bella.

just went to hug Amma and wen I did she laft and I askt her with my heart haow to be a beter persun and she anserd lissen to your hart lissen well becus it is hard to heer. But wen you heer it respand emeadeutly, and you will be a beter persun. That is her respans.

—Sophia.

Portrait of Amma the Divine Mother,
drawn by Sophia Moes

Our family liked staying at Amma's, except for Bella, who *loved* it. She relished meeting people independently of us while she volunteered in the kitchen, and spent long hours sipping mochas in the canteen with another fourteen-year-old girl, who was from London. We stayed close to a week, which meant we got another hug a couple of days later. A resident told me that I could ask her a question if I had one and she might answer it (through a translator).

I had one.

I figured that the difference between Amma, and say, an ordinary woman like me, is ego. My ego kept me focused on me and mine, while hers did not, allowing her to operate from an unconditioned place of love. This place of love has been called the Divine, Buddha Nature, Universal Love, or saintliness, depending on who was talking. I thought, if I could be more like Amma, all my problems would be solved. When I got through the hours-long line for her hug the second time, I asked her, "How do I diminish ego?"

She laughed, then hugged me, then pulled me away and spoke in Malayalam for a long time to her attendant. He explained her answer:

> "If you do work, and have leadership, responsibility, then having an ego is good—it allows you to have authority. When you are angry, for example, at a child who needs discipline, that anger is not who you really are, it is passing, not deeply you. Shine the light, and the darkness will disappear. The ego is like a rope, a tool you can use, then burn it and it is gone. Illusory. The mind is like an old car. It bumps and grinds and knocks about, until it hits something really big and hard. Then it stops."

The ashram had lists of rules posted around, regarding visitors' conduct. In the elevators, on the doors, we were reminded that modest dress was required and that drinking, gambling, gaming, drugs, and smoking were prohibited. Sophia found where the rule-breakers went to indulge in cigarettes, chess, and probably any number of other illegal habits. Visitors were advised to stay within the compound walls during their stay, as touts, temptations, or worse might be outside the gates waiting to prey on the foreigners. I thought the boundary of the ashram gates was absolutely clear for our girls, but apparently Sophia didn't get the memo. Or her concept of "boundary" differed from ours.

Her friends came looking for her one afternoon, and it was a classic Sophia moment—"Wait, I thought she was with you!" Bella cruised the spots she should be: the ice cream stall, the children's library, the plaza with banyan climbing trees, but to no avail. Right before I shifted into full-blown panic mode, Sophia appeared, lips and teeth stained an ungodly orange from candy. "I found the chess games!" she announced, batting her eyelashes the way she does when she notices her mother looks ready to explode and suspects she might be in an itty-bitty bit of trouble.

"Why don't you take us there and show us?" Adam responded.

We followed Sophia behind some outlying buildings and through a hole someone had cut in the back fence. We squeezed through the hole and found ourselves on a squalid, dusty street, where a local family had set up a tarp-shaded Tea and Coconut Shop. Men of various ages and races sat around smoking cigarettes and playing chess. Butts and empty cigarette boxes were scattered all over the ground. Goats wandered through munching on the butts. Every couple of minutes the *thwap* of coconut being split by a young boy with a heavy machete rang out. Hindi pop played from a decrepit boom box. Everything was dusty and dirty, and the ratio of males to females was roughly fifteen to one.

Sophia was delighted by her discovery. "Isn't this great? I have been watching these guys play chess, and they even bought me a soda!"

"And candy," I remarked.

We bought a coconut and stood drinking the sweet water through a dusty straw in the smoky heat.

"Sophia, we are going back in the ashram now, and you are never, ever to come out here without me. Is that perfectly clear?" Adam said.

"Yes, Daddy."

I never did find out how Sophia discovered that spot in the first place.

It was time to do a bucket wash. Bucket wash is how most of India washes its clothes. All that is required is a 15-rupee (25¢) bar of soap and a bucket. At home, laundry was a constant project involving mountains of clothes and linens in our expensive and energy-consuming machines. In travel mode, our laundry fit into the small bucket that we found in every Indian bathroom. After washing the clothes in soapy cold water and rinsing each item well, I carried my bucket to the laundry lines on the roof. The roof was the seventeenth floor, and the laundry fluttered in the breeze against a captivating view. The Arabian Sea sparkled on one side, the vast green jungle dissected by dark blue waterways stretched to the horizon on the other. I leaned over the balcony railing, inhaling deeply, as if I could breathe the beauty into my lungs and keep it with me forever. In this ashram bustling with thousands of devotees, it was a rare, solitary moment.

I felt relaxed. The simple task of hanging laundry, how easy that was without twenty other things on my to-do list. Without being on-call. At home I knew that at any moment I could be called to a birth. And I understood that anything could happen at a birth, and it was my responsibility to keep mother and baby safe. I could be faced with a hemorrhage, or a baby's shoulders could get stuck on a pubic bone after the head is out, requiring swift and intense maneuvers to deliver the child. A baby could be born blue and floppy, and not breathing. The life-line for both mother and baby lay squarely in my hands. Midwifery is what I did, but when I stepped away from it, I could see the background of stress created by being constantly on-call. Then there was my investigation, which I hadn't thought about for weeks. The idea of losing my nursing license and my livelihood left me cold and crushed, even in this heat.

I had been a midwife for most of my adult life. When I was twenty-two years old I lived in New York City, dabbling in theater and waiting tables, and wondering what to do with my life. I wanted to do something meaningful, to help people, but I didn't know what it was, yet. I came from a family of doctors but I had been the artsy kid, solidly resistant to math and science. A career in health care was the last thing on my mind, until my highly intuitive, pagan priestess roommate Judy came home from work one day and placed a book in my hands.

"Here. I saw this in a bookstore and for some reason it made me think of you."

The book cover was a pattern of tiny Buddhas on pink lotuses surrounded by swirling psychedelic flowers. *Spiritual Midwifery, Third Edition, by Ina May Gaskin.* I had never heard the term "midwife" before, but I sat down on the futon couch and began reading. The book contained home birth stories from a 1970s commune in Tennessee and explained basic midwifery skills such as prenatal care and the management of labor and birth. It even had a chart of cervical dilation. Then it described the path of the spiritual midwife.

> *"A spiritual midwife has an obligation to put out the same love to all children in her care, regardless of size, shape, color, or parentage. We are all One. The kid in front of you is just the same as your kid. We are all One.*
>
> *Her religion has to come forth in her practice, in the way she makes her day-to-day, her moment-to-moment decisions. It cannot be just theory. Truly caring for people cannot be a part-time job.*
>
> *A midwife must have a deep love for other women. She knows that all women, including herself, are sometimes as elemental as the weather and the tides, and that they need each other's help and understanding. The true sisterhood of all women is not an abstract idea to her."*

The book explained how confidence in women's abilities to give birth had been undermined by the industrialization of childbirth in the mid-twentieth century. Midwives were making a comeback, to return the power of birth to women. Midwifery was a profession that was part feminist revolutionary, part protector of a sacred rite, and part health care professional. Midwifery was something I could *do*, to actually make a difference in the world. Something deep within me clicked into place; my genetic lineage of Jewish doctors met my radical Feminist soul. I shut the book and stood up.

"Judy! I think I want to be a midwife!"

Judy said, "I thought so."

I visited a yoga retreat center in upstate New York a couple of weeks later, bringing *Spiritual Midwifery* with me. I filled my journal pages with scrawling notes about becoming a midwife, while on solitary forest walks. My last day there happened to be Mother's Day, and mothers came up from the city for a sweat lodge. I helped collect rocks to be heated in the lodge fire. I carried a large stone out of the forest and headed back for another. A couple of women huffed and puffed as they passed me, carrying rocks.

"You can do it—you are almost there!" I told them.

"You sound like my midwife!" one woman said.

"Really?" I said, incredulous. "I just decided to become a midwife."

She set her rock down. "Well, my name is Nancy, and I am the President of the International Cesarean Awareness Network. I had a cesarean with my first baby and a home birth last year. Here is my card. Call me next week and I will give you the scoop about midwifery programs. You should become a certified nurse-midwife so you can get the best training. Got that? A certified nurse-midwife."

"Got it." A nurse—that does not sound like me *at all*, I thought. Yet my friendship with Nancy led to my volunteering on the labor ward at North Central Bronx Hospital, where births were attended by nurse-midwives. I applied to a couple programs and entered Yale School of Nursing's three-year master's degree program in nurse-midwifery a year later.

Every single baby had come with a story. There was baby Ella, whose mother sat in the birthing tub eating a steak dinner one hour before she delivered. There was Shelby, who arrived before I did. I coached her father through the delivery by phone as I drove the freeway to Oroville at 3 a.m., and that birth cost me several new gray hairs. I called her mom "Crowning in Oroville" ever after, because when I phoned my assistant Serra to give her report, she kept repeating "She is crowning? In Oroville?" Baby Jeremiah was born with a cleft lip and palate. His mom syringe-fed him breastmilk until she could see the pediatrician in the morning and get the special feeder.

And of course, there was Kaeda Mae, my best friend Serra's baby. My first birth assistant who stood with me for five years, the childbirth education teacher for my clients, and Chico's prenatal yoga instructor, was finally having a baby. Serra was the friend I considered an auntie to my girls because my actual sister lived so far away. Now it was *her turn*. She rocked her labor for hours, and we both thought she must be at least eight centimeters already, the way things were going. But when I checked her, she was only two centimeters dilated. I had the horrible job of telling her that labor was still beginning. Serra went through a dark night of the soul (*I can't do it! And I am the childbirth teacher!*) and eventually tapped into a source of strength deep, deep within. She sat alone on her toilet for two hours, and when she came out of the bathroom at last, she looked deep into my eyes and whispered, "I can do it." A couple hours later she ecstatically birthed her baby on a futon on the floor.

So many women, more than I could count, have hit *transition* around eight centimeters, which is the point where women at the hospital most frequently request pain medication. Roaring with pain, looking at me with a face that says, "What the hell Ms. Smiley Midwife, you didn't tell me it would be like *this*!"—then they did it. They rallied and pushed their babies out, and loved me afterwards, as if I had performed magic when all I had done was be there and believe in them. Midwifery meant witnessing women find inner strength that they never thought possible. Midwifery was a service of trust, patience, optimism. It was my drug, my passion, my way of life.

"So, what will I do if I can't be a midwife anymore?" I asked myself, a question I hadn't been able to face at home. I stared into the sea for a long time, letting those words sink in. Can't. Be. A. Midwife. The sea, the breeze, some birds whispered at me. I couldn't make out what they were trying to say. I told myself I could let go of the past, and sent it all off the roof, into the sky.

Feb 1

Ah-ha moment anyone? I had a realization. Selfless service brings happiness, but we as humans continually
forget that. Amma taught me that. Now the lock screen
on my iPod is the words "Selfless service brings happiness" so that I will be constantly reminded.

Love, A Happy Bella.

At the end of the week, we prepared to catch a water taxi north
towards Fort Cochin. After a morning spent sweeping the path that
Amma would walk from her home to the stage, we slung on our
packs and went through the ashram's back gates. As we crossed the
long bridge over the river in the midday heat, I noticed how much
stronger we were. It was easier to walk with our packs now, despite
the noonday sun pummeling us. We found the taxi boat stand, and
then lunched in a waterside dhaba on spicy thali. The four of us were
jubilant, full of good feelings from Amma's ashram and also glad
to be heading into the unknown again.

Our boat pulled up and we climbed aboard for a five-hour ride
up the river to Alleppey. We lazed on the upper deck, watching the
world of the Keralan backwaters go by. Sophia read one of her Harry
Potter books, Bella began reading *Life of Pi*, and Adam meditated and
then napped. I gazed at the green scenery, the simple and serene villages, the canoes transporting everything imaginable. As we neared
Alleppey we saw dozens of the high-priced rice-barge turned house-
boats for tourists. We had enjoyed the same scenery that they saw,
but for only a handful of rupees, on this water taxi. Feeling smart and
travel-savvy, my eyes closed and I drifted into sleep.

CHAPTER 11

My Dream: A vision of a world in which women and men progress together, a world in which all men respect the fact that like the two wings of a bird, women and men are of equal value.

—Amma

COCHIN

Take a seaside town with 500-year-old Dutch and Portuguese architecture. Add giant spreading trees making green canopies across the sky. Mix with Kerala's ubiquitous coco-palms and banana trees sprouting up through the pavement. Add art galleries and cafes. Sprinkle with more litter than you would like. Scatter rickshaws, goats, and the aroma of curry freely, and bake until steaming. Voila, welcome to Fort Cochin. The city was a Portuguese colony in the 1500s; the Dutch took it from them in the 1600s and then handed it over to the British in the 1800s. European-designed buildings and parks remained in various states of colorful distress. Fort Cochin boasted a neighborhood called Jew Town because a community of Jews had lived there since 70 AD, when the second temple of

Jerusalem was burned down by the Romans and a single boatload of Jews washed up on the shores here. We discovered that the tiny blue-and-white synagogue built in 1568 was still in use by their descendants.

The homestay was tucked into a narrow alley between houses built in the 1600s. Our hosts cooked us a South Indian breakfast each morning, which had to be the world's best breakfast; either round, melt in your mouth, spongy lentil-flour *idlis* or thin crispy dosas, served with spicy sweet coconut sauces and fat slices of papaya and mango on the side. We booked three days in the spacious flat but planted ourselves for a week. The heat, the charm of the Old City, the airy room, and the sunsets held us in suspension. Our wrinkled clothes were laid flat on shelves, Sophia's art supplies got scattered around the room, and the math books were opened for the first time since Bodh Gaya. Adam spent hours each morning working on math with the girls, while I puttered and found errands to run on the twisting streets—anything to avoid math. Internet in the room meant that Bella could connect with her friends back home via video chatting and snapchat. She believed this contact was essential and made her happy, but I noticed it actually had the opposite effect. It made her miss her friends more. Bella's homesickness was something that traveled with us like an old injury that would sometimes flare up and sometimes be forgotten.

Bella's commitment to selfless service since our time at Amma's included renewed kindness towards her sister. Sophia had always been the president of the Bella Moes Fan Club. My memories of Sophia's babyhood consisted of a grinning, laughing baby on the floor, whose sister sang and danced in circles around her. As she grew into a toddler, Sophia would happily play along with whatever game Bella concocted for them. Our month-long summer camping trips were easy because the girls had each other to entertain, no matter how remote our wanderings were. The three-and-a-half-year age difference meant there was little competition. Then the heartbreak of middle school happened. Bella moved out of their shared room and into an attic room upstairs. She didn't want to play anymore. Even the complicated stunts on the tree swing that could only be done together were abandoned. It was embarrassing to be seen anywhere with her little sister. Sophia had been relegated to the awful position of tagalong.

But now, Bella's internal clock was winding backwards before our eyes. The skinny jeans were left in Delhi and make-up was forgotten. The hair straightener was left behind, and her ponytail was girlish. Adolescent girls in India are kept much closer to their parents than in the US. They stay home until they either marry or go off to college and are not allowed to go out without adult supervision. Because of this, there hadn't been many opportunities for us to meet Indian teen girls. Sophia happily filled the social vacuum. Endless games of Uno, the making of silly videos on the DSi, and tickle fights filled our long evenings and unhurried mornings.

Unlike the girls, Indian boys had the run of the streets.

"I think that I would like to be reborn as a boy in Kerala," Bella told us one day, as a gang of curly-haired boys passed us on their bicycles, whooping and laughing.

"Why?" I asked

"Because they live in such a relaxed place, and as boys, have an easy life and are given freedom. Everywhere we go boys are hanging out and biking around. And you know their moms treat them like kings."

I was astounded that Bella had picked up so much about gender roles and social dynamics already.

"You're right," I agreed. "They do seem to have it pretty good."

The four of us were walking to the beach for our daily ice cream and sunset, along with about half the city. The girls went straight up to an ice cream cart. "Namaste! Pista, please," I heard Sophia say. We had discovered that chocolate in India doesn't taste like chocolate, but pistachio is heavenly, as is Kulfi, a thicker, pudding-like ice cream that tastes somewhat like roses and a bit like almonds.

We passed the camel ride stand and went to the water's edge. We stepped into warm sea and watched Cochin's families splashing in the surf fully dressed, while laughing and snapping pictures. The sun turned red and brushed the sea with orange flames. Suddenly, the same boys we had seen on bikes earlier surrounded us, jostling each other and laughing. They spoke little English, but obviously wanted to play. Bella and Sophia ran around playing tag with them until they were out of breath. Then they sat in a circle with us. The boys sang songs in Malayalam, and Sophia and Bella sang them English songs in return. They started showing off, doing cartwheels and flips. Finally, the boys teased each other, pantomiming what the others' fathers did for a living. *Your father is a chai-walla. Well your father drives a rickshaw! Well yours sweeps the street!*

Adam and I laughed at their clowning. We walked back to our guesthouse with the boys escorting us, popping wheelies and singing all the way.

Across the bay from historic Fort Cochin, in the sprawl of Cochin proper, was a midwife-run birthing center called Birth Village. I had contacted them months ago by email, and a student midwife named Priya invited me to visit. I phoned them up and Priya gave me directions to get there by bus. I found the birthing center down a tree-shaded street in a bustling neighborhood. Priya, and Donna, a midwife from Alabama who was training her, welcomed me in. They gave me a tour of the Western-style labor rooms with birthing tubs and big, comfortable beds, the exam rooms, and their offices. We sat down at a table and the cook served us vegetable curry, chapatis, and tea. As we ate, I learned about birth in India.

"There are only three birth centers in all of India," Priya explained. "Here in Cochin, one in Goa run by European midwives, and one in Hyderabad operated by an obstetrician. I am one of the only modern student midwives in India."

"That cannot be!" I said, thinking of the billion people, the gazillion babies, on the subcontinent.

But it was so. I learned that while fifty percent of India's babies are born at home, they are not cared for by licensed or professional midwives. They are born under the care of low-caste birth attendants called *dais*. The knowledge of the dais is ancient, holistic, and based on sacred Vedic texts and traditions that are thousands of years old. Their midwifery know-how is intertwined with religious beliefs and customs. Concepts such as *jee*, or life-force, guide treatments that include herbs, oils, rituals, and foments. Because the majority of dais do not read or write, their knowledge is passed from generation to generation orally, and is in danger of being lost in the rush of modern development.

Nowadays, families receive financial incentives to leave their homes and go to clinics for childbirth. This is not always a safer option than staying home, due to poor staffing, a lack of basic medical supplies in case of complications, and disrespectful or even abusive treatment of mothers by the medical providers. The increased use of such facilities has decreased the mortality rates for mothers and newborns, but not as significantly as had been hoped. Birthing mothers and their dais have historically been looked down upon due to the ancient idea that a woman's body fluids, especially blood, are "unclean" and "polluting." Birth has been handled by low-caste women so that higher caste people are not "defiled" by the "impure" elements of birth-related blood. Because the dais are illiterate and low-caste, there is little interaction between them and the nurses and doctors working in India's government health-care system. Nor is there much effort to preserve their traditional knowledge. Priya was the first Indian woman to study professional midwifery with the intent to incorporate aspects of modern medicine such as oxygen, life-saving medications, and suturing, with traditional birth practices such as using Ayurvedic medicines, giving birth standing, and heating the placenta to stimulate a baby who is not breathing well. The Birth Village Board of Directors imported a preceptor from the United States to train Priya. She was the first of India's modern midwives, but she envisioned a future with many more.

Donna and Priya asked about my midwifery practice. I told them about my nine years providing home birth services in Chico, my challenges with the local doctors, and the investigation by the Board of Nursing.

"I am traveling to get a break from that stress for a while," I explained.

They were sympathetic. Donna faced similar troubles in Alabama, where home birth was recently declared illegal. She came to Cochin to train Priya and also dodge her licensing problems. "Here in India, no one cares whether a midwife has a license or not. There is no way to get in trouble," Priya said. "But we cannot go into the hospital with our clients at all if they need to transport, and the doctors *slap the mothers around* when they get there. Sometimes they don't let our mothers see their babies for two days, just to be spiteful."

I sucked in my breath. *Obstetric violence* was a term I had heard bounced around in midwifery journals and conferences. Dr. Stern had been verbally obnoxious but that was always as far as it went. "Oh, my goodness. This makes my situation sound like a dream. I would rather they come after me than mistreat my families. Slap the mothers around! Keep them from their babies? That is, thank goodness, unheard of where I am from."

"There is much work to do here, to modernize attitudes towards women and childbirth. Especially doctors' attitudes in a backwater place like this," Priya said, shaking her head.

We sat in silence, sipping our tea. The scale of the tasks that lay ahead for India in maternal/child health was considerable. How to humanize the hospitals, train providers in patients' rights to respect and kindness, and overcome cultural bias against women? How to integrate the dais and document their knowledge, while also creating a class of professional, formally-educated midwives? With fifty million births in India a year, the forty or so that happen in this clean, cozy birth center surrounded by two caring midwives was like a bag of amniotic waters breaking into the Arabian Sea.

Donna interrupted my reverie, saying she had been on call for ten months straight, and wished sometimes that there was someone to cover her. Ten months straight—that sounded like my life back home. I started to offer, perhaps I could cover for a week or two, if Donna needed to get away . . .

The two women laughed at me. "You said you are here to spend time with your family, taking a break from midwifery!"

"You are right. What am I thinking?" I said.

Priya said, "You are welcome here if you decide to come back someday."

"Thank you," I replied. "I *will* come back someday, I've already decided."

Walking back to the bus stand, I thought about fifty million births a year. That is a staggering number of mothers and babies, many receiving less than optimal care. For the vast numbers of them living in poverty, their health is already compromised when they conceive in the first place. They can be overworked, malnourished, or live in degraded environments. They might drink polluted water or be victims of gender violence. My thoughts fell into a single phrase, whispered over and over like a mantra as I climbed aboard a rickety red bus: "There is so much to do. There is so, so much to do."

CHAPTER 12

COORG REGION, KARNATAKA

It usually happened like this. After weeks or months of harmonious married life, something triggered a conflict between Adam and me, which spiraled into a meltdown. Our disagreements were rare, and I had a strange amnesia about them, forgetting how misera ble they were until the next one. When we fought, blinds over my heart snapped shut. With a twist of the wrist, dozens of slats that were open to let in light and goodness flipped closed leaving only darkness. Suddenly our entire history aligned to prove that we were absolutely wrong for each other.

This fight started on our journey to the Coorg region, in the mountains of the Western Ghats. The bus station was chaotic, the buses dilapidated and packed with people. It was *hot*. We found our bus and climbed aboard. Adam went to buy snacks and returned proud to share a strange assortment of sweet ball-things and giant spicy somethings. Bella made a snide remark about their inade-quacy, and that *Mom* should have gotten the snacks. He turned away and took a seat far from me and the girls for the day-long bus trip. That choice made me seethe. He didn't want to deal with his teen daughter's attitude, which left me with both girls for this whole, hot trip. I started down the rabbit hole, my old story bubbling up with a fresh twist; I do more than my share for the family here, just like I did at home. Once I started down this path, my mind chugged like a runaway train. I made the plans, I found the buses, I studied the guidebooks, booked our rooms and trains, and provided structure and schedule to our wanderings. "Here we are, across the world," I realized, "falling into the exact same pattern that I was trying to get away from." I almost laughed out loud, thinking of that ridiculous cliché: wherever you go, there you are.

The bus wound its way down a twisting mountain road through tall green trees and explosions of flowering shrubs. I put Adam out of my mind and focused my attention on the eye-popping scenery. At one o'clock, in the thick of the jungle, the bus engine coughed to a stop. "Lunch stop!" the driver called out. Everyone got off and entered a thatch-roofed stall beside the road. Two old men served us heaps of rice with vegetables and dal on banana-leaf plates. The girls and I sat together in the roadside dhaba while Adam ate with two travelers he had been sitting near. I walked past him without speaking. When we were done, we flung our banana leaf plates onto the ground like the locals did, so dogs and goats could finish the meals.

We arrived in Madikeri, and my plan was to book a trek for the following day. I knew, via the guidebook, that the trekking office closed early. Because Adam had not talked to me for the entire day, he did not know the plan. I stepped into the bus station office with the girls to wait for him. He came over to us and said, "We need to clear the air."

He was right, of course, but I still wanted to book our trek first. "Not now," I responded. "We need to get to the trekking office. It's closing soon. And I don't even know why you are angry."

"I haven't heard anything about this trekking office. Consensus process has totally broken down. If you are calling me angry when it is *you* that is hostile, then I am out of here." Adam put on his pack, turned on his heel, and walked out the door. He was gone. It happened so fast.

The girls and I sat in the office, stunned and scared. I was so angry, my brain spun like a clock guessing where he would go without us. I jumped to the worst-case scenario and assumed he would get on another bus as soon as possible. *Good, I will be relieved to be rid of him. He can travel solo now, like a freewheeling bachelor, while I do double-duty parenting—doesn't that figure.* The slats in my heart slapped completely shut. He *would* walk out on us, I thought, and abandon us in a bus station in the middle of India, without even saying goodbye to the girls.

I remembered he had Sophia's passport, and called him with my Pocket Guru 1200. He came right in to hand me her passport. He hadn't gone far after all—just to the other side of the station. We went to the guesthouse together and then Adam left to book himself his own room in the guesthouse next door. After checking into his own room, he came over to talk it out. As usual, our process involved heated debate. Okay, *yelling*. Bella interrupted and told Adam he was bullying me. They started arguing and I despaired, convinced we had the most screwed up family, ever. After spending way too much time getting absolutely nowhere, Adam and I left the girls in the room and found a place up the road to sit outside.

"I am not going to put up with Bella being rude to me," Adam said, "and that had nothing to do with you. And I wasn't ignoring you, that is your own perception."

"Well, you left me alone to deal with both girls on the bus and I didn't like that. And I am always doing everything, for everyone, and you don't even appreciate me," I answered.

"I didn't leave you alone. I was on the bus, but I wanted to sit up front. Don't assume the worst of me. And you can stop doing everything and let me guide us some. You don't always need to be in charge, and then get pissed at me about it. No one is asking you to do that."

Don't assume the worst. But I did, I always did.

"When you blew off my request to clear the air, didn't include me in your plans, and then accused me of being angry, then of course I got angry. And I am still angry," Adam said.

"Well, you sure seemed angry to me. And when you walked out of the bus office, that was awful. We thought you had abandoned us. Pulling that kind of stunt is unacceptable. If you had listened to me, and come with me to the trekking office, we could have cleared the air right after without this huge blow-up."

Around and around we went. Finally, we made some agreements. Adam requested I step down from my position of Person in Charge of Everything, which, he said, would be a relief to the whole family. He reminded me of his alternative strategy: a consensus approach where we each had equal say from now on, regarding where we went and what we did. I said I was willing to give it a try. But when we returned to the girls, Bella was still irate at Adam for walking out on us in the bus station and then for yelling in the guesthouse. She refused to even look at him, and he left to sleep in the room next door. Bella begged me to send her home. We all slept poorly and began our trek the following morning fractured and emotionally drained.

We should have postponed the trek, but honestly, I didn't know how. Bright and early the next day, our guide, a quiet man in his fifties named Mohan, came for us. He wore slacks, a button-down shirt, and Oxford-style shoes to walk through the hot, sticky jungle. Hardly looking at each other, we reluctantly followed him out into the world. A bus took us out of Madikeri and onto a twisting mountain road. We got off at a spot where there was nothing but trees and flowering foliage, and we followed Mohan into the jungle.

A nasty, hollow feeling scraped out my chest. Adam's face was a mask, which I knew meant he felt attacked, was hurting. We took up barking at each other as soon as we were on the trail. We played the game "Whose Fault is This?" ferociously, seeking the real bad guy, each of us righteous, stubborn. We were a perfect display of how to destroy a relationship. I turned around to see that both Bella and Sophia were crying. Bella begged, again, to go home.

Then I had a sudden moment of clarity. I saw that it was completely in my power to either continue carrying on this way or choose to stop fighting. I saw that this was not some roller coaster I had gotten on—I was actually the driver and I could kill the engine right now, get out, and ride my bike instead. I could drop my case against him and behave in service to the family. I called out to Mohan to stop walking.

I yelled to Adam who had stormed ahead. "Adam, we have to stop fighting! I am sorry. We can't do this to ourselves, and to the girls. Let's choose to be loving and careful with each other for now. I think we can do it."

He stopped and waited for me.

I caught up, breathless, and said, "Look, when we get to the top of that hill, let's hug and promise to forgive each other. Let's start over. Would you try that with me? Please?"

He looked at me, glanced at the girls, and looked back at my tear-stained face.

"Yes."

We got to the top of the hill, where there was a clearing. Adam and I gingerly put our arms around each other. I inhaled Adam's scent, and felt the blinds over my heart open a crack. I made a promise to myself, a vow, that we would not fight like this for the remainder of the trip. At home when we fought it was bad, but at least the girls were at school, or, if not, could go to their room. Here, traveling like this, fighting was untenable. Adam and I had our problems, but dealing with them would have to be tabled, for now. Adam and I stood, holding each other, until the girls reached us.

I told them, "We are done fighting now."

We stood together and then pulled the girls into our hug. "Family, family," I said with a Hinglish lilt, remembering Amma.

"Family, family," Sophia echoed.

Mohan waited for us, undoubtedly pondering the strange customs of Western families. We began walking the trail again, and soon crossed paths with a local man coming the other way. He talked animatedly to Mohan in *Coorgie* for several minutes. I sensed something urgent about the communication and asked Mohan what he had said.

Mohan spoke to us in his soft, gentle voice.

"There has been a wild elephant through here in the night. Somebody has been killed. Many banana trees trampled, much damage done. We must walk quietly, so as not to disturb the elephant if it is near. If a wild elephant is surprised it will charge and trample."

With that, he turned and headed up the trail.

Should we stop? Ask to turn back? But Adam led Sophia and Bella on and I followed. The arguments in my head were forgotten as we walked in complete silence for the next two hours through the green tunnel of dense jungle. Creeping around dangerous wild elephants had not been mentioned in *Lonely Planet*. Every so often Mohan stopped, listening for sounds. Hearing none, he kept on. I pondered what I would do if we were suddenly charged. The trail we were on had a lip of a cliff on one side that dropped into a foliage-filled ravine. If an elephant came running at us on this trail, I decided, I would pick up Sophia and hurl her off the cliff into the ravine. She would be scratched up, but live. I could probably do the same for Bella. Adam didn't think we were in any real danger; he thought Mohan merely wanted us to quit squawking at each other.

We climbed out of the jungle and onto a dirt road. The canopy opened out to reveal beautifully tended plantations of cardamom, coffee, bananas, vanilla, and betel nut. The coffee was in bloom with fragrant white flowers. I had never seen a landscape with such delicate, exotic beauty. We came upon a walled-in house surrounded by bright flowers. Mohan opened an iron gate. "Lunch stop," he said.

During the afternoon we walked several relatively flat kilometers through the spice and coffee plantations. The damp heat and hours of hiking had wrung the anger out of me. The girls ran ahead, absorbed in a game they made up. We were put up for the night in a campground beside a farm, where Adam built a fire. The four of us sat around it and watched the moonrise. Adam's olive branch to me was to start singing folk songs, which he knew I loved. Sophia and I joined in. Bella silently stared into the fire. When we moved to songs from the kids' Waldorf school, she joined in, reluctant at first. "Summer is a-coming in, loudly sing cuckoo!" Louder and louder we sang, the girls blending their voices into harmonies. Afterwards Adam talked about the consensus process. "When decisions need to be made," he said, "we will hold a family meeting where each of us has a turn to speak. We won't do anything unless we all give it a 'yes.' How does that sound?"

"Boring," Bella said. "I vote for whatever Mom plans."

CHAPTER 13

MYSORE AND HAMPI, KARNATAKA

The hotel clerk checked us in and told us we were just in time.

"The Mysore Palace lights will turn on in twenty minutes. This happens once a week, for an hour. Cross Gandhi Square, walk up a block, and you will see the palace."

"Thanks."

Hotel Dasaprakash was a relic from the 1920s. Uniformed bellhops, an office full of still-functioning antiques, a cobblestone courtyard, and a sense that no renovations had taken place over nearly a hundred years cost our usual $12 per night. After days in rustic home-stays deep in the jungle, it was refreshing to be in a city. We found our room, splashed cold water on our faces, and headed to the palace.

Mysore was charming and less crowded than Delhi, but still had the vibrant ingenuity and swirling chaos of urban India. Bicycles passed us stacked high with mattresses, bricks, or mountains of copper pots. Women thronged the roads in bright saris, and rickshaws buzzed past, blowing their horns. Cows relaxing in the middle of the traffic tossed their heads, gazing at us with gentle eyes. Chai stalls, food shops, and markets crowded the sidewalks in front of dirty, aging buildings from the last century and beyond.

The Mysore Palace is a crown jewel of Indian architecture. It is the ancestral palace for the Wadiyar dynasty, which ruled Karnataka from the 1300s until Indian independence in 1947, when the last Maharaj voluntarily stepped down. The palace stands where an older one burned down in 1897. The reconstruction was completed in 1912 and was done in an extravagant architectural blend of Hindu, Muslim, Rajput, and Gothic styles. We arrived at the gates as they opened to let the families of Mysore into the palace courtyard. A uniformed police band played rousing music and people spread out to picnic in the vast courtyard. Vendors sold watermelon slices and balloons. At the stroke of seven, the 100,000 light bulbs outlining the majestic form of the palace switched on.

A soft *ahh* moved through the crowd, momentarily quieting the sounds of *Kannada* swirling around us. I passed my camera to Bella and she snapped pictures of Adam and me with the fantastical lights behind us. I scrolled through those pictures and saw a couple leaning into each other affectionately and smiling against a dazzling, romantic setting. I wondered, not for the first time, how we can be happy together for great swaths of time and then awful and icy at other times. I couldn't understand how those both could be true, but also knew that they were. I realized that anger, my own as well as his, was something I had always tried to dodge until it was literally strangling me and I had no choice but to face it.

On the walk back to the hotel, we came across a Domino's pizza restaurant filled with Mysore teens sporting skinny jeans and smart phones.

"Please, please, please," begged the girls.

I glanced at the menu posted on the wall "Girls, 350 rupees a person—that is almost what dinner for the four of us should cost."

They stopped begging and glumly acquiesced.

"Well," I said "350 rupees *is* only six dollars. I suppose you have earned a treat . . . let's do it."

The pizzas were tiny, but decent. We washed them down with bottles of Coca-Cola, savoring the forgotten flavors of home.

After dinner, Adam and I took a walk while the girls played

Uno in the room. We surreptitiously held hands as we explored dark alleys full of shops and stalls. We came across a paan maker on the street. On a tray of tiny bowls, he spread herbs and pastes into leaves and then folded them into bite-sized packages. A young couple bought some while we watched, and the sari-clad woman insisted on cutting hers in half and sharing it with me. I chewed on the fragrant, slightly sweet bundle, and tried to spit the juices from between my teeth the way Indians did. Perhaps I did get a lift from the paan, or maybe it was the relief of my family feeling stable again that put a bounce in my step.

Feb 18 2014

Dear Diary,

Last night we took the train to Hampi. We sat in our little compartment and enjoyed dried kiwi, plain cashews, and dense crackers. The clean sheets and pillowcases came in a brown bag, along with a thick blanket that I definitely didn't use. The sweet sound of the older lady in a shiny sari speaking lovely Kannada in the compartment next door was very relaxing. I felt happy.

I woke up on the train, and ten minutes later was on the bus to Hampi. It was only a 30-minute ride, but I marveled at the abrupt change in landscape. The palm tree jungles were replaced by red-rock piles, rising like mountains. We got off the bus and found a guesthouse by taking a rickety wooden boat across the river. What a place! It's called Sunny's, and the whole place is full of young Israelis who drink and smoke and watch tons of movies on the massive flat-screen TV. Wow! What a super-duper change!

Love, Bella.

An Israeli red-head named Ariel played chess with Sophia in the guesthouse cafe. Around them lazed scantily-clad Israeli youth. They dressed in skin-tight tank tops and leggings or bootie shorts, completely ignoring the modesty customs of India. We heard them yell at the waiters and watched them leave tables littered with cigarette butts, uneaten food, and spilled beer bottles. They pulled their stashes out, rolling fat joints and then passing them right over my girls' heads to their friends.

Ariel explained who they were. "Seventy-five percent of Israeli youth spend a year in India after discharge from the army. They are twenty-two years old. They all went into compulsory military service right out of high school. When they get out, they just want to go crazy for a year, and they do it in India. They only go a few places: here, and Goa, and a couple spots in the Himalayas."

I contemplated these kids, who shared my Jewish ancestry, who were practically my relatives, and how challenged I felt by their behavior. I imagined them in the military, trained to kill and die for the sake of Israel, of the violence and discipline they had lived with and had just escaped from. No wonder they swung so wildly in the other direction now. We had landed in the middle of their decompression from the army. I noticed flies crawling over the half-eaten plates of food abandoned on the tables and felt my stomach turn.

Hampi is said to have been the site of Kishkinda, the ancient Monkey Kingdom, during the time of Rama, Sita, and the events of the Ramayana. It was the location of the flowering Vijayanagara civilization until the late 1500s. In 1500 AD the Vijayanagara Empire had 500,000 inhabitants, making it the second largest city in the world after Peking-Beijing. It collapsed under Mughal invasion at the end of the 1500s, and then the ruins were discovered in 1800 by a British colonel. Walking day after day across hillsides strewn with boulders and ruins, Adam and the kids and I pretended we were on Star Trek investigating a new planet. We rented bikes and then motor scooters to get to various ruins, spread over ten kilometers.

Ancient carvings of voluptuous goddesses, Hanuman the Monkey God, elephants, archers, and the sacred cow processed along walls, temples, and colonnades, now left to decay under the Deccan sun. A megalithic statue of Vishnu as a giant frog with googly eyes and tongue wagging out drew me to it. I stood transfixed before it until Sophia called, "Come meet this priest who lives in an underwater Shiva shrine!"

Drums beat urgently. Sophia and I followed the sound down a slender trail to find that tribal locals had sacrificed a goat and were chopping it up, blood running on the floor of an ancient temple ruin. Someone lifted a silver platter up. "Do you want to see the head, Madam?" I winced a "no," and we turned and ran. Back at the river, Lakshmi, the temple elephant, appeared to smile as she placidly munched bananas and tree branches in the shade. Locals washed their clothes in the river, traversing the water in round basket boats while half-naked Israelis just discharged from compulsory military service basked and got baked on smooth river boulders. Coconuts, fresh juice, souvenirs, and pakoras were offered every ten steps. Ancient and modern worlds dramatically collided in the beautiful, surreal landscape.

Every evening two hundred travelers climbed a mountain outside of town to drum and dance together as the sun slipped away behind the blood-red hills with their bright green foliage. Local families sent their youngest children up after them, with thermoses of lemonade and chai to sell. Every night after dinner, Bella and Sophia battled it out with drunk Israeli ex-soldiers, until Sunny had no choice but to play a Harry Potter movie for them on his big-screen outdoor TV.

Feb 23

Dear Diary,

Last night Dad got really sick. He lay on his bed moaning and looking pale. Later he threw up. Mom yelled at him for getting it on the rug but then she threw up.

Today I relaxed at the guesthouse all day. I am beginning to feel a bit annoyed with the constant drinking and smoking that happens here. At any hour of the day or night, people can be found polluting the air with smoke and boisterous noise.

Now I am feeling ill and am starting to burp sour cream and onion chip smell. Yuck.

Love, Bella

Hampi was the end of my South India itinerary, and we had a couple of weeks before our flight from Delhi to Nepal. Adam and I were determined to use a consensus approach to making the next plan. We went into a travel office together and discussed our options. Based on our experience of the party-scene here, Goa was out of the question. Adam wanted to go to the Buddhist caves of Ellora and Ajanta, but that would require a *sixty-hour* train ride. I vetoed the idea. The travel agent told us about a beach in Karnataka, with a night bus that could take us there. According to the agent it was beautiful and remote, and the scene was mellow. It sounded great to me, a beach redo since Sophia had gotten sick at the last one. I checked in with Adam to make sure he agreed. He nodded, I nodded, he nodded again. Then we bought our tickets.

CHAPTER 14

A MYSTICAL BEACH
HEREIN REFERRED TO AS LAPUNA

We climbed aboard the bus and saw that the seats had been removed, replaced by beds stacked two high running the length of the bus. Sophia cried because she didn't like her assigned berth, so Bella traded. We unpacked our books, journals, and silky sleep-sacks as the bus pulled out and onto the road. Now, how on earth are we going to sleep on this, I wondered.

Night trains are one thing, gliding along the tracks with a rocking motion, the clackety-clack rhythm lulling one into sleep. But buses are entirely different. First off, rural Indian roads are in terrible states of disrepair, with large potholes and places where the road has broken into dirt and rocks. Furthermore, the bus must constantly swerve to avoid slower vehicles such as rickshaws put-putting, ox-carts crawling, and of course, cows meandering. The road to Lapuna was no exception. The bus swerved, braked, bounced, and blared its horn as we made slow progress into the dark jungle night. There is no way I can sleep through this, I thought.

The next thing I knew, the driver was walking down the aisle calling, "Lapuna, Lapuna!" I turned over and glanced at my watch—it was 3 a.m. I sat up, put my things away, and shook Bella and Sophia awake. "Girls, girls, get up. Make sure all your things are packed up, and *chalo!*"

Sophia whined, "Mom, I threw up out the window!"

Bella cut in, "No, you didn't!"

"I did!"

"Either way, I am sorry Sophia. You must have gotten car sick. Come on, let's get off the bus."

We stumbled into the night and sat outside a roadside café, waiting for a van to take us the rest of the way. After half an hour a van pulled in and the driver told us to get on board. Slowed down by sleepy kids, we were the last to get on. There were no seats left, so we crawled onto the floor to crouch among legs and feet, and the van took off.

Again, we were dropped off on the roadside. The other travelers stayed on, as they were going to a different beach. Our driver told us, "There is no road to Lapuna Beach. You will have to walk the rest of the way. Follow that trail down the mountain. You are just in time for the holiest, most special week of the year. Good-bye."

The van peeled off, leaving us alone in velvety black night. Adam took charge—thanks to our handsome Safety Officer we were equipped for this moment. "Pull out your headlamps, and here we go."

Packs on, lamps on, we headed down a rocky trail. I expected the girls to complain, it was 4 a.m. and we marched in the fog of sleep deprivation, but they hiked bravely through the dark, down a steep hillside. I stumbled on rocks and roots as we passed thick foliage on either side. After what seemed like hours but was probably thirty minutes, we stepped into the sand of a wide beach. We walked out to the center of the beach where we could see the fringe of jungle on one side, and then the sea on the other, foaming into curvaceous, beckoning waves lit with a hint of phosphorescence. I thought I could make out roofs of structures along the jungle fringe, but in the moonless night it was impossible to tell for sure.

Adam said, "Let's lie here in the sand and sleep for a while."

We pulled out our silk sleep-sacks and crawled into them on the sand. Within a few minutes the cold of the night sand crept into our bones right through the thin silk layer.

Sophia sat up. "Mom, the sand is too cold to sleep."

"It is for me too, Sophia. Let's snuggle for a while." I pulled Sophia close to me and put my arms around her bony frame.

As the grey light of dawn flushed out the blackness and revealed where we had landed, other backpackers tromped onto the beach, gathered wood, and lit a fire. We crowded around it, warming our stiff limbs as the sky turned blue and we finally saw that we had, in fact, arrived in our own version of Shangri-La.

There is a sense that travelers can get, of having arrived where they are supposed to be. India, with its intense, chaotic energy, keeps a traveler from landing in any one place for too long. There is an initial wonderment, when you first get off the train or bus, at the beauty, fresh palette of vibrant colors, newness of a place. Then, after a few days, the heat, touts, trash fires, or sheer crowdedness make you want to leave and head onward. This sequence of falling in and out of love with each place propelled our journey forward, until we landed in Lapuna. After two months of travel, we felt "home."

The as-of-yet roadless location of Lapuna beach meant it was peaceful and under-developed. A dozen temporary restaurants made of bamboo and palm fronds with names like Namaste Rocks and Om Shanti lined the mile-long perimeter where the jungle met the sea. Each one had a collection of coconut-thatch and mud huts behind it, tucked into the trees, to rent out as lodging. The cost to rent these huts was cheap—three or four dollars' worth of rupees a night. In the mornings, a parade of gorgeous, muscular women in saris hiked onto the beach from town, baskets of food balanced on their graceful heads, delivering supplies. The food in the cafes was remarkably good and included wood-fired pizzas served on banana leaf plates, fish coconut curries, chocolate-coconut ice shakes made with potable ice from pure spring water, and *limonana*, which was a blend of ice, lemon, mint, and sugar.

The travelers wintering in Lapuna were European students of Buddhism and Hinduism, musicians, massage therapists, artists, and yoga teachers. They were similar to the people who attended Rainbow Gatherings, and we felt among our tribe. There were home-schooled children Sophia's age who welcomed her into their friendly circle. There were few teens beside Bella, but she spent her days playing cards at Om Shanti cafe with friends she made. With the children thus occupied, Adam and I were able to spend time together, the two of us. We rented a hut behind Om Shanti Cafe and I asked our cook/landlord Aadesh what the van driver meant about this week being special.

Aadesh explained, "This week is Shivaratri, Shiva's birthday. In the town a twenty-minute walk from here is one of the most holy Shiva temples in India. Hindus from all over come for *mela*. There is a free classical music concert nightly. A week from today, the thousand-year-old chariot will roll through the main street. You must not miss it. It is taller than the tallest building. The chariot has rolled every year on this day. Thousands of people come to toss bananas at the monks and priests in the chariot. If your banana hits a monk, then it is an auspicious year for you."

I loved it: hippies, perfect surf, ancient temple, and tossing bananas at monks in a sacred rite. It seemed the perfect place to regroup for a week before heading to Nepal. I raised my eyebrows at Adam. "Whaddaya know—we are just in time!"

Feb 27

Dear Diary,

Today I woke up in a thatched hut on the beach. There was a rat in our room last night, chewing on the thatch. I didn't sleep much even though we hardly slept the night before. I got up and showered by bucket. The cold water woke me up and made me feel alive! I sat in the cafe sipping a strawberry ice and listening to the relaxing sound of waves crashing on the shore. Soft improv music wafted to my ears from the hippies with dreadlocks and exotic accents. We moved into a nicer room with no rats and I realized my iPod was missing. I must have left it on a table for a second and it got stolen. I am strangely okay with that.

I learned how to play the game "Hearts" and won second place among four adults who have been playing for years. Pretty good, huh? Before I knew it, it was sunset and Mom came running over to take me to the water to watch. After dark we went into town which was alive with lights, flowers, Shiva's birthday music, and the sweet smell of street food.

Love, Bella.

Ocean swims, boat rides to remote beaches, music and song in cafes, and walks into town to see music concerts and the colorful mela filled our days. Nights were quiet, with candlelit dinners in the electricity-free cafes, and sound sleep in the quiet jungle. Sophia attended a Montessori morning program and Adam and I used the time to visit shrines and temples in town. And there was potable *ice*. For the first time in two broiling months, ice stung my lips, crunched between my teeth, numbed my tongue. Limonanas with ice, chocolate ices, chocolate-coconut ices. I appreciated the loose, modest salwars of South India that hid my sugar-softened waistline.

At sunset, international travelers, Hindu pilgrims, and locals gathered on the beach. One evening, an orange-robed sadhu named Rama approached Adam and me. He took each of our hands in one of his and talked to us in lilting English. He stared intently into our faces for several minutes, as if he was reading our story in them. Then he told us, "It is good you take your children to all the sacred pilgrimage sites. But the holiest pilgrimage site of all is *home*, when you are loving to each other." I looked at my husband, radiating smiles and openness in this moment, and felt the dusty, cracking blinds over my heart fall away. The clear directness of his gaze seemed to say, this is always here, how it truly is, even when we forget and get angry and disconnected. I wished I could keep this feeling in my mind, and not let my anxieties and anger poison our family anymore. *Love—it is so simple, isn't it? But I had to cross the world and make my way to this cow-patty strewn jungle beach to get it.*

"The holiest pilgrimage site of all is home- when you are loving to each other."
Adam with Rama, an advice-giving, wandering Sadhu, in Karnataka, India.

March 2, 2014

Dear Diary,

Yesterday we saw a five-story tall ancient chariot roll, full of monks, through the small town of Lapuna. To top it off, the monks were being pelted by bananas from the crowded street. The streets were full to bursting, and the family and I had a lovely view from a third-floor balcony. When the cart began to roll, a shout of pure joy rose up through the streets. Hundreds of people helped to pull the cart, using rope as thick as tree trunks. It was so tall, the top teetered way above the rooftops. Bananas flew and the drums played to the beat of my heart. The cart was lovely, like a towering cupcake draped with leaves and flowers and full of smiling monks. A once in a lifetime experience.

In the week I have been here, I have fallen in love with Lapuna Beach and with one of the kitchen boys at my main hang-out, Om Shanti Cafe. His name is Manish and he has big dark eyes and a sweet face. We only spoke once and it was very minimal. We spoke way more through secret eye contact and shy smiles and a sure and unexplainable knowing that he liked me and I the same.

Leaving today was hard for me. I did get his email though. As I walked away, I turned back, almost out of sight. I turned around and waved to him. He blew me a kiss.

Love, Bella.

It took us four buses, a short flight, and a night train to get us from the Karnataka coast to the desert state of Rajasthan. On the bus ride, I stared at the lush green scenery of South India for the last time. Winter was ending and the hot season would bear down upon the jungle, followed by monsoon. We were told that the monsoon rains were so heavy here they call them vertical lakes. It was time to head North.

CHAPTER 15

UDAIPUR & JAIPUR, RAJASTHAN

The night train stopped in the Udaipur station just before dawn. A chai stand stood on the platform before us. The chaiwalla had a long, twirled mustache that was hennaed bright red, and wore an orange turban. He served us Dixie cups of the creamiest, most fragrant chai we had in India yet, and for only five rupees a cup, half the price of anywhere else. We each had three cups while shooting admiring glances at the tall dashing chaiwalla with his fabulous mustache.

A rickshaw took us into the center of the Old City to find a hotel. Udaipur was founded in 1559 as the new capital for the Rajput Mewar kingdom. It was built around a series of man-made lakes, the oldest in the world. Lake Pichola is the central lake around which eleven palaces were built. Today, hotels, temples, palaces, art galleries and shops fill the whitewashed buildings of the Old City. Udaipur's tag of "the most romantic spot on the continent of India" was first applied in 1829 by Colonel James Tod, the East India Company's first political agent in the region. It has been a popular tourist destination ever since.

We found a hotel and ate breakfast on the high roof top over-looking the lake, palaces, and the jumble of ancient and decaying white buildings crowding the lake shore below us. Cows wandered the narrow lanes and monkeys frolicked, leaping from roof to roof. We were captivated. The girls fell asleep in our tall, soft bed and I luxuriated in a hot shower—my first in two months.

We set out to wander the city, and I was quickly discouraged by how the shop keepers and gallery owners stood outside their shops calling to us to *come and see, come and see* their best-priced wares. "Henna designs, Madam? Miniature paintings? Fabrics, purses, carved boxes? Just step in and look?"

"They think they are drumming up business, but it really just makes us want to get away from their store," Bella said.

"Exactly. Maybe I will write a letter explaining that and pass it around. I think they just don't know that hassling tourists isn't good for business."

"Mom!"

"Just kidding."

The central temple was a tower of intricately carved stone that looked right out of Hampi, except that here it was in the middle of a bustling city. We took off our shoes and stepped into the courtyard to learn that this was a Vishnu temple and a service was in progress. Inside the temple we sat among beautiful women while a priest sang to us, accompanied by rousing percussion with drums and *zils*. When he finished, he threw flowers and colored powders over all of us.

We continued toward the main palace, stopping to snack on pizza, chai, and then ice cream along the way. A gang of Muslim schoolboys in fez hats and long shirts all ordered the same faintly pink ice cream flavor, and we decided to try what they were having. Sophia tasted hers and her eyes grew large.

"Mom, I think we are eating roses!"

I licked mine and sure enough, my cone was topped by rose ice cream, which tasted as sweet as a fresh rose smells.

At the palace gate we were told we needed to hire a guide, and one was assigned to us for a small fee. Our guide, Vikram, was a tall, muscular Rajput wearing dangling earrings, a wide pointy mustache, and hand-made leather shoes. His English was impeccable, and his tour entranced us. The city palace was built in 1559, but additions were constantly made over the next four hundred years.

The compound was a labyrinth of courtyards, formal sitting rooms, shrines, completely mirrored bedrooms, and fantastical ladies' quarters and bath houses. The current Maharaj is the seventy-sixth in the Mewar dynasty and rents out parts of the palace for weddings and events. Our guide told us stories of the Mewar family, a history replete with intrigue, invasions, victories, and harems full of wives.

In a courtyard surrounded by massive blue and green glass mosaic peacocks, each one representing one of the seasons, Sophia sighed and said, "You know, I think I'd like to live in a palace."

Vikram turned and smiled his wide under-that-twirled-mustache smile at me. "You know, of course, the Maharaj of Jaipur is a boy of sixteen, unmarried."

In that moment, an entire movie of a possible future flashed through my mind. Jaipur! We would be there next week. I looked at Bella. Every teen boy we have met in India thus far has been bewitched by my confident, tall daughter. *Perhaps, if we could just arrange a meeting, a friendship could begin . . . pen pals via email over the next couple years . . . there could be worse things . . . he is probably very smart and well-educated . . . and then of course we could live in the Jaipur palace, at least for part of the year, and have family ties to India forever . . .*

I shook my head. Vikram had led my family into the next room while I stood there, daydreaming. I chuckled as I hustled to catch up. Me, who has always prided myself on not being a "material girl," thinking this way. Is there such a thing as palace fever?

The palace aside, there was something vaguely off about the tourist infrastructure in Udaipur. We searched the Old City for good places to eat. Good, meaning lively with local customers, and fairly priced. Every other storefront was a restaurant, completely empty and overpriced. When we finally resigned ourselves to eat in one, we ordered and then the food took an hour and a half to arrive at our table. We took to bringing books, games, and cards with us to restaurants, anything to make the wait for food bearable.

Adam had his theory. "What happens is, we order, and then they send a boy out to the market in another part of the city to purchase the ingredients. Then they cook."

I knew he was right. "So where are all the tourists?"

We found out the next day, in an art gallery. The gallery owner told us, "This city used to be full of European tourists, coming to shop, eat, buy art. But since the European economy took its downturn, only a fraction of the people who normally come are here anymore."

During the interminable wait for dinner that night, I pulled out *Lonely Planet* and announced, "It's almost Holi and we have an invitation in Jaipur. Time to move on!" Everyone nodded in agreement, and consensus was achieved.

I clutched a dirty, bent business card in my hand as the taxi wove through Jaipur traffic. I dialed the number and a woman answered.

"Vicki? This is Dena. Can I pass the phone to our driver so you can tell him where to go?"

We had met Vicki at Amma's ashram. She was a Spanish woman who lived in Jaipur with her Rajasthani husband, Raj, and their daughter Anila. Before we left the ashram, Vicky had handed me her card.

"If you happen to be near Jaipur for Holi, come and stay with us. We live in an old, respectable neighborhood where Holi is for the children. Please come."

The driver pulled off the busy thoroughfare and took us into a neighborhood of wide streets and large houses. He rounded about ten corners, and then stopped in front of a three-story, stately yellow house with a gated front yard. Eight-year-old Anila, thick black ponytail bouncing, ran to greet us with fistfuls of Barbie dolls. Bella rolled her eyes and groaned as Sophia leaped out.

"Once again, no one *my* age. This is the theme of my life."

Vicki showed us into the two-bedroom apartment above her family's first-floor living quarters. The apartment had several empty rooms and big windows letting sunlight in. Bella cheered up when we told her she could have her own room. She went in and shut the door.

Holi is the Hindu festival of spring. It is an ancient Vedic harvest celebration, occurring yearly on the full moon prior to the vernal equinox. Holi is a three-day festival, but the final day is the day for color play. The celebrations start the night before with sacred bonfires around which people gather, sing, and dance. The next morning is a free-for-all of colors where participants play, chase, and fight each other with dry powdered colors and colored water, either in water guns and or water-filled balloons. Anyone and everyone is fair game, friend or stranger, rich or poor, man or woman, children and elders. It is traditionally celebrated in high spirit without any distinction of cast, creed, color, race, status, or sex. To many Hindus, Holi festivities mark the beginning of the new year as well as an occasion to reset and renew ruptured relationships, end conflicts, and rid themselves of accumulated emotional impurities.

I had listened to travelers' stories about Holi, many of which included warnings. In tourist areas, the free-spirited celebration has been used by some men as a chance to grope or bother Western females who are normally off-limits. It had gotten so bad in some places that hotels warn their foreign guests to stay off the streets altogether, offering private Holi play within the hotel grounds. I was grateful to have Holi here with Vicki's family.

At sunset we climbed onto the roof to watch the bonfires. All around Jaipur, enormous bonfires were lit right between buildings and in the middle of the streets. We watched the fire blaze on Vicki's corner, as women fed sacred herbs, palm fronds, and flower offerings into the fire. The sun slipped away and the sky turned smoky purple.

March 17, 2014

Dear Diary,

Today was Holi. It started early, with only the youngest children in the street. Sophia and I watched Anila throw colors with the neighbor girls from behind the gate. When Sophia and I stepped through the gate, we each got a sweet and gentle facial caress by a hand covered in colored powder, and the whisper, "Happy Holi." Afterwards, we all threw colors. Bigger boys joined us, and then a group of teen girls showed up with very, very bright powders. I was invited into numerous homes where mothers hand-fed us sweets and salty cashews because our own hands were covered. It ended with a finale of a colored water gun fight in which everyone got soaked with purple water. Loved Holi. Final step: shower and shower and shower.

Love, Bella.

The sight of traditional Indian families and elders covered with colored powder made me laugh and cry at the same time. After doing our best to follow Indian cultural norms for months, the breaking of social conventions and formalities for the day was cathartic. Mainly the neighborhood children played, but then entire families drove by on their motorcycles, covered in colored powder. Even the women, so proper in their saris and head-coverings, played. Adam and I stepped out of the gate to join the fray and became walking rainbows. A group of elderly gentlemen strolled the neighborhood getting a Holi color-rub at each house, along with sweets and nuts to snack on. Everyone was blessing each other with colors in a spirit of joy and new beginnings. Spring!

Delhi in late March was in the height of spring. The polluted winter fog was gone, gentle breezes kept the days cool and the sky blue. The park across from Amy's house was full of flowers. Even the people were slightly tinted in spring colors of red, pink, and purple. Stains from Holi remained on faces and hands for days. It was a joke that everyone shared.

We were relieved to be "home," ready for a break from hotel living and hotel eating. Amy had called me and asked, "So, what food do you miss?" She filled her kitchen with cheeses, wine, pasta, grapes, and apples for us. I bit into some sharp Cheddar, a glass of cabernet in my hand, and then slowly ate the entire block of cheese.

Amy and I clinked glasses. "Amy, you are my hero. All that is missing is bagels and lox and cream cheese."

"Well, there are a few things impossible to get in India, even in the capital. Lox would be one of them."

In the bedroom, the girls squealed over the treasures found in our two suitcases.

"It's like Christmas!" I said as we pulled out fresh, clean favorite clothes from home, as well as art supplies, books, recorders, knitting supplies, Adam's ukulele, and shoes other than the one pair we each had worn for the past three months. I remembered lugging those suitcases through San Francisco, which seemed like a million years ago. Ananya ran from room to room, carrying handfuls of Adam's earplugs and making piles of them under the table and in the cabinets of her toy kitchen. We emptied our backpacks out to clean and re-pack them for the Himalayas. I reached into the bottom compartment of mine and touched an unfamiliar electronic gadget. I pulled it out and realized that I was holding Bella's stolen iPod. The thief was me, rushing around the morning we moved houses in Lapuna.

"Bella," I called out, "get in here right now! Come see what I have."

Bella and Sophia sprawled through the house, knitting, drawing, browsing our stacks of books. Lalli washed our threadbare clothes and silk sleep sacks. Adam sat at his laptop, uploading photos and videos. I ate cheese as though it was my personal cure for homesickness. Vandana cooked her usual fragrant Indian food, which had somehow lost its appeal.

In the evening, Amy took Adam and me to a party hosted by a journalist for the Washington Post. When we walked in the door of the swanky apartment near Lodi gardens, we were informed by our hostess that this was a French cheese, olive, and wine party. I couldn't believe my good fortune. We were introduced to Amy's friends: the India correspondents for *Time*, the *New York Times*, the *Wall Street Journal*, the *Guardian*, and the BBC. I am sure they were lovely, fascinating people, and I observed Adam getting into deep conversations about the Indian economy and whether or not Modi would get elected and what that would do for the country. But, as for me, I cannot recount a single conversation because I stood by the table all night shoveling bites of brie, goat cheese, and camembert into my mouth, gulping crisp pinot grigio between bites. When it was time to leave I teetered out the door and into the car, laughing.

We flew to Kathmandu to re-set our tourist visas, and of course to see Nepal. Tourists in India have to leave within six months but can then re-enter. Although it had been only three months, we wanted to re-set our visas now so we would be able to stay in India through July, when His Holiness the Dalai Lama was leading a ceremony in Ladakh. At the Delhi airport we splurged and lunched at McDonalds. One remarkable thing about India is that even franchise restaurants are sourced locally. Also, meals from a chain like this cost three or four times what a thali plate of rice, curd, curries, dal, and papadom would cost. This McDonalds was beef-free; the menu options were McCurry Chicken on a bun or McCurry Veg. We choose the McCurry Chicken and the meal was a huge disappointment to the kids. But then, as our final boarding call was made, we passed a Starbucks. Bella had recently informed us that her One Wish, the Only Thing on Earth She Pined For, was the taste of a Starbucks caramel mocha frappuccino or some such nonsense. There it was, the fulfillment of her wish. How could I say no? We nearly missed our flight and ran to be the last ones on, but Bella got her wish and Instagrammed it, so Chico's teens would know she drank a Starbucks frappuccino on her flight to Kathmandu.

CHAPTER 16

May I be like a guard for those who are protectorless,
A guide for those who journey on the road.
For those who wish to go across the water,
May I be a boat, a raft, a bridge.

—Shantideva

KATHMANDU, NEPAL

MOPS ADRN read the sign, held by a diminutive man outside the Kathmandu airport.

"There's our driver, Pradep," I said, pointing and steering us towards him.

"What, how can you tell?" Adam said.

"Mops Adrn. That's Adam Moes, with a couple of wrong letters and also in the wrong order." I started to giggle, and then could not stop for the first part of our ride through the city. I asked for the sign and folded it into my journal. A friend had recommended this taxi driver, whom I had called from Delhi to arrange the pick-up. We observed Kathmandu from the taxi window, congested with traffic, pedestrians on the street wearing facemasks as barriers to the diesel fumes. Pradep told us, "A few years ago Kathmandu was not like this, but now so many cars and vehicles, so crowded. And Kathmandu valley is like a bowl, holds the pollution."

We were headed to Boudhanath, a village at the top end of Kathmandu Valley. The center of Boudhanath, Boudha for short, is the Great Stupa, one of the most important Buddhist monuments in the world. It is located on the ancient trade route between Tibet and Nepal. An elderly poultry woman built the stupa around 500 AD. She had a vision and asked the king for land to construct a shrine to the Buddha. The king agreed and offered her as much land as she could cover with the skin of a water buffalo. The woman proceeded to cut a buffalo hide into thin strips and placed them end to end to form a huge circumference. The king realized that he had been tricked by the old woman, but the stupa was constructed according to these dimensions.

The woman's four sons helped her build the massive white stupa complex, including the pure gold top that is decorated with the Buddha's eyes gazing out in the four directions. Of the four sons, one is believed to have been reborn as the Tibetan King, Trisong Detsen, who first brought Buddhism to his country. Another was born as Padmasambhava in the Swat Valley, which now is part of Pakistan. Padmasambhava visited Tibet at King Trisong Detsen's request and established Vajrayana Buddhism there in the eighth century. Since the Chinese occupation of Tibet in 1959, twenty thousand Tibetan refugees have steadily trickled into Nepal from China, and many of these have settled in Boudha. Boudha is now an enclave of Tibetan culture, with over thirty Tibetan Buddhist monasteries, nunneries, and learning centers within a few blocks' radius from the Great Stupa.

We booked ourselves into the PK Guest House, attached to a Tibetan monastery and a block from the stupa. No cars are allowed in central Boudha, so diesel fumes, noise pollution, and traffic were diminished on these narrow cobblestone streets. There was a kitchen on the rooftop for guest use, and a Buddhist library with internet. The room came with two beds, enough for all of us, and big picture windows overlooking the charming street below.

The girls chattered happily as we settled in. I could tell they were excited, in a "this is it, we are going to love it here" way. But also trying not to be, because months of travel in India had taught us that first impressions could be misleading.

Adam suggested we go see the stupa first off, so out we went. The ancient street was lined with shops offering food, vegetables, goods, and sacred Tibetan objects, but no one hassled us or asked us to come in. Monks, nuns, and Tibetan families in traditional long wool dresses and braids filled the streets, as well as Nepalis and foreigners. Everything was so clean and appealing, I felt like we were on the movie set for *Seven Years in Tibet*.

"I am glad to be back among the Tibetans!" Bella said.

We came to the end of the street, where the stupa begins. I looked up at a twelve-foot-tall white tower with the Buddha's eyes on top and said, "It is pretty, but somehow I imagined it would be bigger."

A few more steps and I realized that I mistook one of the directional markers along the stupa's border wall, for the actual stupa.

"Ok, wow, never mind," I said, taking in the smooth white immensity of the monument.

The golden peak of the Great Stupa rises 120 feet above the street, and the whole structure would fill a small city block. Pilgrims, monks, Tibetan families, Nepalis, and tourists were slowly walking clockwise around it, chanting *Om Mani Padme Hum*, *Om Mani Padme Hum*, the mantra of compassion, the best-known Tibetan prayer, which is said to purify anger, pride, jealousy, greed, ignorance, and aggression with its six syllables. Our family joined the slow, inspired parade around the stupa, making the three requisite circumambulations. We entered through a gateway and climbed onto the structure itself, where fragrant cedar offerings were burning in a giant ceramic pot. Tibetan Buddhists believe that coming to this stupa generates peace and contentment for the world. Tranquility and joy surrounded us, penetrated us, became us. Adam pulled us in for a group hug, and Adam and Bella began to softly cry. Sophia patted their heads. Bella sniffed and said "We are not tourists here. This is where we actually belong. And I am proud of that."

The uppermost layer and golden spire of the Great Stupa in Boudhanath, Nepal.

March 26, 2014

Dear Diary,

My day today began with a note giving me freedom from Mom and Dad who were attending Dharma teachings, and fifteen dollars of Nepali rupees, which goes a long way here. I felt like that was the start of a truly wonderful day. Sophia and I roamed the cobble streets, marveling at the shops and smiling at the monks. We walked around the Great Stupa, which furthered our good moods. We bought a few things, including a blended mocha, heavenly. For lunch we met up with Mom and Pop and I got an amazing buffalo burger. At the restaurant, we ran into some folks from Chico! Positively astounding and delightful.

Since today happened to be Dakini day, after dark the whole stupa was wonderfully lit with thousands of tiny candles. Hundreds of Buddhists with dark almond eyes thronged the butter-lamp lit streets. The stupa towered above, spectacularly pure. A big puja went on, involving a mountain of tsok offerings the size of a car, with candy, fruit, nuts, and popcorn. Mom bought some popcorn to throw on the pile, for blessings for our friends back home. The monks chanted rapidly in low voices and blew decadent horns and beat their drums. Then the food was divided up and given away to the poor. It was a lovely thing.

Love, Bella.

The girls and I woke up to the sound of gongs, drums, and chanting from the monastery next door. Adam was out already, so I went downstairs and bought groceries from the shops on our street. We ate German cornflakes and milk from a box, and I drank instant coffee, on our rooftop terrace under the unblinking gaze of the Buddha's eyes on the golden-topped stupa. Adam bounced up the stairs two at a time, and told us, "I ran into a friend from San Francisco. He says Chokyi Nyima Rinpoche is here, at his White *Gompa* a block away. Let's go see him this morning. There are teachings and events going on all week."

Chokyi Nyima Rinpoche was one of Adam's closest spiritual teachers, whom he met twenty-three years ago. He met him in Bodh Gaya and then came to see him again here in Nepal during his year abroad. Over the years the whole family had gotten to know him at his annual retreat in California for his American students. Chokyi Niyma's father, a famous *Tulku*, founded his Boudhanath monastery in 1972. Now Chokyi Nyima ran it with a nunnery, a monastery, a PhD program for Western students, and a service organization called "Shenpen." Because Chokyi Nyima was such a beloved and dynamic Buddhist teacher who visited San Francisco every year, it was no surprise to run into other Californians here.

We walked into the monastery compound and a monk told us Rinpoche was upstairs in his shrine room. When we entered the room Chokyi Niyma grinned, beckoned us over, and gave us each a friendly tap on the head with a metal *dorje* as we bowed in greeting. Students from Malaysia were with him, and he was about to perform a ceremony that they had requested. Adam sat down to be a part of it, Sophia went outside to play with the young monklets kicking balls around the grass, and I took Bella to the Shenpen office to see if she could sign up for volunteering. Anika, a Nepali woman, offered to take Bella to help with various children's programs in Kathmandu throughout the week. Bella lit up like a butter-lamp to learn that she could do this on her own, without the rest of the family.

"It's nothing personal," she explained as we went back to the shrine room, "but after doing *everything* together for months, I really need to do my own thing for a while."

"Bella," I replied, "I understand. You don't have to explain."

"I love you Mommy!"

"I love you too."

After lunch I took Sophia around to see if I could find an activity for her. On the plaza beside the stupa I noticed signs for *Thangka* (Tibetan sacred painting) classes, and we climbed the stairs and peeked into a studio. The room was full of young adults, Nepali and Tibetan, quietly working on canvases of Buddhist deities and mandalas. The teacher, a soft-spoken man named Poorna Lama, introduced himself. He showed us the studio, including his own exquisite, detailed paintings in progress, and I watched Sophia's eyes grow huge with admiration.

I cleared my throat. "So, my daughter Sophia here is an artist." I looked at her, a fifty-pound duckling in a baggy salwar. "I know she doesn't look like much, but she is very dedicated, and would work hard if you would take her as a student."

"Sure, I will take her as student. But she must come every day for a week. And it will cost 3000 rupees ($30)."

"Sophia, do you want to study thangka painting?" I asked.

Sophia nodded enthusiastically.

"Okay she may start tomorrow," Poorna Lama said.

The Garden Cafe, with its almost-like-American buffalo burgers, generous bowls of Tibetan thenthuk soup, and clientele of international Dharma students, would become our daily lunch spot. On the bulletin board in front, overlapping fliers announced Dharma talks, Buddhist teaching series, visiting lamas, ceremonies, and celebrations. I scribbled dates, times, and names into my journal, and compared notes with what Adam had heard about.

I considered the bounty of thirty Tibetan monasteries in one village. In Tibet, these monasteries would have been spread out over vast distances, taking days or weeks of travel to get from one to the other. "This must be the center of the Vajrayana Buddhist universe," I told him. "What surprises me is that twenty-three years ago, you ever left."

"I had no choice," Adam said. "This was the last place I came after a year of travel. I ran out of money."

My mornings had a routine. I crept out of the room before the girls woke up and did my *kora*, or meditative walk, around the stupa. I did kora twice a day, in the morning by myself, and in the evening with the whole family. "*Om Mani Padme Hum*," I chanted, as I passed friendly monks and Tibetan families along the way. The enthusiasm of the prayerful Tibetans was contagious. Joining the circle around the stupa was like entering a warm mind-bath. As I walked, I spun the ancient prayer wheels that lined the border walls, prayer wheels that sent additional *Om Mani Padme Hums* out into the world which each spin. The devotion of the hundreds of people walking with me washed away whatever doubts, worries, or obsessive thoughts I woke up chewing on. *Blah blah blah, girls, blah blah blah, Adam, blah blah blah, breakfast, blah blah blah, next travel plans.* They dissolved, leaving my mind clear and my heart feeling full of love. When I came back to the guesthouse and found Adam deep into geometry lessons with Bella, that love spilled over into a full-on gratitude gush. *We are here in this incredible place AND Bella will complete geometry. Now, that's some rock-star parenting.*

Sometimes I sat up on the stupa and meditated. I met a young lama named Norbu there, who gave me a spontaneous teaching one morning. He guided my meditation, and helped me glimpse something within, underneath the layers of mental habits, emotional patterns, and my individual personality. I listened to him and saw through the illusions, to the bliss and clarity of the way things actually are. "Who we really are is the same as the Buddha: pure, clear love. We don't recognize it, because we are so distracted by mental habits. The spiritual path exists to lead us to what is already there, within everyone." As Lama Norbu spoke, I felt myself grow lighter and lighter, until my heart felt like a balloon, filled with air instead of solid matter. *I am light! I am love! Everything else is an illusion!* I floated back to the guesthouse, stopping to buy breakfast supplies along the way. Before enlightenment, cornflakes and coffee. After enlightenment, cornflakes and coffee.

March 30

Dear Diary,

Yesterday we all woke up early and took Pradeep's taxi up the hill into a neighboring village called Pharping. We went to this cave where Padmasambhava actually meditated on his way to Tibet. He left his handprint in the rock wall. It was powerful in that little cave. I guess that when Mom and Dad were married in 1996 they were told to come and pray there together. Eighteen years later, they finally made it. We also saw Chokyi Nyima visiting the monastery next to it. He was teaching in Tibetan when we walked in, but I was enraptured. He is so extremely beautiful. We were taken to meet this 100-year-old yogi that has been in retreat for FORTY YEARS there. He was so old he could barely speak, and he spoke no English. He poured us apple juice into dirty cups, and waved his hands, telling us to drink. He had this light in his eyes and was so beautiful.

I have been volunteering at a school with Anika and I took a series of Dharma teachings called the eight verses of training the mind. Then I went to a puja in Boudha. Monks wore giant masks that embodied deities. One threw gasoline sand stuff onto a fire, making it flame towards you, while another flicked ice-cold water with a branch of pine. Walking through the heat and cold at once was an enrapturing sensation. Then, sitting in the center of gongs, drums, monks, nuns, golden horns, hundreds of each ringing with rich sound through my ears, I felt my heart beat in time with the deepest pulse of the noise. Tears came to my eyes, I felt reborn, a smile stretching across my face. What is the point of this precious human life if we cannot benefit all sentient beings?

Love, Bella

Adam and I spent a few afternoons a week in the home of a lama named Tenzin Rinpoche, and his beautiful wife Khadro. Rinpoche gave a series of teachings in the afternoons, translated into English by one of Chokyi Nyima's PhD students. He taught on ancient Tibetan texts, with names such as "Restoring the Ease of the Mind." These texts use poetry to describe the true nature of things, which is beyond words or concepts.

"Everything is beyond extremes, beyond mental elaboration," he told us again and again, using different metaphors. "Mind is like the empty sky, vast. Thoughts are like clouds. They don't change the sun. If you spend your time scheming for happiness, all that happens is more clouds. When one's mind is relaxed, one's experience becomes like a river, flowing."

Khadro helped with the translation and saw that students were comfortable. She carried a tiny baby in her arms and her older children peeked down the stairs from time to time.

After teachings one day, I asked her about her babies.

"I have four children under five years old," she told me.

"Four under five," I repeated, surprised. Tibetans are not particularly known for large families. I was concerned, in my midwife way. "You need to take care of yourself, to recover from so many births in so little time."

"Yes," she said, cheeks rosy and eyes clear. "I have two women live with us to cook and care for the children and I get an hour's massage every day. All I do is rest."

"An hour's massage every day?" I repeated, sounding like a broken record.

"Every day. That is why I feel so good." The apartment was small and spare, and this family poor by American standards. There was no furniture other than a bookshelf, no TV, and no car. But Khadro had support and help that is unheard of back home in economically rich California.

"That is wonderful." In my mind, I chanted, *two live-in women and a massage every day, two live-in women and a massage every day.* Khadro did not need my expert advice, I needed hers. The following morning during my kora I observed the Tibetan and Nepali mothers out with their babies strapped on. Every single one was accompanied by at least one other adult, often several other women. My mind scanned through scenes in India, and I realized that there, too, a woman with small children always had other people with her. *Mothers are not supposed do everything alone, the way we do the West.*

I sat on the stupa and thought for a while. *Two live-in women and a daily massage, two live-in women and a daily massage.* I remembered the first Rainbow Gathering we attended as a family of four. Bella was four and Sophia had just turned one. She was not yet walking, so I carried her in a sling, often over vast distances to get from one place to another. The morning of July 4, which was the climax of the gathering, Adam left to meditate in the main meadow as part of the prayer circle. The plan was that I would take the kids to Kid Village for breakfast and face painting, and we would meet up at noon when the meditation silence was broken by the children's parade. It did not occur to Adam to stay with his wife and children during the biggest, most hectic day of the event. I did not ask him to skip the meditation, *just this once, since we are here with two small children, one of whom does not walk yet.*

On the rugged hike to get breakfast in Kid Village, four-year-old Bella quickly got cranky and hot. She was a solid, chunky girl, and I couldn't carry her with baby Sophia already in my arms. Brambles on the trail shredded her satin-and-tulle ballerina dress, which she wore special for this day. The "parade" from Kid Village to the prayer circle turned out to be almost a mile walk in the blazing noon sun at 8,000 feet elevation. When we got there, amidst thousands of hippies dancing and drumming and having the time of their lives celebrating *freedom*, I could not find Adam.

"I'm tired, I want to go back to camp," Bella whined. I searched for Adam, but he was nowhere to be found. We were now sunburned and out of drinking water. I craned my neck, hoping Adam would appear, hoping to run into any number of people I knew, and then gave up. Bella and I began the long trek back to our camp without him. My bones felt like they were disintegrating after carrying Sophia for so many hours, Bella howled her high-pitched litany of complaints as we trudged, and I slipped into self-pity, tears stinging my eyes. And anger, *where was Adam?*

A tall, muscular man wearing a tie-dye strolled by.

"Need some help, Sister?" he asked.

"No, we're fine!" I answered automatically, marching on. Then I stopped and said, "Actually, wait! I, I . . . we could use some help."

He turned and waited for me.

I spoke. "We are exhausted from the sun and need to get back to camp. I wish someone could carry my daughter. I couldn't find my husband."

"No problem, let me walk you back."

He scooped up Bella and placed her on his shoulders like she was a bag of feathers and carried her to our camp. As we hiked together, I cried bitter tears. I was upset that I had to get help from this stranger because my husband hadn't known how to show up for me. I also cried for a deeper loss—I mourned the autonomy I had in my life until that point, the weight of all I carried now as a mother suddenly clear. *I would have to start asking for help.* The man comforted me with gentle chit-chat but it was no use. When Adam finally arrived back at camp, he had no idea why I was angry at him with a rage that seemed to come out of thin air. He had, of course, looked for us too, and was glad we had made it safely back to camp.

"Two live-in women and a daily massage, two live-in women and a daily massage." *Where's Adam,* felt like the refrain to my life when the kids were little. There were a thousand moments when I needed another set of hands but didn't have them. I often faced dinner burning, a child crying, a diaper dirty, the electrician here, the dog escaped, the bath overflowing, and the phone ringing all at once. Adam would be at work, or else at home, but maybe out back either fixing something or just avoiding the mayhem inside the house after his long day at the office. "Where's Adam?" I would ask the toddlers, the dog, the burnt pots piled in the sink, overwhelmed with longing for more adult assistance in my reality. *Where's Adam* was my cry for a village, for in-laws, for anyone. There seemed to be an inverse correlation between the chaos whirling around me and Adam's availability. Thus began my hard time asking for help without sounding desperate and demanding. Adam took to critiquing *how* I asked for help. He would tease me for "being an emergency," or he'd say "*Yes, dear*" in a sarcastic tone.

Now I saw those years with a new perspective. Perhaps Adam did not help me enough because he was not *supposed* to be my only source of help. It had always been a set-up for struggle. Observing life in India and Nepal, I saw that humans are not necessarily designed to live the way we lived in America—one woman and one man, isolated and alone, responsible for their entire castle, their children, earning a living, without other human support. Until the recent past, humans always lived in communities such as extended families or close-knit villages, like the Tibetans, Indians, Nepalis, and probably most people on the planet still do. We Americans, for whom independence is like a religion, are the exception, not the rule. I needed to forgive Adam, and I needed to forgive myself. I wondered how I could clear myself of the lingering resentments I had toward him. They seemed to have burrowed into my very tissues, and they rose to the surface to whisper doubts about my marriage during our most vulnerable moments.

Adam was stir-frying onions in our rooftop kitchen while I chopped greens and carrots. Rice bubbled on a burner. Lama Norbu, the young yogi I had met at the stupa, was coming over for dinner and a puja with us.

Adam said, "I heard about a seminar for Western students in Dharamsala with a highly respected, up-and-coming teacher named Chamtrul Rinpoche. He lived with and studied under Jigme Phunchok, one of the greatest masters in Tibet. Now this young lama is beginning to teach, and it is a very precious opportunity to get in with him." He raised his eyebrows slyly. "The seminar is free of charge. By donation only."

"Sounds great," I said. "I wanted to go to Dharamsala anyway, after our trek."

"Well, there is a catch."

"What's that?"

"We have to be there by April 20. If we are not there for the first day, we cannot attend. And the seminar is four weeks."

"April 20! I don't think we can make it there that soon." I counted on my fingers. "If the trek is five days, and we leave here in three more days, that would give us only three days to get there after the trek. Let me do some research."

"We may have to skip the trek."

"Uh, no, we did not come all the way to Nepal to skip the trek. I'll figure it out. Here are the greens."

Adam tossed them into the wok, and the sound of sizzling filled the room.

The following day I got on a computer and did some research. How could we get from Pokhara, Nepal to Dharamsala, India in a couple of days? I found two options. For a few thousand dollars we could take three flights: Pokhara-Kathmandu, Kathmandu-Delhi, and Delhi-Dharamsala. The second option included a bus to Lumbini, crossing the border on foot, an overnight train to Dehradun and then an overnight bus from there. The overland route would cost only $150 dollars total in travel expenses and included another important pilgrimage site: Lumbini, the birthplace of the Buddha. Pankaj, Amy's travel agent in Delhi, booked us 2AC berths for the night train from Gorakhpur to Dehradun on April 17. Well, sort of booked them. We paid for them but the beds were sold out; we were wait-listed numbers 8-11.

"Don't worry," Pankaj told me, "By April 17 they will have beds for you."

"I sure hope so. We will need them for the eighteen-hour ride."

Poorna Lama used a ruler to map out the sacred geometry for drawing the Buddha's face and body in perfect proportions. Sophia felt shy and asked me to sit in on her first lesson.

Sophia will never be able to do this, I thought, as we watched him work. This is way beyond a ten year old . . . he will have to do the geometry for her, and then she can paint it.

Sophia took Poorna Lama's sketches home with her, borrowed a ruler, and spent the evening practicing the measurements and angles. Each time she did it, she came closer to getting it right. The following day she told me I could leave her on the stairs, she was ready to be there alone. When I came to pick her up she had sketched the geometry onto her canvas by herself, with guidance from Lama, and the Buddha's form was emerging from the angles.

For two weeks Sophia worked on her thangka, sometimes for five hours a day. Poorna Lama chose a classic Buddha sitting on a giant lotus for her, with swirls of halo and color around him. After the figure was drawn and painted, she spent days on the green halo, filling in the space with tiny, individual brush strokes, almost like an impressionist, or pointillist, would.

"Poorna Lama told me that painting is a meditation," Sophia explained. "To do these brush strokes takes total concentration. Through them I can purify anger and hatred, and also send love out to all beings. It trains my mind."

"Oh Sophia, that is beautiful. No wonder your Buddha is turning out so well."

On the last afternoon, an elderly Tibetan couple was sitting on the stoop when we returned to the studio from lunch. They were the oldest-looking people I had ever seen, faces wrinkled like dry fruit, bodies shriveled, their little remaining hair in thin strands, and even their clothes faded and falling apart. The woman was weeping as they sat there facing the stupa. I was astonished that tears could even fall from the eyes of such a dry and withered person. She seemed so old that she had crossed over and become like a small child again. I wondered what she was crying about. Had she crossed the Himalayas on foot to get here, a last wish of her life fulfilled? Was she grieving a child or grandchild, and come to the stupa to pray? She wiped her eyes with a plastic bag of leftover rice that she was holding. I would never know why she was crying because we had no common language. All I knew was that wiping one's eyes with a plastic bag of food is not pleasant or effective. And I had something for her.

"Wait a minute," I muttered, reaching into my purse. I pulled out a carefully folded wad of clean toilet paper and handed it to the woman.

The woman's face lit up and broke into a smile of rotting, brown teeth. Her sorrows seemed to transform into glee as she dabbed her eyes with the tissue. "You made her so happy Mom!" Sophia said, before she stepped around her to enter the building. As I walked away, I thought, No, she made me happy. At pick-up, the Buddha was carefully rolled into cardboard, the lama was paid with a generous tip, and after bows all around we made our final kora at the Great Stupa.

Sophia with her thanka *painting of the Buddha, in an art studio across from the Stupa in Boudhanath, Nepal.*

CHAPTER 17

The journey itself is my home.
—Basho

THE POON HILL CIRCUIT, NEPAL

"Annapurna Peak is 26,500 feet," Bella read from the guide book, as the car bumped along. "Everest is 29,000 feet, so really, it is almost as tall as Everest. It is the tenth highest mountain in the world."

Our family and a hired guide, a twenty-five-year-old, third generation porter named Isur, were on our way to the trailhead for a five-day trek on the Poon Hill Circuit. Our route would take us along a ridge of mountains in view of the massive glacial peaks, without going above 10,000 feet elevation. This made the trek suitable for beginners and families, of which we were both.

"This day will be easy for the first three hours, then we will climb 4,000 stone stairs to get to our lodgings," Isur explained.

I asked, "How do we climb 4,000 steps?"

Isur didn't answer, so Adam did. "One at a time."

The modern world slipped away in fragments. First, we walked along a dirt road, jeeps and trucks passing every so often. Even then, the green, lush landscape called to me. "Where have you been all my life?" the soft hillsides, verdant glens, blossoming rhododendron trees seemed to sing as I walked by. After two hours the road ended. Now we were on a rocky, uphill trail, the original mountain road. People have walked these trails leading to remote mountain villages since at least 550 BC. Above us, high peaks played peek-a-boo with strands of fog. Butterflies and bubbling creeks gave the scenery a tropical feel. Wobbling steel suspension bridges spanned roaring rivers. These terrified Sophia, who crossed them with her eyes squeezed shut. Every hour or so we passed a village. Subsistence farms on tiny terraced plateaus, low stone walls, stone houses, healthy-looking chickens and dogs, ruddy-cheeked children, and anything we could want for sale—soda, snickers, pringles, chai.

The narrow trail was a thoroughfare for hikers from all over the world. Sherpas passed them, heavy gear and supplies in baskets tied to their heads. Ancient local women briskly traversed the steep trails in plastic flip-flops and saris, dusting everyone with their speed and grace. Once in a while the tinkling of bells warned us to step aside and let the donkey trains loaded with food and supplies go by.

Sophia complained, "Mom, all the hikers have walking sticks but us."

She was right. To a person, every foreign hiker had a high-tech trekking pole in one or both of their hands.

"Sorry, I didn't get the memo about trekking poles," I said, tripping over a rock. A walking stick *would* come in handy.

We rounded a bend and a Nepali family sat by the trail, brightly painted sticks of bamboo in their hands.

"Walking sticks, Madam?"

"How much?"

"One hundred rupees each ($1)."

"Fine, we will take four. Pick yours first, Sophia."

We got our sticks just in time to face the 4,000-step ascent. Throughout the five days, Adam, Bella, and I relied heavily on those sticks to assist us along the rocky trails. Sophia, however, only used hers when she was tired. Then she would put it between her legs like Harry Potter's Quidditch broomstick, get a burst of energy, and go running up the trail ahead of everyone.

Dear Diary,

Sunrise on the mountain
Yes, the birds they sing so sweetly.
Distant hints of silent giants
Otherworldly snowy peaks
Shrouded in mist the world slumbers
The waking dawn bring adventures anew
In the blue light, the donkeys pass
the light clip-clopping of their shoes.
And there she is, now bathed in pink.
A graceful mountain, tall and true
The cock plays a soundtrack to my soul
And all the world seems cloaked in blue.
But not her majesty, she shines bright,
brighter far than all the stars.
Towering above the new daylight
Like a silent vigil for near and far.

By Bella Moes

The night before the Poon Hill ascent, I didn't sleep well. Perhaps it was the altitude, but I tossed and turned, anxious I would miss the 4:30 a.m. wake-up. I didn't. Up and out of bed in the freezing cold, I woke up the girls. Bella glanced at the clock and yelled at me for not waking her up at four on the dot, so we would go at the exact same time as the German family we met yesterday. I woke up Adam and he sat up groaning, his face green. He had been sick since the day before when he chugged the raw yak milk a farmer had offered him. *Note to self; don't drink a stranger's raw yak milk out of a dirty bucket.*

We bundled up and were on the trail by 4:40 a.m. We had to go without Adam or we would miss the sunrise. The trail was already packed with people. Sophia was freezing but all I had as an extra layer for her was her neon rain poncho. "At least it will cut the wind," I told her. It was pitch black, with our headlamps giving us thin circles of light. The trail consisted of steep steps, straight up. I hurried to keep up with Isur and the girls and stay ahead of a wolfpack of hikers behind me. I was so strained and out of oxygen that when I tried to speak my words came out as gobbledy-gook, as though I had pebbles in my mouth. Gasping for breath, we made it to the top as the sun was beginning to rise. Isur fetched us hot chocolate and coffee from the chai-stand conveniently located on the 10,000-foot summit.

The peaks, Annapurna and Dhaulagiri, soared above the clouds, appearing to be floating in the ethers untethered to the earth. The Poon Hill summit was an international madhouse of cheers and the wrangling of tripods and massive cameras with lenses like long tongues reaching out to lick the view. Most of the people here had come all the way to Nepal for this sunrise. The mountain peaks turned bright pink, and then appeared to be lined with golden fire.

At breakfast back at the lodge, Adam moaned and belched and made sad faces. I choked on my eggs trying to stifle the "I told you so" that rang through my head. Adam went back to bed, Isur left to find him medicine, and I watched as within an hour, every last one of the hundreds of hikers cleared out of Ghorapani. The bustling village was deserted, and I had the view of the peaks, clouds forming and dancing around them, all to myself. Bella stomped around, positively livid that her new friends had left while she was stuck here alone again, thanks to her sick Dad.

"It figures when I finally meet some kids my age that we could be hiking with, Dad has to do this."

"You're right, Bella. I am sorry you have learned the truth; Dad got sick to torture you."

After a two-hour nap, Adam got up, took the Flagyl that Isur had found in the village pharmacy, and announced he was feeling better. I could hardly walk with my muscle fatigue, but out into the Himalayan sunshine we marched. Sophia placed her stick between her legs like a broomstick and zoomed off on the trail. Bella glowered at me and walked along, head hanging. Adam went silently, bearing the sickness he had brought on himself with dignity. I let them all get ahead of me, and as I walked it suddenly hit me that I was not responsible for anyone's happiness but my own. I brought them out here, I thought, and I am always trying to "fix" things for the three of them. I don't have to do that anymore; what experiences they have is up to them. I need to look at myself now—where am I at, what am I bringing to this?

Sore and exhausted, that's where I am. To keep going forward, I attended to the placement of each footstep along the treacherous, rocky trail. I leaned heavily on the red and yellow bamboo staff. Step, step, stick. Step, step, stick. In rhythm with my clumsy footfalls, pat, pat, pat, cold raindrops began to fall.

"Girls!" I called out, "Put on your rain ponchos!"

I looked up from the rocky trail and noticed the yellow twilight that had fallen. The icy mountains that had been in view off to the left were gone. A wall of dark gray replaced them. We were racing a massive storm across the ridge and losing.

Isur and the family were ahead, out of sight. The rains turned to blinding snow, and I was suddenly alone in a blizzard, at nearly 10,000 feet elevation. My mind skimmed through an encyclopedia of emotional states, feelings storming through me in rapid succession and then falling away.

First, my automatic whiny California response: *Shit, I don't want a storm on my trek. Now I can't even see the beautiful mountains. We were supposed to have perfect weather.*

Then, fear and blame: *I am sure this is dangerous and I should be alarmed. How terrible— whose idea was this? Oh yeah, mine.*

Maternal fear: *My girls! I can't even see them, what if they fall or get lost? No, I have to trust they will be fine. What kind of mother does this make me?*

Awe: *Wow, this is actually beautiful. I am experiencing the fury of Mother Nature in all her glorious power. Look how heavy the rhododendron flowers are, sagging under their coating of snow. I am so high up here, I am practically IN the clouds.*

Gratitude: *Thank goodness we are in Nepal, where there is a village every few kilometers up here. If we were in the West, where the vast wildernesses are devoid of human civilization, we would be toast.*

Grief: *How sad. I have lived my whole life thinking that mountains should be empty of human habitation. At home the indigenous people were disappeared off the mountains. If there hadn't been the genocide of Native Americans, American mountains would have villages in them like Nepal.*

Concentration: *One step at a time. Don't slip. Don't wander off the trail. Don't worry that my sneakers are soaked and squish like a sponge with every step. Doesn't matter. Keep Going.*

Silence. My mind empty of thought. Clear and still like pure mountain air. Just. Walking. Just. A. Step.

Freedom and euphoria: *This is so real. I am here. I am not at home paying the bills. I did it! I got back to myself . . . I AM ALIVE!*

Dedicating this joy to others: *May all beings be happy. May they all be free from suffering and the causes of suffering. I am sending love out from the top of the world, to all of the beings on this beautiful Mother Earth, especially my mom-friends at home who are probably driving around taking kids to school right now. A-ho!*

I ran, sobbing, into the tea house that suddenly stood before me.

I peeled off my wet clothes, ordered a chai, and noticed that Bella was ensconced in a card game with her long-lost German friends. Sophia had also made a friend, a British/German girl named Zsa Zsa. She had twinkling green eyes and a mischievous grin, the European doppelganger of Sophia. Adam and I introduced ourselves to the two sets of parents and we sat together in the cozy house to wait out the storm.

Adam pulled his ukulele out of our pack and we sang "Free Fallin'," "Hotel California," and Bob Marley's "Three Little Birds." This brought the entire multi-generational Nepali family out of the kitchen and bedrooms. They sang Nepali songs to us in return. The

German kids had also attended Waldorf School and knew the same songs our kids did, so they sang some of those together in a jumble of German and English. Isur found a rickety boombox, popped in a cassette tape, and pulled me up to dance a traditional Nepali dance with him. When the storm had blown itself out in the late afternoon we decided to continue the trek with the other two families, as a group. Bella and Sophia were practically delirious from having kids their ages to hike with. The Nepali family sold us warm woolen mittens and hats, we put on our now-dry shoes, and headed out into the slushy forest with a band of children chattering like monkeys and leading the way.

CHAPTER 18

LUMBINI, NEPAL
BIRTHPLACE OF THE BUDDHA

I peered at the rock in the dimly-lit temple, trying to see the carving. This was the holy relic, the statue of the Queen Mayadevi holding onto a tree branch and giving birth to Gautama Siddhartha, who would become the Buddha. Mayadevi gave birth on her way to her parent's home in Devdaha while resting in Lumbini under a Sal tree in May of 642 BC. A stone in a glass case on the floor had a sign that read MARKER STONE, THE EXACT BIRTHPLACE OF BUDDHA. The foundations of ancient temples lay inside the walls of a modern temple in the center of a vast park.

I could barely make out the figures. A woman, reaching up to a branch above her, a child, standing beside her (the Buddha is said to have gotten up and walked several steps, immediately after his birth), and three female attendants. The carving had been stroked by the hands of so many devoted pilgrims over the interim 2600 years that the figures were melting back into the stone.

Adam whispered, "I imagine any woman who wants an auspicious birth will come and rub this statue. The hopes and dreams of all those women have washed Queen Maya away." Down a wide, sunny walkway through a forested park we came across a 2,400-pound bronze baby Buddha statue. He stood twelve feet high, smiling and pointing at the sky. In 2013, Thailand gifted this statue to Nepal as part of an effort to turn Lumbini into a global hub of Buddhism, similar to Bodh Gaya. However, the vast parks of Lumbini were mostly deserted, and the business district in town consisted of a shabby, mostly deserted road two blocks long.

The baby Buddha's giant head dwarfed its stout body—kind of adorable, kind of weird. We photographed the giant babe with puffy white clouds behind his head. The girls imitated his posture and stood beside the statue pointing at the sky.

I said, "It's only fitting that a midwife visits the Buddha's birthplace."

A forested preserve surrounding the temple and the baby Buddha housed temples and monasteries from Buddhist countries around the world. Vietnam, Japan, Bhutan, and even China had a monastery there. It resembled a set for a live-action Mulan. We walked back to the Korean monastery where we were staying for the night. Dinner was served, and we sat down to a meal of miso soup, tofu, rice, curried vegetables, and kimchee.

A Nepal-wide strike to protest elevated gas prices meant we had to get up at 3 a.m. and travel to the Indian border before dawn, crouched on the bottom of a cargo van. We arrived at the border at 5 a.m. when the sun was starting to pink the sky. A ragtag collection of international travelers stood at the border office. Stamped passports in hand, we crossed the hundred-foot, no-man's-land border between Nepal and India and passed through a gateway that said, WELCOME TO INDIA. It was guarded by soldiers holding long guns.

"This is surreal," I said to Adam as we walked across the border at dawn with our rucksacks on, our intrepid daughters leading the way. Bella and Sophia strolled past the heavily-armed soldiers, walking strongly and confidently under their bulky packs, uncomplaining despite the early hour and lack of breakfast. We had been saying how glad we were to be going back to colorful India, but when we stepped onto Indian soil, all hell broke loose. The shabby streets of Sonauli, India, were full of mammoth, parked trucks, because the border closes overnight to motorized traffic. As we wound our way between them, touts came slinking out of the shadows, dusty and dirty as the streets.

"Change money?"

"Jeep to Gorakhpur?"

"Belts, jewelry, handkerchief?"

"Boiled eggs?"

"Raw plutonium?" (*Okay, not really.*)

No, no, no, I shook my head. "Girls—get over here! Stay right next to me!"

The agent at the Indian border office operated at a snail's pace, as if he got satisfaction from making sleep-deprived Westerners stand out on the street for unnecessary hours while he studied each passport like it was a Nursing Board exam. As the sun climbed into the sky the trucks slowly roared to life and a deafening cacophony of engines and horns surrounded us.

All that would have been fine, and we were in good spirits about the whole adventure thus far, until the trash fires started burning around us. Dawn—time to burn the plastic trash in the middle of street. I lost my sense of humor and *insisted* that the children be allowed to sit inside the office, out of the fumes from burning plastic. Mr. Super-slow said, "No," but when his colleague arrived to speed things up he let us come in.

After bargaining with a couple of jeep drivers in an unfortunate manner that led to a fist fight between them, we were packed into a jeep and ready to *chalo*. Bella counted thirteen of us crammed into the jeep, including six "in the boot." Even the driver shared his seat. Ah, India. We drove out of town and within minutes were in pastoral village-and-farm India again. Bullock carts pulling loads of children to school, women in saris with water pots on their heads, thatched roof huts beside mustard fields. The jeep let us off at the train station in Gorakhpur. It was only 11 a.m., ten hours before our train departure. The heat was already coming in waves off the black-top. We had not been in the plains of India during the hot season yet and I was glad to experience it—for a few minutes. We stood on the busy street where the jeep dropped us. People stopped to stare at us with expressions that said "What is this, a real live *white family?* How shocking. They look strange, like they do in pictures."

"Well, we made it off the tourist track," I said to Adam.

Our plan was to find a hotel across the street, take a room for the day, and camp out until the train. To do that we had to walk a few blocks with our big packs on, in blazing heat, navigating an obstacle course of rickshaws, cars, mounds of trash, giant cows, and countless street vendors frying pungent unidentifiable things in huge sizzling woks. Again, the girls moved along as though this was a normal stroll.

We found a hotel room with two beds and a swamp cooler (working only while the power was on). We took it. We napped, watched Bollywood music videos, laughed at Indian TV commercials, and in a crowded local lunch spot found the most delicious curry yet.

I went to the railway station to find out about the status of our wait-listed berths. Internet had been down in Lumbini while we were there, so I didn't know if we were off the wait-list or not. The mustachioed Station Officer checked his sheaf papers and said, "You are now RAC."

I asked, "What is RAC?"

"Reservation Against Cancellation."

I asked, "Does that mean we have beds?"

Head bobble in response.

I tried again, "So, will we have beds on the train tonight, on 2AC?" Head bobble response again. "Can you give me a yes or a no because I don't understand if we have beds or not?"

"Yes, Madame."

"Yes, you can, or yes, we will?"

"Yes, Madame."

End of conversation.

I decided to relax, because as usual in India, absolutely nothing was under control.

At 8 p.m. we stood on the train platform, ready to go. A seating chart was posted, assigning two of us beds. Once we boarded the train, the conductor found a third bed for us, and thus the Moes family slept soundly while traveling across India, the littlest Moes sharing one bed, sleeping end to end like puppies. In the morning I woke up to Adam presenting me with a row of tiny Dixie cups full of chai. We sipped the warm tea together and watched the magenta sunrise. Adam photographed the dawn landscape and then turned to snap photos of me.

"Stop," I giggle-whispered, running my fingers through my matted hair. "I look terrible."

"You are the Rolling Dawn Goddess," he said.

It was a golden start to a long, lazy day on the train. The girls awoke, and more 10-rupee cups of chai were procured. Bella asked Adam to tell her the story of his adoption, and about the first time he met his birth mother, Rachel, at age twenty-eight. Sophia sat quietly for a long time doing something in her journal. She mostly drew in it; her dyslexia made writing not so easy.

"I've written a poem," she announced.

"Let's hear it."

Sophia tentatively began, "I wrote this because I was watching the wheat fields go by."

"Okay."

She cleared her throat, nearly changed her mind about reading it to us, and then sheepishly read:

This delicate, tender blade of grass
That even I know will never last
Will soon be plucked by a gentle hand
Before it's beaten into sand.
But before it's eaten, even I know
It must be softer than white snow.

Our train delivered us in Dehradun, and after driving around the city in circles for an hour, we found and caught our bus right next to the train station we had arrived in. The bus was freezing cold but our warm clothes had been stowed away beneath. This night bus did not have beds; we were expected to sleep in hard tilted-back chairs. Sophia slept soundly, but Adam, Bella, and I only dozed on and off for a few minutes at a time. And so, we arrived at dawn in Mcleod Ganj, above Dharamsala, India, on April 19, the day before our seminar was to begin.

We found a sunny studio apartment in a guesthouse. The studio had a kitchenette, *hot* shower, and soaring views of the snowy mountains and the town below for a hundred dollars a week. Bella walked into the room and fell onto the wide bed, looking wan and fatigued.

"Mom! I am tired of bus rides and train rides and arriving at new places and searching for a new hotel. I want to stay in one place for a while."

"Me too, Bella-boo. And guess what! I have rented this studio for a month, and maybe we will even stay longer."

"Yay, Mommy. I think I am going to really like it here."

Outside the window, a hawk sat in her nest in a nearby pine tree and a monkey nursed her baby on our balcony ledge. I knew that further on down that hill was the residence of His Holiness the Dalai Lama.

"Yes, I think we all will."

CHAPTER 19

MCLEOD GANJ
(OTHERWISE KNOWN AS DHARAMSALA)

In 1959, the 23-year-old Dalai Lama fled from Tibet amidst the tragedy of an unsuccessful Tibetan uprising against communist Chinese occupation. His exodus was driven by warnings that the Chinese were preparing to assassinate him. The young spiritual and temporal leader of Tibet slipped out of Lhasa in the dead of night, dressed as a Chinese soldier. His party traveled through the mountains at night only, to avoid being seen. He arrived at the Indian border sick and exhausted from his perilous two-week journey across the Himalayas, and the world breathed a collective sigh of relief that he made it out alive. The Indian government gave His Holiness land in McLeod Ganj to build a residence, temple, and housing for monks and nuns. A couple thousand Tibetans arrived as refugees and settled there each year thereafter, and the town became a "Little Lhasa." Now the town was predominantly Tibetan, with schools, the Tibetan Children's Village orphanage, nunneries and monasteries, cultural centers, and the Central Tibetan Administration, Tibet's government-in-exile. The

Westerners were largely here with a purpose: to study Buddhism, Tibetan language, yoga, or to volunteer with NGOs. McLeod Ganj was everything I loved most about India. The narrow streets were jammed with shops and the feel was bustling and international but not "touristy." In restaurants, we found cuisines that we had not tasted in months, including real Italian pasta, Korean, and vegetarian Japanese. A five-minute walk from our studio brought us into pristine forest where monkeys tracked us from emerald branches. Himachal Pradesh must be the cleanest state in India, I thought, breathing in the clear mountain air as I huffed up the steep street leading to our guesthouse.

Mornings, I rose with the sun to meditate on the roof. I could see the rooftop of the Dalai Lama's residence peeking through the trees. *That's the Dalai Lama's house. He is probably meditating too.* A Tibetan woman lit a clay stove each morning on the roof next to ours to make smoke offerings of juniper branches. Colorful prayer flags breezily shuddered in a sky fringed by the snowy peaks of the Dhauladhar range. Hawks swooped into the valley below. The Himechali brothers who ran our guesthouse cooked our egg breakfasts to order, and we ate out on the balcony. I took our laundry to be done by the man across the street, and then we each went our own ways, to our various schools for the day.

School—my job here was to learn Dharma. A trail through the forest led Adam and me to Chamtrul Rinpoche's house. Chamtrul Rinpoche was an angelic-looking monk in his thirties, with a serious air about him. I was both intimidated and entranced. We sat with him every day, taking notes while he gave detailed philosophical lectures in his packed living room. As I scribbled, I figured that I could study this material for years to come. Rinpoche taught the precise minutiae of karma, cause and effect, emptiness, impermanence, and how to meditate. His explanations made perfect sense. He would look around the room and say, "You don't have to take my word for it—follow the reasoning—it is *logic*." Bella attended afternoon seminars with Rinpoche after working on math in the morning. She finished geometry and would be ready for Algebra 2 in the fall as planned. Then she met some teenagers who taught Tibetan language. They told her that their language was endangered, because in Tibet only Chinese is taught. She decided to take Tibetan language immersion classes for the rest of our stay.

"Good idea," Adam told her, thinking *way* ahead. "Then we can bring Tibetan masters to Chico and you can translate for them."

Ignoring Adam's lofty expectations, I said, "I think it is a great idea. You will get an introduction to the language and it can be something you can pursue later, if you choose."

Someone told me about a school for kids Sophia's age in Upper Bhagsu, the next village over. Sophia and I walked the road out of town, followed a trail through a verdant forest dotted with houses, and found the house we were looking for. We opened the garden gate and entered an enchanted garden. Flowering shrubs bloomed. Beautiful, healthy trees canopied the yard. And up in those trees, chattering high in the branches, were not birds, not monkeys, but playful Western ex-pat children. I signed Sophia up for six weeks of school. In addition, she joined a Bollywood dance class two afternoons a week in a dance studio with a spectacular mountain view.

April 24, 2014

Dear Diary,

Two days in a row a monkey ran into our room whilst my sis and I were here doing math and stole mangos and bananas off our counter. I screamed so loud that the manager came running.

Today, I began Tibetan class. The Tibetan alphabet is very complex and beautiful. My teacher is this young guy with tiny hands and a fantastic enthusiasm for my ability to memorize the sounds of 34 different characters in a very short amount of time. I really enjoy putting my mind to something difficult; it makes me feel much more worthwhile and alive. I love Mcleaod Ganj. I love the people here and the food here and the view. I love the ancient cow that can barely walk that hangs out outside our guesthouse. I love being out of contact too, it makes me less homesick.

Love, Bella.

We finished our lunch of mo-mos and noodle stir fry at the Tibet Kitchen. I went to pay our bill and the restaurant manager asked me, "Did you go sign up yet?"

"For what?"

"For the public audience with the Dalai Lama this Saturday, for international visitors and local Indians only."

I had heard about these famous audiences, in which the Dalai Lama came out and blessed people in the courtyard of his home. I also heard that he stopped doing the audiences a decade ago, on his physician's orders. The Dalai Lama was seventy-nine now, and his doctors recommended he slow down to preserve his health. When he traveled, the Dalai Lama spoke to stadium-sized audiences; when he was home he needed to rest.

I felt my heart jump in my chest.

"I thought he doesn't do those anymore, for health reasons."

"He hasn't for twelve years. But he announced that he will hold one this Saturday. Go around the corner, with your passports, and sign up."

A few days later my alarm went off at 6 a.m., and by 6:30 we joined the rapidly increasing line in front of the Dalai Lama's residence. The Indian government was committed to his safety; it took two and a half hours to get through security. We handed over our bags to be searched, walked through metal detectors, and then received a pat-down. We were guided into a courtyard and told to wait. The courtyard grew more crowded as the hours wore on, and the din of excited voices resounded off the flagstones. Bella and Sophia lost their patience; our lack of breakfast was a serious oversight. This was the one place in all of India without a chai stand. At 9 a.m. we were instructed to arrange ourselves into groups of twenty or so people by country: Indians here, Americans there, Germans over there, and so on. It took another hour for us to sort ourselves into groups. Now Bella had her "Feed Me or I Will Hurt You" face, and even my blood sugar had hit the pavement. *Maybe seeing His Holiness in person is not such a big deal, anyway. We could go get some breakfast and still have a lovely day.* I was about to give up and suggest leaving when Bella called out, "There he is!"

His Holiness the Dalai Lama came strolling into the courtyard from his house, looking like he stepped off the cover of *Time* magazine. He went to each group and stood with them while a professional photographer took pictures. Our group of Americans crowded together, ready for our moment. Sophia and I kneeled in front. I held a *katak*, a white satin scarf which is a traditional Tibetan offering to a lama, in my hands. Suddenly the skirts of his burgundy robes were in front of me.

My eyes followed the line of his robes until I gazed into his face. His full-hearted smile. Something happened. There are not exact words to describe it, but this image comes to mind: an enormous meteor crashing to earth in a Siberian forest. The force of the meteor's strike is so great that mammoth trees instantly fall in a vast circle around it, flattened by the impact. The Dalai Lama's infinite, unconditional love for all of us was the meteor. And I was a tree, flattened by the impact.

He looked into my eyes.

"*Tashi delek.*" I stuttered the traditional Tibetan greeting, holding up the katak. He took my hand in his and asked, "How are you?"

I felt the expanse of his love wash through me, beyond me, filling all the space in the universe, and answered him by bursting into tears. I knew in that moment that the Buddhist words, the vows, the poetry about love and compassion were not pat slogans, not pretty sayings. Infinite love is real, and I witnessed it, fully present, in a living, breathing human.

He turned and stroked Sophia's cheek and I watched her melt under his touch. Then he stood for his photo, clutching Bella's hand for support. These photos were later uploaded onto His Holiness's website, for the 1500 of us in attendance to download, print, and hang on the wall, a once in a lifetime picture. And so, we got a portrait with His Holiness, sunshine glinting on us, everyone radiantly smiling around him except me, whose face is contorted by a sob.

"The monkeys show me where I came from, the monks show me where I want to go," I told Adam. I was trying to explain why I loved it here so much. Not only was I studying with Chamtrul Rinpoche for four hours a day, but I met Tibetan monks and nuns wherever I went: the chai stalls, the grocery stores, and while having lunch and dinner. They were friendly, and easily struck up conversations with me. I learned so much from these interactions, I felt like I could eventually get enlightened running errands around town. Two young monks met with me several times, sharing stories about their families and their escapes from Tibet. I asked them leading questions, trying to provoke an admission of anger towards the Chinese. I could not elicit any. I thought about how we in the West hold onto our anger and resentment like they are precious gifts. We are *victims*, these feelings are our *right*. The monks explained that holding onto anger is like holding a hot coal in your hand with the intent of throwing it at someone. You are the one who gets burned. But from them, this was not just a saying, it was who they were, all the way to their bones.

One afternoon a Tibetan friend told me, "You were Tibetan in a past life."

I was honored by that thought. "I was?"

"Of course," He answered. "That is why you feel so at home here. But at the time of your conception you saw how things were and chose to be born, this time, in the Golden West. To be born in Tibet now leads to too many problems. I think there are many of you like that."

I considered what he said all afternoon. We were lucky to be here as Americans, with US dollars to spend and US passports. The Tibetans did not have the luxury of knowing that when they tired of this adventure, they could return home. We had the benefit of it all: air-conditioned cars and hot baths back at home, as well as access to profoundly spiritual and beautiful places. Adam and the girls and I, we seemed to have been born in the perfect place, at the perfect time. We lived within what was perhaps the pinnacle of the human condition, the flowering of human civilization. I felt immense gratitude, and also the weight of knowing that I enjoy an absurd standard of living that only a fraction of the world gets to have.

But the conversation about privilege quickly changes in the Buddhist context. As my friend reminded me, I was born into privilege *this life*. Yet this life is transitory. Who knows when it will end, and what the conditions of my *next life* will be. It all depends on how I use this one. According to Buddhist teachings, people born into material luxury tend to squander their lives away, worrying about protecting, and seeking to increase, material gains, none of which lasts or comes with us when we die. We bring only our karma, the energetic results of our actions, into the future. I almost sensed that the Tibetans took pity on us Westerners, who easily fall apart without our excessive material comforts. Our reliance on our abundance of *things* makes it hard for us to understand that things do not actually cause happiness. My Tibetan friends often reminded me that people in the West suffer too. It is just a different kind of suffering.

Like the Buddha taught, our own material circumstances changed overnight. Impermanence. I was a midwife today, but tomorrow I would not be. Wishful and optimistic me, I had begun to think that nothing was going to come of my investigation. It had been four and a half years since the complaint against me had been made. I had held the vision that the Board of Nursing would drop the charges. I had prayed for that outcome in Bodh Gaya, at Amma's, at the Great Stupa. I had pictured the letter, the "Complaint Was Dismissed Without Merit" letter, time and again. If they thought I was a menace to society, how could they justify taking years to come after me? When I read the email from my lawyer, which came a week after our audience with the Dalai Lama, my heart plummeted through my chest and landed somewhere in my colon. The panic that rose up blinded me. When the fog of freak-out cleared enough, I read again that the California Board of Nursing had formally charged me with six counts of gross negligence and incompetence and intended to revoke my license.

"Shit! Fuck! Oh, Fucking Shit!" I yelled at the computer.

"What? What?" Adam asked.

I couldn't even say the words aloud. Gross negligence? Incompetence? How could those labels be applied to me? Me, who has had a hundred percent healthy babies born under her care. Me, who is goddamned smart, not to mention Yale-trained. Me, who has been responsible and committed and has worked for a decade to build my reputation. Me, the main provider for my family, whose income creates the situation my family calls home, who has earned her living this way since she was twenty-five. Revoke my license?

I spat the news out and heard a high-pitched tone to Adam's voice. "On what basis are they making those charges?"

I skimmed the pages and tried to make sense of the legalese.

"Um, on the basis that the two clients in question were VBACs, vaginal births after a cesarean."

"Aren't those legal? I thought you were within your protocols."

"I thought they were, I was following the guidelines the California Medical Board has for licensed, non-nurse midwives, because there ARE no guidelines for nurse-midwives on the books."

"If there was any question, why did you take VBACs at all?"

"You know why I did. I had to. It's a human rights issue. I wasn't going to let hospitals force women to have unnecessary surgeries. I attended VBACs because that is who I am. When the doctors in our county let insurance companies dictate their practice, and refused to allow women natural births, who stood up for the women? Midwives."

Adam was quiet for a moment and then asked "And weren't the two babies in question born safely, after hospital transport?"

"Yes, both babies were born healthy, by cesarean section, after I brought them in."

"So, what, exactly is the problem? How could that be incompetence? Why would they shut a good midwife down?"

"I don't know. I have to read through all these papers. It seems that the board interpreted these two clients as out of my scope of practice, because that is what the Chico OB doctors told them when they came up to investigate the complaint."

"Well you better get with your lawyer. It sounds like the docs and the board are in cahoots with each other." Adam sounded frightened. I knew he was not ready to support our family with his low-profile acupuncture practice; I had never asked him to. We were both counting on my business to stabilize our finances upon return to the US. All that we assumed we had back home was suddenly uncertain.

"That's right, that is why I have a lawyer. Damn! I am not ready for this."

"Don't worry." My lawyer Peter said in his deep, bass voice. "They are not going to take your license. You may get probation of your license for a few years. And pay a fine. But I won't let them take your license."

"They can't take my license? You won't let them?" I asked, wanting to hear that again and again, on repeat, for about twenty hours, to erase the dread that had turned my gut to stone since seeing those charges.

"How much longer will you be out of the country? Two months? Okay, then enjoy the rest of your trip. I'll file a notice of defense and then make sure no court dates are set until after you return. Try not to worry."

Try not to worry. I thought of the hundred thousand dollars my colleague near San Francisco had paid her lawyer already, for a similar complaint. I thought of losing my RN license, earned through a forty-thousand-dollar education, the bread and butter for my family. Right.

When I meditated in the mornings after that, facing the direction of His Holiness's home, I imagined the doctors and the nursing board in front of me and sent them rainbows of light with my prayers. *May all beings be happy, may they all be free from suffering, especially Doctor You Know Who and the California Board of Nursing. They are people like me, trying to do their best. Like the Chinese in Tibet. Now I can practice what I have learned.*

Sophia's eleventh birthday fell on a Wednesday, and Adam and I brought cake to her enchanted forest school. The town plaza had a bakery where I would buy the girls soft serve ice creams after dinner. I ordered a cake with a fruity middle layer, a crème frosting, and Sophia's name in curly script. We took a rickshaw, cake in Adam's lap, to her school. The children were sitting in a circle in the garden, finishing lunch. The cook had made them rice and dal and vegetable curry, which they sopped up with chapatis. We sang "Happy Birthday" to Sophia, cut the cake, and shared stories while eating it under the trees. It was the simplest birthday celebration she had ever had, and remarkably, it was enough.

A few days later Sophia performed with her Bollywood dance class at the Tibetan Institute of Performing Arts. She had joined the class just in time, her teacher Drolma told us. They were preparing two dances for a performing arts festival. Sophia picked up the

Young Bollywood dancers prepare for their show, at the Tibetan Institute of Performing Arts, founded by the 14th Dalai Lama, in McLeod Ganj, India.

choreography and was ready to perform but needed a sari to wear. I found one, a tiny pink sari that shimmered with sequins and silver threads and gave it to her for her birthday. During a furious late spring hailstorm, Sophia danced to the Hindi pop hits "Dhoom Taana" and "Nagada Tam" with her class for a packed auditorium, fog machines rolling, strobe light flashing, and the rowdy audience shouting with approval.

I lay in bed while my family slept, thinking about VBACs. I always said that VBACs were my favorite births. A woman who has previously given birth by major abdominal surgery appreciates the experience of a natural birth: every contraction, every sensation, every push. Afterwards, when she is in her own bed with her baby in her arms and the endorphins pumping, instead of laying in OR recovery groggy and gutted, she radiates euphoria. She knows, then, that there is nothing fundamentally broken or wrong with her, and the trauma from whatever happened last time to land her in the surgical suite begins to heal. As a midwife, I witness the birth not just of a baby, but of a stronger, more confident mother. In those moments I know my work has a purpose. I am helping the world become a better place.

When I was a student midwife at North Central Bronx Hospital in the mid-nineties, VBACs were treated like any other laboring patient. Then, in the early 2000s, VBACs were suddenly banned and women with prior c-sections were no longer "allowed" to have natural births. The primary reason was that some studies showed that when drugs to induce labor were used, complications were more likely with VBACs. Instead of limiting the use of those drugs, the American College of OB/GYNs recommended banning VBACs instead. This recommendation resulted in nationwide hospital and insurance policy changes and caused an epidemic of surgical births. By the time I left for India, one in three American women were giving birth by c-section, half to two-thirds of those medically unnecessary. The World Health Organization recommended a ten to fifteen percent c-section rate for the United States.

VBAC women had to seek me out and convince me to take them as home birth clients. There was Heidi, who planned to drive to San Francisco, four hours away, to birth at a hospital that allowed

VBACs. In the final months of pregnancy, she decided to birth at home instead. It was a good thing because her labor was only two hours and she would have given birth on the freeway. There was Melissa, having her sixth baby, and only two of her other children had been born by c-section. She gave birth in a pool of warm water in her living room, surrounded by her husband and five older children. Aimee was a fitness trainer and author, who had both a cesarean and a natural birth previously. We sat around her after her short and sweet birth and toasted her with fine champagne. The two VBAC clients I transferred to the hospital for blood pressure problems needed surgery to deliver their babies, and then medical interventions to control the blood pressure. Their blood pressure complications had nothing to do with the fact that they were VBACs. But that was what the board was coming after me for, nonetheless.

May 12

Dear Diary,

Today I was extremely tired because last night I slept over at this sweet girl named Ella's house. She is American but has been living in India since she was three. We watched funny videos and played cards and laughed. It was so fun.

My afternoon teacher, Wang Bhumo, took me for a walk to the Dalai Lama's temple. There were lots of Indians at the temple for some reason, and they seemed terribly ignorant, asking silly questions and being almost rude. Wang patiently answered each question and then as they were walking away, I waited for her reaction of annoyance, frustration, or anything. But all she said was "These were good questions. It is important to think about why we are Buddhist." I was deeply inspired by her reaction. Then her friend asked if we wanted to do an offering with him to the spectacular gold Buddha statue. It was very powerful and I am feeling very alive. My aspiration was to speak kindly to my parents and have patience.

Love, Bella

I booked our return flights with a heavy feeling. There was now an endpoint. Our final destination in India was the Himalayan kingdom of Ladakh, where we would attend the Kalachakra Ceremony for World Peace with the Dalai Lama. Then we would fly to Thailand for a couple of weeks, arriving home in California the week before Bella started high school. The house, the cars, the need to find health insurance, and now my legal troubles would require our attention immediately. Food would cost what it costs in America, again. *How can I pay four dollars for a coffee drink again, when I am used to our whole dinner costing that much?* We'd have to get our businesses up and running right away. I would be grocery shopping, scheduling appointments, planning dinners, taking the girls back-to-school shopping, and pulling our crap out of storage. Or maybe we could stay here in McLeod Ganj, I thought. Adam had started giving acupuncture treatments to Chamtrul Rinpoche's students during the daily lunch break. We could probably live off a few treatments a day. Sophia could stay at her forest school. But there were no high schools for Bella. Our dog, our renters, our friends, and a cadre of pregnant mothers, who had been receiving prenatal care from another midwife, were awaiting our return.

At our last morning seminar Chamtrul Rinpoche relaxed, looking around the room and smiling at every one of us for the first time. I hadn't noticed he had dimples before, he always seemed so stern. He admonished us to go home, and not to even consider running away to India to become Dharma bums. "Go home to your jobs and your families. Dharma practice doesn't mean running away from your life. It means to be in your life, every challenge and obstacle an opportunity to develop more love, more compassion, more patience. Be of benefit to your home communities."

I bowed my head, tears stinging for the zillionth time. *I am going. I got this.*

CHAPTER 20

TSO PEMA TO KULLU VALLEY

My dread of returning home was a stone I had swallowed and could not pass. I need to sort this out, I thought. I need to figure out what the problem is and find a solution. I looked out the greasy window on the hot bus and squirmed in my seat, feeling crampy all of a sudden. Crampy, and irritable. The obvious stressor was my nursing board charges; being Chico's midwife was not just a job, it was *my life*. Yet I didn't want to admit how much it mattered. I looked for the source of my anxiety elsewhere. I have been spoiled by India travel, I thought. I figured the trip would be enough of a break, that I would be glad to go home and get back to it. But it hasn't worked out that way. Maybe I don't want to go back to cooking and cleaning and driving the carpool, to mountains of paperwork and housework.

The bus ride was long and hot. We were headed to Mandi, and from there would catch a bus to Tso Pema, with its sacred lake. When Adam was in India twenty-three years ago, Tso Pema was one of the pivotal places of his trip. In the caves above the lake, Guru Padmasambhava, the founder of Tibetan Buddhism, did extensive retreat on his way to Tibet. Still today, nuns and yogis retreat for years in caves there. The lake is sacred to Buddhists. Hindus, and Sikhs.

The girls were quiet, but Adam got strangely irritable. It seemed to me that whenever I felt grumpy, Adam got even more so, as though PMS was contagious between spouses. Perhaps this was the natural outcome of being married so long, or of traveling in India together for six months with all of us always together in one room, or both. I watched Adam grab Bella's fleece sweatshirt to use as a pillow, and saw the sleeves blowing out the open window. It appeared that the fleece would blow away and be lost as he drifted off. When Bella asked for it back, he turned around, bunched it up, and tossed it at her. Bella rolled her eyes. I shrugged at her, determined to be patient with our collective funk and then forgot all about it when I got an unmistakable feeling of warm, wet blood between my legs. It was my period, ten days early—surprise! When the bus driver pulled into a station and called out "fifteen-minute lunch stop," Adam jumped off. Here we go again, I thought. Adam walking off in a hot and chaotic bus station.

"Wait!" I called. I climbed out after him. "Don't walk off! I need you to stay with the girls. I have to go to the bathroom right now." I said.

This was one of *those moments*: me asking for help in a pushy, desperate tone, inwardly building my case as if I already knew he would balk at how I had asked. Time froze, and I seemed to observe the two of us from above, watching to see if I had asked him *right*, waiting for his reaction.

"What do you think I always do, dear, and I don't appreciate how you asked."

Whatever.

I ran and did my business and got back on the bus.

Bella asked "Why was Dad wagging his finger at you?"

"Was he wagging his finger? I didn't notice."

"He was."

I didn't want to answer her because I knew how she'd react. "I guess he didn't like how I asked him to stay with you while I run to the bathroom."

"What the *hell*, Mom. You don't deserve that. What is wrong with him?"

"I don't know Bella." I tried to defend him, make it seem okay.

Bella, with her keen sense of *fairness*, often pointed out when things between Adam and me did not seem fair, and usually ended up siding with me. I tried to deflect her involvement in this situation, but my words sounded hollow. "It's me. I am not good at asking for help . . . he is irritable sometimes. We're both irritable today. After a long, hot bus ride leaving a place we loved, with my legal troubles looming over us, it's not surprising. None of us are at our best today."

Her eyes narrowed. "Whatever."

Tso Pema was small and shabby, dusty and hot. I felt anxious and PMS-y and unsure exactly what we were doing here. I wanted to encourage Adam to take care of us, but could feel him wanting space, to get his own mind clear. Again, I heard myself sound like I was pulling, begging him, even though I tried not to. I said, "I'm nervous about what to do with the kids here. We all miss Dharamsala. This is your special place, so I hope you will take charge and be the guide for us."

He spoke without facing me. "I am going to set you and Bella up in your own room and then leave you two to it. I'll take Sophia and we will rejoin you in a few days after your periods."

"What? I don't know if I like that idea."

He still spoke to me while looking at something else. "Well, you put me in charge and that is what I am doing."

"Oh."

We rented rooms at the Nyingma Monastery. Adam and Sophia took a room on one end of the monastery, with me and Bella at the other end. Adam placed Bella and me in the "fancy" side, where our room had a private bathroom, wide windows, and TV. He and Sophia stayed in a small, TV-less room on the "monastic" side. Regardless, Bella and I felt banished. We cheered ourselves up watching Indian movies on TV for a few hours until the novelty wore off. Then we took a walk in the dusty heat around the sacred lake. The monkeys were so vicious, they attacked people, jumping on them and tearing food items right out of their hands.

I tried to make the together time with Bella fun, but it was hard in this place that neither of us really wanted to be. Bella was hurt by Adam's attitude towards her. I was too. I did not want to say anything negative about Adam, but Bella did enough talking for both of us.

"Sometimes I think Dad is the most selfish person I have ever met."

"Don't say that, it isn't true."

"How can you say that? I think you know it is true. You do everything for me and Sophia and for him. You're so giving, you deserve someone who can love and care for you as much as you love and care for them."

"No, that is not how it is. Dad does love and care for me. Women just . . . naturally . . . well, not naturally but culturally, or maybe, yes, *naturally*, take care of everyone. Look, I can't even think about one of us without thinking of all of us. It's like you are all a part of me. Men are different. It's not just Dad." I sighed. "I hope that changes by the time you have kids someday."

"I'm never having kids, so it won't matter."

June 5, 2014

Dear Diary,

I am currently sitting on the shore of Lake Rewalsar, at sunset. The sounds of children laughing and birds chirping floats on the breeze, along with the muddled splash of fish fighting for food. Tibetan monks sit with their malas, praying to the giant Guru Padmasambhava statue and being stared at by extremely numerous Indian tourists. Highlights of the day:

• Baby monkey attempting to eat bread dough, stuffing its mouth, wondering why it is so hard to eat and sticky, looking around at all the people, including me, who are laughing at it, then making tiny squeaking noises

- Being let into the spectacularly intricate temple by a monk who spoke no English
- The beautiful, often toothless smiles of the Tibetan elders whenever I greet them in Tibetan

Love, Bella

Bella and I ran into Lama Gelek, the yogi from Bodh Gaya with solar eyes. He was also staying in the monastery, and with a few words of broken English he invited us into his room for coffee. He was exuberant, and I guessed that he had been in meditation retreat for days or weeks and had reached the blissful state of a Buddha. He boiled water for coffee, and then gave us prayer flags, Tibetan trinkets, and herbal medicine pills from the Dalai Lama. He laughed with delight as he gave us his things, as if giving us stuff was the most fun he'd ever had. He held my cold, clammy hands in his strong, warm ones. I was disconcerted and not sure what to make of it. Later, I decided that he had been exhibiting pure love and generosity, and it was hard for me to be on the receiving end of it. He even wanted to give Bella the slippers off his feet. "No, no Lama-la. Bella has shoes in her room. She has shoes."

As we walked upstairs to our room I said, "Wow, that is what the practice of generosity looks like."

"Yeah," Bella answered, "I sure wish Dad would learn some."

That night I had an erotic dream about beautiful Tibetan men. In the dream I enjoyed the male attention and woke up aroused. It hit me that Adam and I had not made space for a romantic connection in way too long. I went straight to his room, thinking that this was it, I know what to do to fix us. I found him reading on the bed, and Sophia on her DSi. I told him I missed him and asked if we could snuggle. I imagined that Sophia could skedaddle over to the other room, where Bella was watching TV. But he was busy reading and said he would stroke my arm after I stroked his first. "Stroke your arm? I am craving physical connection!" He wouldn't have it. I stroked his arm half-heartedly, and then he stroked mine even less attentively, and I left, spurned.

I told Bella that I needed to be alone and went for a walk. A temple nearby housed a fifteen-foot golden statue of Padmasambhava sitting on a lotus. The temple was deserted, and I sat down before the statue and watched my breath until the raging voices in my head settled down. Then I prayed for clarity.

"What can I do to embrace returning to Chico? And what is the truth about me and Adam?" I asked silently, to the sacred statue before me with golden skin and blazing lapis eyes.

I sat in the dark silence for a long time, questions swirling around my head, unanswered and unanswerable. This was a familiar place—wondering if Adam and I were truly meant to be together or not and wishing someone could tell me what to do. In 2007 I considered leaving him, and even emptied his Random Access Method closet contents onto the driveway. I had been seething about various aspects of our living together but was also brokenhearted with love and frightened of living apart. Friends intervened with intensive couples counseling and we ended up working hard on our issues together, and the family stayed intact. In the dim temple I stared at the whirls and twirls in the halos around the statue's head, and at the spirals within the colorful lotus petals. The color and the intricate designs dazzled me. The beauty of the statue overwhelmed my senses and drained my head of thoughts and assumptions.

Slowly, slowly, out of the darkness, out of my intense concentration of sitting and staring at the statue, an answer came. Your biggest attachment, a voice inside me said, is to your idea of marriage. You cling to the hope that your marriage is working, and to the notion that it is good for your kids if you stay together. You are fearful, because you think you "need" Adam, and you can't survive alone. If you cut away that fear, which is only an illusion, perhaps you both would be freer. What are you teaching your girls if you do stay with him, and what are you teaching them if you don't? Your ideas about marriage are merely concepts. Stories. This could be the final chapter of a beautiful eighteen-year cycle of your life, and a new beginning for you both.

Holy. Shit. I sat immobilized by the message that had come through. And startled by how clear and happy I felt. For the first time since the kids were born, I knew that I could make it on my own. I didn't have to stay with him for *them*. I realized I was power-ful instead of helpless, strong instead of defenseless. The world was wide open with fresh beginnings. I could choose to stay married or I could not. I chose not.

A few days later Adam and I sat together on the dark balcony. I had been waiting for the right moment to tell him. I had gotten an email from a friend back home saying, "Your place looks beautiful, the ladies are taking great care of it." Those words started me thinking that I could ask our renters to stay on as housemates with me and the girls. A house full of women was what I wanted, to help with the cleaning and cooking and gardening and raising teenage girls. It wouldn't be me feeling so alone anymore!

I had been thinking about things from Adam's side, too. I was certainly no one's definition of a saintly wife. Our marriage had pretty much revolved around me and my wild schemes. When I needed to pay off my student loans, Adam moved from beautiful Sonoma County, California, to Leavenworth, Kansas, for my first job. When I had baby fever and wanted kids *now*, even though Adam was a year into grad school and really needed to focus, Adam said okay. For years, my being the home birth midwife had been the most high-maintenance, high-drama aspect of our life, and Adam backed me up unfailingly. When I was harassed by the doctors and couldn't stand up to them, I would let my anger out on Adam, later.

"Don't project your hatred of patriarchy onto me just because I am the most conveniently located white male," he would request.

And when I decided we should spend a year in India, Adam started packing. Without me, his life would be much more stable and calm. He would probably progress on his spiritual path quickly with me out of his hair. I wanted to free him up for that. I chewed my cheek and wrung my hands as we sat in silence, staring out at the dark waters.

"Adam, what the hell were you doing over these past few days?"

"Look, after six months of living in one room with you ladies, I wanted space from you during your periods. That's all. Like a 'red tent.' You don't realize it, but you both get emotionally labile. I wanted to give Sophia and me a break."

"Well, the way you went about it was wrong, all wrong, to be so cold like that, out of the blue. A red tent is something we would *choose*, not have you force it on us in an unloving way."

"Unloving? Farthest thing from it," he said.

"Well, that is how it felt to us. And while you were 'red-tenting' us, I thought a lot about us. I had this vision in the temple . . . I want to tell you about it."

Adam stared out at the water, his face relaxed. He had no idea what I was about to say. Or did he? I was sure that deep down, a break was what he wanted too. I took a breath. "I saw that it could be beneficial to us both if I set you free. I realized that I am not good for you. I am over-controlling and I seem to lack the ability to fully trust you, even after all these years. I think we both can do better, we can both be happier. I want a divorce."

Adam's voice was surprisingly calm. "Okay . . ."

I told him that our return to the US seemed like an auspicious time for a new chapter to begin. But that I wouldn't push him out the door, of course. I cannot remember what else I said, but when he finally spoke, I could hear his disbelief.

"Too bad," he said, "because during these days apart, I had been thinking about how I was going to change when we got back. Cook more, clean up my stuff, and even remodel the house for you."

I stared out over the water and tried to picture that. But all I could see was a change that would be much, much bigger. "Oh, well."

I went to bed feeling courageous and clear.

Somehow, despite the fact that I was bent on separating as soon as we got home, we carried on together into Kullu Valley. We were waiting for the Manali-Leh highway, the road to Ladakh, to open. The snow was still twenty feet high in spots along the "highest motorable road on earth," we heard. But the Border Roads Organization was working to clear it. The Indian government was air dropping cooking oil into Ladakh, newspapers said. Because the road was so late to open, people had run out. We would be among the first to visit this year, to attend the Dalai Lama's Kalachakra Ceremony for World Peace.

The bus ride to the Kullu Valley region was otherworldly. We traveled through mountain canyons, along rivers and across gorges, to Manikaran in the Parvati Valley. Adam remembered it as a pristine, sleepy village in the mountains, with beautiful hot springs in the center of town. As we got close, however, the roadways were jammed with giant buses and snaking lines of taxis, honking their horns.

"This is not how I remember it, there were no buses, hardly any cars at all," Adam said.

"I guess a lot can change in twenty-three years."

The town was across the river from the road. We needed to descend steep concrete steps to the bridge over the rushing Parvati river. But there were so many people coming up the steps from town we could hardly move. It was a traffic jam of Sikh Punjabis. We walked against the tidal wave of humanity with our bulky backpacks, trying to follow Adam. The quiet, beautiful village Adam remembered was gone, replaced by an overcrowded Punjabi tourist destination. We booked a room in a hotel that had its own hot spring pool, and the soak almost made the hassle to get there worth it.

"Let's trek up to Kheerganga tomorrow," Adam said.

"Where is that?" I asked

"It is a ten-kilometer hike from a trailhead, not far from here. There are a couple teahouses with beds and food. It is beautiful up there, and I remember the hot springs as pure magic." He glanced about forlornly. "Of course, things change."

The next morning, we left our big packs locked up in our hotel and hitchhiked out into the hills along a bumpy dirt road. Where the road ended, an enormous dam was under construction. The dam tore a mammoth hole of concrete and industrial machinery into an otherwise postcard perfect mountain view. "The dam has been sitting in this condition for five years now. I think that they do not plan to finish," our driver told us, bobbling his head in dismay. I could see Adam's heart breaking, the mountain hideaways of his memories demolished by the march of progress.

We found the trail and hiked into the mountains. Once the dam was out of sight, we were in lush green forest, tiny hamlets of farms here and there, and an occasional herd of goats in otherwise pristine wilderness. The trail followed a narrow mountain canyon with waterfalls and gorges along the way. The walk was strenuous and uphill, but we were strong from our Nepal trek and the month-long stay on the steep hills of McLeod Ganj. Halfway, we stopped in a meadow where a waterfall sprayed horizontally out from the rocks, resembling a cobra of water, ready to strike. A Hindu priest sat by the sacred site to ensure that people took their shoes off near it and treated the area with respect.

The final few kilometers were straight up hill and bone-grindingly hard. Adam led the way, but the girls and I lost sight of him and fell behind. The trail was slippery with mud and in places turned into rocks scattered across dangerously ice-cold, rushing streams. The girls were losing steam, plopping themselves onto boulders as we rounded each bend. "Come on girls, almost there!" I panted again and again. I was both freezing cold and drenched in sweat. And, of course, I was angry at Adam for not walking with us and leaving me behind on the trail to hike with the girls alone. From his point of view his pace was naturally brisker, he would meet us at the top. But for me, it was that familiar feeling of being let down, wanting help but not getting it —and maybe for the last time. The sky was darkening, and we had lost hope that we would ever get there when we emerged from the trees onto a vast, high mountain meadow ringed by snowy peaks. Above us we could make out a few structures, people, and herds of sheep. We stumbled upon Adam laying on the meadow grass, watching the stars come out.

There were six squat, haphazardly built restaurant/lodges, and the girls picked the one called Fire and Ice. Bedding and pillows were piled along the edges of the long room. Two woodstoves blazed against the mountain cold. Guests pulled the bedding out and slept in the restaurant to stay warm by the fires. The other visitors were a diverse crowd of Israelis, Europeans, and enthusiastic Indian youth from Delhi and Mumbai, out having their first wilderness experiences. The lodge was a party scene, with delicious food, hot drinks, card games, music, and hash and marijuana being smoked by Indians and non-Indians alike. *This would be a hoot if we weren't in the middle of breaking up.* Adam and I ordered honey ginger lemon tea and lay down on pillows. He opened a Dharma book, I pulled out my journal. But the girls loved it and immersed themselves in card games with new friends, young adults from around the world.

The next morning, I got up and went to the hot spring pools, up the hillside from the lodges. They were separated into Gents and Ladies, as they had been in use by traditional Indians for millennia. According to legend, Lord Shiva stayed here and meditated by the pools for 3,000 years. A Shiva temple and ashram had been built beside the pools, and the Shiva priests maintained them. The Gent's pool was broad and beautiful and open to the majestic sky. The Ladies' was small, with wooden walls around it and a tarp roof over it, to keep us ladies modest and out of view. But it also took the views from us.

I went inside the wooden bath house and changed into my swimsuit. Hot spring showers washed the dirt off my weary body before I stepped in. I slipped into the very hot water and greeted the three other women in the pool, Israeli and Argentinian. Steam rose around us. We soaked in silence for a long time. Bella and Sophia came in but the water was so hot they mostly sat on the edge with their feet in. Then the bathhouse door opened and a group of Himachali shepherdesses entered in faded saris and plastic sandals, chattering loudly in an unfamiliar dialect. I watched them wash their saris in the showers and then thoroughly wash themselves. Then they got in the pool with us. These women lived their whole lives up here in a tiny village, tending flocks of sheep and goats. Their lives were strikingly different from my own, yet we were bathing together, nearly naked, in sacred waters on a remote mountain slope. I wished I could hear about their lives and their relationships with their husbands to gain some perspective. I guessed that they lived in such close proximity to each other in their tiny village they didn't need all their love and support to come from one individual. But there was no way to ask.

Adam and I were able to get away for an hour. I followed him up the hill from the hot springs to a remote, high ledge where we could talk alone. The vision of living in our big home with a community of other women had wormed its way deep into my mind. I flashed to memories of living with Judy in New York, and then other girlfriends in grad school; the days when cooking and cleaning meant laughter, conversation, and companionship. In India, there would be at least six adults sharing a home the size of ours, helping with the upkeep, the cooking, the children. There would never be only one man and one woman. I would finally have my village, my extended family, and I would not be isolated and alone any more, staring into the maw of my fridge trying to muster enthusiasm for making and cleaning up dinner in a dirty kitchen after an already exhausting day at work. I would be a better mother, a better midwife, a better *everything*. All I needed was to settle Adam and his stuff in another house. Maybe we could eventually be lovers; we simply wouldn't live together any more. The solution seemed obvious.

Adam led me on this walk with the intention to forgive and reconnect and make love under the soft shade of the pines. He lay his foam pad on a patch of grass and wildflowers and gestured to me to sit. We were silent for a couple minutes, and then I spoke. I did not trust myself to communicate this very well, so I took a deep breath and cut to the chase.

"So, I want the house, for me and the girls. You will have to move out, and take your acupuncture clinic, elsewhere."

Adam stared, stricken. "Wait, what?"

"I get the house. It is the perfect home to raise the girls, and with your things out, there would be room for housemates, which is what I want. But . . . I'll help you find a place. Let's talk about where you think you will want to live."

Adam gazed across the valley, at the black granite peaks prodding the sky.

"I can't believe this," he said. "No really, I cannot believe this."

The girls were having a great time. They befriended Bhupal and Mowgli, two bespectacled and skinny college boys from Delhi, learned Indian card games from them, and then stayed up playing for half the night in the smoky lodge.

"I think the girls are getting a contact high from being in this room," Adam said. "Bella doesn't seem right."

"I think it is us that aren't quite right," I responded. "The girls seem fine to me."

Adam and I listlessly orbited each other. I felt ready to fly away from him, ready to start my new life. Travel with him was now going through the motions. Adam was aching inside; the sooner we could physically be apart from each other, the better. He would be able to develop himself in new ways, too, without banging himself against my anger and resentment. Late at night, lying on our beds unable to sleep, Adam whispered that he heard there was a small Indian Rainbow Gathering ending soon, a half hour's walk away. I encouraged him to go without us and have a great time. We could check back in by phone at the end of the week, when we both got back to town.

Adam got up at dawn and left before I was out of bed.

As the morning unfolded, the truth of what I had done slowly dawned on me. *I have sent my husband away, up here, in the remote Himalayas. I am alone now with my two girls.* Being a single mother had always been my biggest fear. I didn't think I could hack it, I get too easily overwhelmed, my girls are way too spirited for me to handle on my own. When the girls woke up, I called them to me. We sat on the floor and I told them that Dad loves them but had to go. It was the three of us now and I would need their excellent cooperation.

"You can do this Mom," Bella said. "We will be fine."

"Yeah." Sophia chimed in, but she didn't look so sure.

"I know we will," I said, and wished my stomach would stop cramping.

My stomach had been off since Tso Pema, but I hadn't been paying attention. Several days ago, I'd had the trots, but my digestion never got completely back to normal. Now, my stomach took a turn for the worse. I told the girls to prepare for leaving early tomorrow. I was sick and needed to see a doctor. They were disappointed and wanted to stay but were willing to comply. By evening I was running to the bathroom every hour, and the same through the night, racing into the freezing outhouse down a winding trail, praying I would make it there in time.

By morning I was depleted and exhausted. I faced an all-day hike, alone with my children, to get to town and a doctor's care. I wondered, my goodness, is this too much? Do I *need* Adam? I could send someone to fetch him. Then I thought, no, I don't. Other trekkers gave me Imodium, rehydration salts, and two bananas, which I ate for breakfast. The Imodium helped, and I felt strong enough to walk. We headed down the trail and I experienced an uncanny, soaring kind of relief. Without Adam, I could focus on what I needed to do to take care of myself, not hoping for or expecting assistance or care. That felt surprisingly good. Welcome to the first day of the rest of my life, I thought.

We hiked under beautiful sunny skies, but by midday I was dehydrated and weak. I took a second pill of Imodium, and soon after we reached a village with a cafe. We joined other hikers at the long, low table, ordered lunch, and sipped Sprite. As our rice and curry arrived, we noticed gray storm clouds moving in overhead. The rain began as we started walking again and got heavier throughout the rest of the day. The trail was slippery with mud and I had to slowly pick my way along. Bella led the way, helping Sophia and encouraging me. We were soaked, and I worried we would get sick, but who was I kidding, I was already sick! A part of me wanted to fall into whining and doubt—I can't go any farther through this mud and rain, I am too sick! So, I gave myself a pep talk instead.

Come on Dena! Look at you! Trekking through the rain, alone with two children for ten kilometers in the Himalayas while sick as a dog! What a rock star! This is your moment! See, you don't need Adam. You are your own best help, fully capable to make your own way. Think—if you can do this, you can do anything!

"Come on Mom, come on! You're almost there!" Bella and Sophia cheered me on. And, after about five years of my life went by sloshing along the trail, I made it to the road. And because it was India, a taxi sat there—wouldn't you know it?—waiting for a fare. The driver took us to Manikaran to retrieve our big packs, then to a quieter town called Kasol, where he left us in the care of a family. We were given a sparkling clean room in a garden setting, beside the Parvati river. We took hot showers and went out to have tandoori chicken dinner in a fancy restaurant up the road, a splurge we had thoroughly earned.

I awoke at dawn, bloated and cramping and excreting more yellow sludge. The guesthouse phoned up a doctor to come make a house call. Within an hour, a handsome young doctor arrived at our room. He took my medical history, examined me, diagnosed bacterial dysentery, and gave me antibiotics, rehydration salts, and something to "calm the colic." He talked with me about Buddhism over chai and then left, charging 300 rupees, which is five American dollars, for the whole visit including the meds.

"Now that's what I call healthcare, girls!" I said as we watched him go.

I rested in Kasol for a few days, recovering from my illness. I was feeling a numb euphoria about leaving Adam. But the girls were driving each other crazy. Without Adam's stabilizing influence, they swung from one ferocious tantrum to the next. It is the stress of the break up, I thought. It is the fact that we are ready to go home. Whatever it was, when Adam called I decided to take the girls to see him where he was staying in a village above Manikaran.

"You must come have lunch in the Gurdwara," the friendly Sikh on the bus said. "Otherwise you haven't really been to India."

"Well, we have to get off the bus there anyway," I replied. "Girls, shall we have lunch before going up to Dad?"

"Yes!" Sophia answered.

Sikhism was founded in 1469 by Guru Nanak in Punjab, with community service as a central tenet. Sikh leader Guru Amar Das created the first Sikh community kitchen in the 16th century. Its purpose, he said, was to place all of humanity on the same plane, regardless of caste, creed, gender, or religion. Still today, Sikhs are renowned for the massive free lunches served in their temples to everyone and anyone who comes. The temple in Manikaran, I learned from my Sikh bus-mate, is on the site where the founder of Sikhism actually prepared the first community lunch, using the hot springs to cook chapatis.

We entered the frenetic Gurdwara and were directed up the stairs to the dining room. We left our shoes among hundreds of pairs at the door and stepped into the long marble hall full of Indians in colorful dress. People sat in rows on narrow mats, talking and eating. We were each given a large metal plate, found seats, and were served rice and dal and vegetables out of steel buckets. The kindness and generosity were touching, but the racket in the room was astounding. A massive dish-washing operation took place by big open windows. Clean metal plates were tossed in a giant metal bin one by one with a resounding and constant "Ka-clunk! Ka-clunk!" Silverware was tossed into another metal bin "Ching! Chang! Ching! Chang!" Pots and serving buckets were banged. The sound of voices and clanging metals echoed off the marble floor and bare walls.

After the meal we were sent to the other end of the hall for chai. On the way we peeked into the kitchen and saw a bare-chested man stirring dal in a pot the size of an automobile. Sophia stood on tiptoe to see and he grinned at us. I sat down next to an old man, dressed all in white. We drank our chai to the crash, bang, and throng of this beautiful bedlam.

The old Sikh smiled and spoke to me. I could barely hear him through the din. "First time? Isn't it so peaceful here? So very peaceful and quiet?"

I was ready to chuckle at his joke, but he wasn't kidding.

I answered him, "It is very beautiful here."

Adam was staying in a decrepit farmhouse-turned-hippie-guesthouse. We sat down in the attic and he served us apple juice fresh-pressed from the neighbors. One glance at Adam's face and I could see he was hoping to reunite the family. I felt for him, my whole chest ached looking at him, but I didn't share that feeling. My decision was based on cold, hard facts, and I was ready for our lives to be different. He should be relieved to be cut loose from pain-in-the-ass me, always asking him to do things he didn't want to do, always running the show and cramping his style. Adam asked me for my list of reasons why I was leaving him. Fine. I had lots of them. I pulled out my journal where I had been scribbling reasons for days, pages and pages of them painstakingly articulated, and read them to him. He rarely cooked. His clutter filled our house and yard. He rarely volunteered to drive the kids, saying that this and that activity of theirs was my idea and not his problem. I had to remind him when he did agree to drive. But above all, when I did ask for help, he made how I asked such a *thing* that I regretted asking in the first place.

Adam listened to me, and then he promised to change. "I will take cooking classes as soon as we get home, get rid of at least half of my stuff, and never say 'Yes, Dear' in that tone you hate, again. I'll drive the kids more and remember to appreciate you."

"Humph. Will you attend to what I ask, instead of analyzing *how* I ask it? That is the most important thing of all. WILL YOU NEVER TELL ME YOU DON'T LIKE HOW I ASKED, AGAIN? I refuse to live with that anymore."

"I promise," he said. "Just give me the chance to show you."

I stared out the window at the grassy hillside dotted with flowers, at the haystack, the cow, and the charming wood and stone Himachali house next door. I stared and stared, feeling terribly conflicted. It *was* nice to be four again. The kids felt so much more settled with him near, and we have always worked our problems out. Minutes ticked by. I nearly capitulated . . . and then didn't.

"No deal. I am happy to see you, but I don't believe you. Words are easy. Make those changes, and then we'll see."

I couldn't believe myself—I really said that. I stood my ground, for the first time in my life. I did not give in, in order to keep the family together. I felt hollow, light, and clear as a bell. Adam couldn't believe it either. He was stunned, choking back tears. Sophia spilled apple juice everywhere.

I brought only Bella back to Kasol with me because Sophia decided to stay with Adam. We would travel separately to Manali, the gateway to the Manali-Leh highway, and then take it from there. It dawned on me that we may not travel to high-altitude Ladakh together, and it may be up to Adam to get Sophia there on his own. I knew he was sensible, but he had also been talking about the glorious adventure of hitchhiking on the Manali-Leh highway. Out of the other three of us, only Sophia had been enthusiastic about that idea.

As we walked away, I turned to him one more time. "Please don't hitchhike to Ladakh. Hire a safe and dependable ride."

Adam just looked away.

My Mom and Dad have been fiiting. My Mom told my Dad that wen we get home he has to move out. Today Bella and Mom are going there oun way for awile. I am siting in the sun room with my Dad. I'm knetting and Dad is plucking on his ukulaly. My Dad starts plucking a toon, and he starts to sing 'Leeving on a Jet Plane.' He only gets to the secend verce when he bersts into tears. Starteld I drop my kneting and aske him why he is crying. Through spluters he ses, "I just love dena moes so much. I don't want to lose her." I tell him, "You just have to sheow her that." I lean over and give him a BIG hug. Sophia.

Bella and I shared a taxi with two other travelers to Naggar, a village near Manali. From there we planned to book seats on some kind of bus or van to take us up to Ladakh, which literally means, "Land of High Passes." We still didn't know if the road was open yet or not; there had been record snows that year. The two-hour taxi ride, instead of our usual crowded bus ride, was a luxury that put us in a good mood. Getting out and on the road with only Bella was easy, and my feeling of lightness and freedom grew with the distance between myself and Adam. We found a mountain-chalet style guesthouse and went sight-seeing for the afternoon.

Naggar had a Himachali castle built in 1460 out of thick pillars of wood and stone. It stood on a cliff overlooking the Beas river, and had been converted into a heritage hotel. We admired it both inside and out and then wandered up the road following music we heard in the distance. "You are just in time," someone told us. "The All-India Music and Dance showcase is starting in the park."

Bella said, "Let's go, Mommy."

We spent the afternoon at the show. Our favorite performances were the athletic all-male Punjabi dance troupe wearing enormous neon hats, and the uncannily precise, acrobatic children's group from Rajasthan that danced twenty minutes of complex choreography without a single slip. We stopped at a cliffside cafe at sunset and tried locally-made lychee wine. Bella and I chatted about our day and then about the boys at home she hoped to see again. The sun slipped behind the mountains across Kullu Valley and the whole view turned to gold.

"Today was a beautiful day!" I said.

"Yeah, I am happy to be traveling with you, Mommy."

"I think we are going to have a good time getting to Ladakh," I responded, and I felt my stomach clench as I hoped that Sophia and Adam would have a good time too.

We grabbed our fleeces before climbing to the guesthouse roof for dinner. Two other guests were up there, Indian men with a bottle of expensive whiskey. They were drinking whiskey and sodas with the hotel owner, who stood over their table beaming at them. We took the table next to theirs, and soon they offered me a whiskey too.

"Thank you," I said, turning to face them. "That would be lovely."

We introduced ourselves. They were Sanjay and Budhu, two physicians from Delhi on their way to Ladakh. Sanjay was an anesthesiologist, and Budhu, a general surgeon. Sanjay traveled the Manali-Leh road yearly, usually on a Royal Enfield motorcycle with a posse of other doctors. But this year he had knee problems, and so was driving his friend, Budhu, who had never been to Ladakh, in an SUV instead.

"The Rohtang pass opens tomorrow at 5 a.m." Sanjay told me, "and we will be on it."

Both of them had families at home, wives and children around Bella's age who were not interested in such adventurous travel. They asked where we were headed and I told them Ladakh as well, in a few days.

"We have an SUV, and the whole back seat is empty. May we offer you a ride?"

"That is kind of you, but no, thanks."

We ate our meals together and talked. They were witty conversationalists, and Bella and I both enjoyed ourselves in their company. Another whiskey later, I reconsidered their offer.

"Take a look at the vehicle," Sanjay said. "It is parked right below in the drive."

I peered over the rooftop's low wall, at the sparkling black SUV below us. I could see it was a new model in excellent condition, with hefty 4WD tires.

"It looks like a limousine after the decrepit buses we've been riding," Bella said.

"Yeah, it's no tin bicycle rickshaw, is it? Well, what do you think, Bella?"

"I think, there is our ride."

I listened to my gut. Could these two men be kidnappers? Axe murderers? Risk-taking maniac drivers? Could they be lying about being doctors? No way. One hundred percent, no. I have lived long enough, worked in the medical professions, and traveled enough, to recognize two nice doctors when I meet them. Maybe this is how I am going to heal my relationship with physicians, I thought. I dialed up Adam to check in. My only hesitation was embarking on the trip without Sophia. Was I sure I wanted to leave her with Adam? I told Adam the news; we had been offered a ride to Ladakh in an SUV, with two doctors, leaving tomorrow at 4 a.m. Should we wait around in Manali for him and Sophia, or go ahead and take the ride? "Take the ride," Adam said. "Have fun."

CHAPTER 21

MANALI-LEH HIGHWAY

The alarm went off at 4 a.m. and Bella and I sat up. There was a knock at the door and a kitchen boy stood there, a tray with two glasses of chai in his hands.

"The gents ordered chai for both rooms," he said.

"Wow." I said, taking our glasses. "I could get used to this."

We gathered our things while my stomach jumped around. I was excited but nervous. The Manali-Leh road was something I had been anxious about, even back when we were planning the trip.

"Maybe we shouldn't go to Ladakh," I had said to Adam. "I think I am afraid of that road. It sounds so dangerous, and what if one of us gets altitude sickness?"

"I took a bus to Ladakh on that road and it was glorious," Adam answered.

I read up on altitude sickness, or acute mountain sickness, which is caused by the lower partial pressure of oxygen at high elevations. People can get it even at 8,000 to 10,000 feet. The Mana-li-Leh road has six passes above 16,000 feet. Mountain sickness can come on rapidly, I read. It can cause a host of problems, from headaches, dizziness and disorientation, to pulmonary edema and death. Between the hazards of treacherous roads in potentially poor condition and mountain sickness, Ladakh didn't seem worth it. Then I discovered that His Holiness the Dalai Lama would be giving a ten-day Kalachakra empowerment there the first week of July. According to his website, His Holiness has a special connection to Ladakh. It is as close to Tibet as he can get, as he is banned from returning to Chinese territory. There were rumors that this might be the last time he would ever give the Kalachakra. The timing would be right for us to attend.

I went back to Adam. "You know what? I changed my mind. Shocker, I know. Let's go to Ladakh after all. The Kalachakra can be the conclusion of our trip."

Adam watched me pencil LADAKH onto our itinerary.

Sanjay stuffed our backpacks into the car's trunk in the darkness. We climbed into the back seat, Bella ooh-ing and ahh-ing at the soft leather upholstery. I had told Adam not to hitchhike, and here I was doing just that. Sanjay and Budhu took their seats and we pulled out. They adjusted the heat and soft music played on the stereo; everything was classy and comfortable. We were still sleepy, and I appreciated how low-key and unassuming the two men were.

As we drove past Manali, Sanjay gave us a run-down of the game plan. "We are going to hit traffic on the Rohtang pass. Last year we waited five or six hours in traffic there. That is the first pass out of Manali, and today it opens. Tourists from Punjab will be going up to see the snow and snarling the roads. Once we are over that pass there will be not much traffic for the rest of the way. We will see a lot of oil trucks on the road, bringing oil to Ladakh and also returning empty.

"We will drive two high passes today, and sleep near Keylong in Lahaul. Tomorrow we will drive for twelve hours, over four high passes over 16,000 feet, all the way to Leh. There is nowhere to stop for the night between Keylong and Leh. It is all above 14,000 feet and trying to sleep at that elevation gives people mountain sickness. It is best not to sleep until Leh, which is down at 11,000 feet. Then, most people rest in Leh for two days to adjust to the altitude before touring around."

My heart raced with excitement and nerves. I was elated to have landed this ride, in such a good car, with a knowledgeable, competent driver. Even so, I closed my eyes and said a quick prayer.

Manali was behind us now, and the road began to ascend. There were thousands of white, identical taxis heading up the mountain too, and soon the road cut through deep snow. After an hour or two, we came to a complete stop on the mountainside, the line of taxis and trucks on switchbacks above us as far as the eye could see. Here and there, clusters of guys in black leather straddled motorcycles, bulky with camping gear. Sanjay cut the motor and said, "This is the four-hour wait."

We got out of the car and stepped to the edge of the road to gaze down at the soaring view of Manali, the Beas River a lapis snake curling through the forest. Above us, colossal snowy peaks cut at the sky with sharp granite edges. Punjabis in rented snowsuits hopped out of their vehicles in impossible numbers, like clowns out of circus cars. They posed for pictures, threw themselves down the steep hillsides on sleds, nearly crashing into the vehicles on the switchbacks below, and picnicked in the morning sun. My phone rang.

Adam's voice sounded terrible. He told me he was suffering from both neck pain and diarrhea, simultaneous onset since the moment I had walked away. I didn't want to let him get to me, but my stomach churned. I told him I was sorry, I hoped he felt better soon, and asked about Sophia.

"She is fine," he said. "She is learning macramé from the women here and playing in the forests around the house, making flower crowns and fairy forts."

"That sounds good."

"I am taking good care of her," he assured me. "And I am grateful to have her with me. But we are not going anywhere until I feel better."

The traffic started to move. I hung up and stood on the mountain's edge feeling a choice point. I wished that Sophia was with us. I imagined that we could somehow go back and get her. But they were still in the village by Manikaran, hours away. And we were about to take the Rohtang pass into the mountains and lose cell service for at least two days. Besides, Adam enjoyed having her with him. It was not within my rights to take that away. I surrendered control of my baby girl, then, to Adam, to the universe, to the unknown vagaries of the highest motorable road on earth. I imagined my fears and worries being pulled out of my body and thrown off the cliff, where they dissolved into a spray of snowflakes and disappeared. *They will be fine*, I told myself. *He won't let anything happen to her. I am not going to worry for even one more minute, because it is out of my hands now.*

I got in the car and it slowly, slowly made its way up the mountain. Behind us, the line of white taxis stretched into infinity.

Sanjay and Budhu were cheerful and attentive. We talked about our lives, our homes, our travels. When I mentioned that I had just decided to divorce my husband, they said "Let's not talk about that right now," and changed the subject. As we neared the pass, we came to a spot where a flood of snowmelt turned the road into a rushing stream. One at a time, each car or motorcycle stopped and then sped up and raced over the rushing water and large boulders that jutted out.

"Ah, there is the hold-up." Sanjay said. When our turn came, he clicked on the 4WD and expertly navigated the watery obstacle. We cheered. Sanjay would safely traverse many snowmelt waterfalls and washed out places over the next two days. Traffic was moving and we were on our way. With each curve in the road I felt I was getting farther away from what was beyond my control and deeper into the here and now. We drove right over the Rohtang pass without stopping. Bella and I laughed at the sight from our window—the world's biggest snow-day mela. The Rohtang pass was a broad, flat expanse of thick snow, and thousands of people in bright snow suits were out playing in it. Hundreds of temporary restaurants and shops had been thrown up out of tarps and corrugated metal, dozens of yaks for riding stood at the ready, and the hills were covered with children sledding recklessly through the crowds, literally landing on top of people.

"I've never seen so much chaos in the snow," Bella said, laughing.

"This is snow day in a country of a billion people!"

We whizzed over the top of that crazy, crowded pass, and suddenly we were in a vast, empty range of high snowy peaks all by ourselves. I gasped at the dazzling beauty and the startling solitude.

"They all stopped there," I said softly.

"Yes, they all stop there. Now it is only us," Sanjay said.

Bella, Budhu, and I pulled out our cameras. We were up at nearly 13,000 feet elevation, and the road had high walls of snow on either side. It was high elevation winter wonderland. We were not looking up at the snowy peaks, we were right in them, in our cozy car. Sanjay pulled over every few minutes and we jumped out to snap photos. We were as light and high as the mountains around us.

Throughout the day, the landscape changed bit by bit. It gradually grew drier, with less snow. The only signs of human civilization were occasional oil trucks, small gangs of motorcyclists, and the Border Road Organization's yellow road signs with safety messages such as, "If you are married, divorce speed," "Be Gentle on my Curves," and, "If you sleep your family will weep." Sanjay had a diverse music collection in his car, and the soundtrack to our journey ranged from Hindi pop to Mozart. We stopped for lunch where the snow was only a couple of feet deep. We ate fried noodles and mo-mos with cups of hot chai in the sun outside a dank little dhaba. When Bella ordered the mo-mos the server brought dipping sauce, which had been sitting out in its grungy bowl for who knew how long. I didn't think it looked good.

"Maybe don't use that sauce," I warned her.

She tasted it. "It's fine," she said, and dug in.

In the late afternoon we dropped into the valley of Lahaul, down at 10,000 feet. Soft green grass draped the hillsides in emerald, and snowy peaks rimmed the sky. The four of us were talking and laughing as if we had known each other for years. We passed a hamlet called Jispa, and then turned off the road at a sign that said "Jispa Journeys." We drove down to an upscale camping resort standing among giant boulders beside the Chandra river. A group of round canvas tents stood in a circle, a dining tent nearby. Sanjay and Budhu had reservations, but after a quick conversation in Hindi, a tent was arranged for Bella and me, as well. Our tent had a huge bed stacked with soft blankets, and an attached bathroom with its own little water heater.

We were informed that the buffet dinner began at eight.

Bella lay down to rest and I walked down to the wide, cold river. I sat on a boulder overlooking the water and said my Buddhist prayers. I prayed for all beings, especially my family, scattered as we were now across the Himalayas. I prayed for India, with its growing pains, and my friends and family back at home. I still felt good, so darn good. Clear and strong, and as though the world was opening up for me.

I walked back to camp and found Budhu and Sanjay sitting with some other fellows drinking whiskey and soda. I joined them, and Budhu mixed me a drink. The other men were cute twenty-somethings, also from Delhi, traveling by Royal Enfield. One of them had longish, curling hair, an Indian version of a hipster, dressed in black leather. He started flirting with me right off and I giggled at his attention, certain he had no idea that I was probably twenty years his senior. He wanted to take me for a jaunt up the road on the back of his Enfield, but I declined. The whiskey warmed us up as we watched twilight fall. Bella got up from her nap and joined us. More travelers arrived, middle- and upper-class Indians, from cities throughout the subcontinent. A spicy, lavish buffet dinner was laid out, and a large bonfire set. We made plates, with multiple curries and *sabjis* and naan out of a tandoori oven and sat by the warm fire to eat.

Bella suddenly had no appetite and wanted to go to the room. I went to check on her and found her writhing with stomach pain, tears in her eyes.

"Oh no, shit!" I said. "The goddamn dipping sauce!"

Whatever it was, it took Bella through the ringer. Sanjay and Budhu came in and insisted on starting her on an antibiotic right away. Budhu also gave her "something for the colic," which she took and then slept.

In the morning she still had diarrhea, but the pain was mild and would come and go. I had to make the call—should we stay and rest here, and let Sanjay and Budhu travel on without us? We could probably catch a bus tomorrow from Keylong, the nearest town. But Bella wanted to keep going. She had no appetite, but was on antibiotics, staying hydrated, and said she was feeling better, only tired. And we were traveling with two *doctors*. Sanjay stopped at a medical clinic on the way out of town, where I think Budhu bribed the nurse to let him take a box of emergency meds that included IV supplies. *Just in case.*

Bella sat in the big bucket seat in front beside Sanjay. He covered her in a blanket and she proceeded to sleep for about seven of the twelve hours of driving. Budhu sat in back with me, and we were off on our drive over four 16,000-foot passes to the "Land of High Passes."

"I'm curvaceous, but please take me slowly," the sign said as we pulled out of Jispa. Later, I saw "Better Mr. Late than Late Mr." and "Don't Gossip. Let Him Drive."

The day was dreamlike and indescribable, the effect of being up above 15,000 feet for hours. The first pass we traversed was Baralacha La at 16,500 feet. We were in wet, snowy mountains, the roads bordered by walls of plowed snow. In the crystal blue air, the granite snow-covered mountains undulated into infinity in all directions. Heaven is reachable, I thought, looking around at the most impressive mountain views I had ever seen.

As we ascended higher and higher, I started feeling the altitude: dizziness, mental fuzziness, and then I found it hard to breathe. I started to panic a teensy bit and was grateful to see that Bella was fine and fast asleep. My mind grew so fuzzy then that I couldn't think straight. I wondered, how do the drivers function up here? I asked Sanjay this, and he answered me in a calm voice, "We go up, and then we go down again."

Which would have been true, except we got stuck behind a broken-down oil truck at the 16,500-foot summit. With the walls of snow lining the road, there was no way to pass. We sat there waiting while the drivers of four other oil trucks worked on the truck. I tried to say something and heard my words come out garbled—and then I freaked out. *We will all die up here, our driver will be unable to think clearly too in a few more minutes!* In a slurred voice, Budhu said, "I think you are panicking. Stop thinking and relax. Thinking uses up oxygen." *Stop thinking!* I told myself sternly and focused on deep breaths. In a million years, or maybe a few minutes, the trucks moved and so did we. Then Budhu panicked, telling us with slow, jumbled words that he was *dizzy, very very dizzy, feels so off now, ohmygoodness.* I told him to relax and stop thinking, focus on his breath. Sanjay silently, steadily drove on. The road dropped us to a cool 14,000 feet, and our hearts, lungs, and brains normalized.

After Baralacha La, the passes were easier because we were out of the snow. There was room to pass on the roads, in the high, dry desert of the Himalayan rain shadow. The eight remaining hours of travel were tinged with addle-headedness and enacted in slow motion, because swift movement of any kind resulted in dizziness, disorientation, and getting out of breath. In slow motion we stopped for lunch, facing gale force winds to step into a yurt and crawl onto some pillows where we ordered noodle soup and chai. We lay down in that yurt after the simple meal and rested, stoned by altitude, until Sanjay told us, here we go! *Chalo!*

After lunch the sky was bluer than any sky I had ever seen, contrasted with the red sandstone formations rising along the road. We saw ibex, marmots, and yaks grazing in the hills. The expansiveness and clarity of the beauty was almost more than I could bear. I wanted to weep with joy, I wanted to capture it somehow, so I could take it home with me and remember it forever. I wanted my head to clear. Bella woke up every so often to see and say *wow,* take pictures, and then fall asleep again. I worried that there was something wrong with her, but the doctors reassured me she was fine. I lay my head on Budhu's lap and slept for a bit too, my mind spinning out confused dreams. Sanjay was the only one of us who did not seem affected by the altitude. Later he told me that he was affected, but he knew how to handle it.

The final pass, the second highest pass in the world, Tanglang La, approached. "Fast Won't Last," the road sign warned us as we began the incline. The ascent was gradual, and after being above 14,000 feet for seven hours, being at 17,582 feet was not so bad. We pulled over on the summit, next to a *chorten,* or Ladakhi stupa, wrapped in hundreds of strands of colorful prayer flags that sent prayers for peace out into the wind. Like astronauts walking on the moon, we stepped out into the cloudless sky and snapped photos. We found we could walk six to eight paces before our brains started floating away. *We did it! We made it!* I thought, triumphant. Bella stood by the Border Roads signpost and I snapped her picture, which became her most popular Instagram post yet. In it, she is wearing jeans and a tee shirt, leaning casually on the yellow sign reading,

TAGLANGLA. 17,582 FEET.
YOU ARE PASSING THROUGH THE
SECOND HIGHEST PASS OF THE WORLD.
UNBELIEVABLE, IS NOT IT?

The sun was setting as we made the slow descent into the Indus River valley to Leh. The sky was pure lavender, the dry hills golden. As we neared the valley plain, we saw an oil truck that had flipped and gone over the edge and had been left upside down on the steep hillside below the road. It seemed a sign, a reminder, that our safe arrival was nothing to take for granted. The highway ran along the river now, and I saw the rustic, square Ladkahi houses made of stone and wood clustered in villages. Ancient white chortens lined the roadsides, signifying that we had entered a Buddhist kingdom. Bella and I stayed the night at a hotel Sanjay knew. I ordered potato cheese soup for Bella and brought it to our room. She ate in bed

The views are literally breathtaking in Ladakh, the Land of High Passes.

and then again went to sleep. Sanjay, Budhu, and I sat in the hotel garden late into the night, eating chili chicken and drinking our last rounds of whiskey and soda.

In the morning, Bella was back to her normal self. She and I moved into our budget backpacker style guesthouse where we would stay for the next couple of weeks. We said goodbye to our companions and promised to keep in touch. It felt like a lifetime of travel that we had shared, although it had only been two days.

I phoned Adam, to let him know we had safely arrived, and give him the address and phone number of our guesthouse. I also gave him the name of a company that ran 4WD van trips up to Leh. I had seen the van on the road and it seemed legit. I girded myself, ready to deal with whatever he had to say. Adam thanked me for the info, and then told me about himself and Sophia. He was still recouping from a bad stomach, but his neck was feeling better. They had moved to a guesthouse in Manali that was serving as an artists' cooperative. They were ensconced in a community of friendly European artists where Sophia was helping to paint a mural and learning anime drawing from a professional cartoonist. Adam planned to wait a few more days before taking the journey to Leh. He had something else to say.

"What is it?" I asked.

"I have had a revelation about us," he said. "If it would make you happy for me to move out so you can live in the house with the girls and some lady roommates, then that is what I will do. I want to give that to you and make you happy."

"Oh." I felt relief washing over me. I was surprised and didn't know what to say. There was silence for a few moments. "Thank you. And I want to support you, to do whatever it is *you* want. If you want to live in Nepal with Chokyi Nyima, or go back to Bodh Gaya and do a three-year retreat and get enlightened, or study acupuncture in China, whatever you wish to do, I want to support that. Consider this your ticket to anything, anything that you want to do. We can each be free to really be happy, and not be limited by each other's expectations."

Adam answered, "I don't know what it is I want to do, but I will sit with it, and let you know." Then he told me about this morning.

He woke up thinking he needed to work more with Sophia on her multiplication tables and feeling guilty about it. "Then, Sophia talked in her sleep. She rolled over, eyes still closed, and said 'six times three is eighteen.' She did that, really, as if to assuage my worries."

The conversation ended peacefully, and something in me settled. Bella and I rested in our guesthouse for two days as advised, acclimatizing our bodies to life above 11,000 feet. Our room was spacious and sunny, with a full wall of windows open to a layer-cake of a view. Below us were the guesthouse gardens with lush green farms beyond. Above those we saw the graceful trees cultivated beside Ladakhi homesteads, bordered by purple desert mountains in the distance. Snowy peaks towered above those topped by exquisite cloud formations that danced in the crystal sky. Bella read me *The Fault in our Stars* over those two days. We lay in bed together hour after hour, sobbing over the love story of two teens with cancer, talking and observing how the light changed over our view throughout the day. Our hosts brought us pitchers of mint tea and we ate dinner downstairs with other travelers who were trickling in to attend the Kalachakra. In the evenings, I caught myself wishing that Adam were here too. One night, Bella rolled over in her sleep and mumbled, "I miss Dad. I guess I want him back, just improved."

I took walks around Leh, which was more like a village than a capital. The sprawling terrain of Ladakh has only 250,000 people, and 40,000 of them live in green, quiet Leh. The Ladakhi language is a Tibetan dialect, and Buddhism was brought to the region from Tibet in the eighth century. Ancient Buddhist monasteries are ubiquitous in Ladakh, like mini-malls are in the West—every village has one. Prayer wheels are found along the road and Ladakh elders wear long braids, longer wool dresses, and travel with malas in hand. The people are friendly, with a spirit of community born from living far above the tree line in one of nature's harshest environments. Everyone hitchhikes, cars automatically stop and pick up pedestrians on the road, neighbors help each other with their gardens and farms, and resources are shared. The barter system worked in Ladakh for centuries, cash has only been used here since the 1940s. Similar to Tibet, Ladakhi women enjoy high status and relative emancipation in their society. Unlike the rest of India, a young married couple in Ladakh can choose to live with the bride's family instead of the groom's.

Bella and I took a day trip with some other travelers to the monasteries outside of Leh. A hired taxi-van took a group of us across the Indus valley to Hemis Monastery, founded in the eleventh century. The monastery was up off the valley floor, nestled into the curvaceous red ridges of high desert hills. We stopped along the way to look at the spectacular views of the valley, the hills, and snowy mountains beyond. The stark landscape was endless and ever changing with hues of golds, greens, and purple. But the sky, the sky! I understood, then, why so much Tibetan Buddhist poetry speaks of the vast spaciousness of empty sky, of our minds' true nature as being luminous, clear, and pristine like the sky. There was something so clarified and pure about the skies above Ladakh. Clouds, of every shade from white to nearly black, flitted like birds across that rarified blue, making perfect shadows on the hills. I felt pulled by that sky, as though I could become more clear and expansive too by drinking in the view.

When we entered the ancient stone courtyard of the monastery the monks were practicing sacred dances for an upcoming festival. They wore big red hats that matched their robes and spun around and around in the sunlight to the pounding of gongs and drums. The gompa, or temple, was built in 1630 in Tibetan style. It was the oldest Tibetan temple we had seen, and the power of four hundred years of Buddhist chanting and prayers clung to us like the blue trails of incense smoke pervading the air.

Bella grabbed my arm and whispered, "I feel like we are in Tibet!"

I thought about how much Adam would love this.

I placed my pillow on the floor of our room each morning and meditated while gazing out at the distilled Ladakhi sky. The storm of intense emotions about Adam had blown itself out. I loved this time with my eldest daughter, but I also kept thinking about how much

Adam would bring to our time here, how much I would like to be here with *him*. His softness during our last phone call undid some knots in me, old stories about him being angry and dangerous. Now I had been the one angry and dangerous. I did not regret the stance I had taken, the exploding of our home life status quo which we would have gone back to. I was not roiling in hatred, nor languishing in sorrow. I was simply here, feeling clear and steady, hoping I hadn't done irreparable harm to anyone, as open to the unknown future as the empty sky.

I surprised Bella one morning by returning from my walk with a rented motor scooter. Bella was in front of our guesthouse, feeding a very pregnant cow leaves that she was tearing off high branches.

"Cool, Mom. What are we going to do with the scooter?"

"Well, I thought we would take a little excursion around Ladakh on it. We have a few more days before Dad and Sophia get here. There are some villages with thousand-year-old monasteries only a couple hours away."

Bella was skeptical. "We are going to ride on this for a couple hours? Is it safe? Can you drive it?"

"The guy I rented it from went over everything. Of course, I can drive it. Come on Bella! After seeing folks travel the high passes on motorcycles, having the time of their lives, the least we can do is tootle around on this scooter for a bit."

"I don't know, Mom."

"Bella! I'm your mother! I will keep you safe. It will be a blast, you'll see."

"All right. You've talked me into it."

A couple hours later I got on the scooter with Bella behind me, we both put on helmets, and I nervously turned over the engine.

"Ok, here we go!" I sang out, sounding way more confident than I was. "Hold on!" I pulled us out onto the narrow road, and the bike somehow ended up facing the wrong way. After an awkward few minutes getting the bike turned around, we were on our way.

"Are you sure you know what you are doing?" Bella yelled into the wind.

"Woo hoo!" I answered. Within minutes we were in the outskirts of Leh. We prepared to turn right, and head west towards Alchi. I glanced to the left, looking eastward across the long valley for a moment. I could see the massive peak of what I guessed was Tanglang La in the distance, wrapped in a swirl of dark clouds. *Looks like a snowstorm has hit the pass,* I thought. *I sure hope Adam and Sophia aren't in that.* I wasn't quite sure when they were arriving, so why worry that it would be today? Then Leh was behind us, and we sped along a winding, mostly empty road that followed the Indus river through one of the most majestic and pristine landscapes in the world.

June 26, 2014

Dear Diary,

Yesterday we rented a motor scooter to ride with me on the back. It was scary, at first. But as the day went on we both became more and more comfy on the bike. For lunch we pulled into the first place we saw, which was a totally empty place. The man who greeted us was strangely familiar. When I pulled off my glasses and helmet, he flipped out, saying he was our waiter at Jimmy's Italian in McLeod. I recognized him at once, and he smiled and said he was very happy to see us. We had an absolutely amazing lunch of chili chicken and veg fried rice.

Afterwards, we went up this high pass and the wind was so strong, it started blowing our bike which scared the crap out of both of us. But we survived. When we arrived in Alchi, we found a beautiful, real family who invited us to stay with them, complete with daughter (Achen), Mother, (Sonam), father, and Grandpa. We visited a 1000-year-old Buddhist temple that still has the original murals painted all over its walls. The monk who showed us in looked 1000 years old, too. It was AMAZING. Then Achen showed us around her family's farm which is ancient too and hasn't changed much in centuries. We ate dinner with the whole family, sitting on the floor on rugs in a big open room, which is how Ladakhis always eat. I loved it.

Today we got up and had breakfast in the warm kitchen. Sonam had already been up for hours milking the cow and brewing a pot of chang, or homemade beer, over a fire in the yard. Breakfast was Ladakhi bread and butter and homemade curd. Afterwards, I tried on Achen's satin garment of traditional Ladakhi clothing, kind of like a chuba. Then, Mom and I took the motor bike. The two-hour ride to Lamayuru was gorgeous. We ate lunch at a tiny place in a village—rice and egg curry and dal. Then, we resumed our ride. We passed Moonland, an area that really, truly, does look like the moon. We arrived at the Lamayuru monastery, perched on top of this steep hill we walked up, just in time for lunch. The monks were so friendly and welcoming, we decided to eat with them—rice and dal.

Again, after lunch, we climbed another hill, and found this secret place where there was a puja. Yogis, with long matted hair and beards and sparkling eyes had come down out of their secluded caves and meditation spots for this puja. We sat with them in the tiny hidden temple for a few minutes, and then they took LUNCH BREAK. So, out of politeness, we ate a third lunch with them. And guess what it was? Rice and dal. We said goodbye and then headed back down to the monastery for one more kora around it, spinning the 1000-year-old prayer wheels. There was an ancient, ancient, ANCIENT Ladakhi woman doing kora with us. She offered me to sit next to her after, and Mom gave her some candy and some rupees and took a few pictures and the woman started crying and said, "Thaku, thaku Bella."

On the ride back to Alchi, Mom let me drive the scooter. SO FUN! Went back and stayed with Achen's family. And dinner? Rice and dal!

Love, Bella

Bella and a Ladakhi woman rest together at Lamayuru Monastery, Leh District, India. A hand-held prayer-wheel, filled with mantras for world peace, spins in the foreground.

CHAPTER 22

Examine the nature of hatred; you will find that it is no more than a thought
When you see it as it is, it will dissolve like a cloud in the sky.
—Dilgo Khyentse Rinpoche

LEH, LADAKH

The beautiful, wrinkled grandmother, Jule, was in the guesthouse garden when we returned to Leh. She stood up from her planting and smoothed her long wool dress. "Your family here. Your baby upstairs," she said. *My baby.* I raced up the steps, heart thumping in my chest. I stopped at the door to our room and caught my ragged breath, trying to calm down. Then I opened the door. Adam was writing at the desk, Sophia was drawing on the bed. They were here, alive, in one piece, *here.*

Adam turned to me. "Hello," he said softly.

"Hello," I said. He looked so good to me—soft-spoken, graceful Adam. I felt my gut clench with sorrow.

"MOMMY!" Sophia yelled, leaping into my arms. I squeezed her against me and covered her soft, apple cheeks in kisses.

"You're here, you made it!" I gushed. "You weren't caught in a snowstorm, were you?"

"Oh yeah. On the highest pass," he answered.

Damn, I knew it. "But you didn't hitchhike, did you?"

"Of course, we did!" Sophia sang.

"But by the time we were in that blizzard, we were on a regular bus," Adam said, "with bald tires and no windshield wipers."

Sophia wanted to be the one to tell their story. I climbed onto the bed to listen to her. "First, we stayed where we were for a few nights. Then we went to Manali, and that is where dad got super-duper sick. I met this couple that would make me chai and teach me how to draw. And, there was a restaurant where they had a tiny puppy I would play with."

"You must have liked that," I said.

"Yup. I miss that puppy. Do you think we can get a puppy when we go home?"

"Probably not. You know my rule is one dog, one cat. So, then what happened?"

"Well, after Dad got better, I made a sign that said LEH in all sorts of beautiful colors. In the morning, we went outside and put the sign on the street. In a few minutes a big car pulled up. In the car was a bunch of Indian men and they said, 'Hop on!'"

"Men?" I asked. "What kind of men?"

"Young men. Really nice. We noticed there were parachutes. They were going parachuting. But instead, they decided to go to Leh with us. They drove us up closer to the mountains, and then dropped us at another guesthouse. They were going to drive back down, drop off their parachutes, and then come back for us. They were gonna meet us at eight in the morning, but they didn't know which guesthouse, so they went right past us and we lost that ride. That was really disappointing."

"What?" I asked, "I'm confused."

"We saw them go by us—they didn't know where we were."

"Oh."

"So, we hitched a ride with a school bus with only four kids left on, going to Keylong. We rode on that till we were near Keylong, when all the kids got off. We were pretty high elevation and I started to get a headache. Then we waited for a half hour and no rides came, or they were full. Finally, Dad said, get on your pack, we will start walking. We started walking. Fifteen minutes and we got there. It was the hardest fifteen minutes of my life.

"In Keylong, Dad got the most fancy stay we could find. I got to wash my hair in a hot shower. We ate a fancy dinner. While I went upstairs to try to get some sleep in our room, Dad went outside to find a bus that could get us to Leh. He found a bus, but it started at 5 a.m. We went to sleep, then he woke me up. We put on our packs and it was freezing. The bus was blue and old-looking, with cracks in the windows and it was not heated at all. I got to sit in the front near the driver. Near me was a happy, jolly Sikh man that reminded me of Santa Claus. He had a big nice iPhone with a game called Hill Climb Racing and I played it to get my mind off my headache. The bus started to rumble. It creaked as he pulled out. We were off!

"The first mountain pass was easy. It snowed a bit at the top but not much. We rode for hours and then stopped for lunch at a tarp with sticks holding it up. Every time the wind blew the whole thing jolted. We ate Maggi noodles. Dad fell asleep. We stopped for a rest in a tiny town. I got off the bus and the Sikh man bought me a candy bar. We got back on the bus and started driving. Over the first pass, there was this big ditch, a stream of ice melt going over the road and we had to go through it. So, all the people had to get out and help it across. The next hardship was that we had to move these giant stones off the road to clear the way for the bus. My headache got way worse. I felt like I was going to barf. Over the second pass, it was easy-peasy. Over the third pass, it started to snow. Over the fourth pass, it really started to snow, so thick that the driver could not see ten feet in front of him. There were no windshield wipers. Every so often the driver got out and wiped the windshield with a rag."

Adam interjected, "The snowstorm was intense, I knew about the bald tires, and I watched the conductor leaning out the window to wipe the windshield with a rag. I honestly thought we might not make it."

"Dad! Let me tell it!" Sophia said, "At the very tippy-top of the pass, the bus stopped. I got really worried. It was snowing so hard outside. I worried that the engine would fail and we wouldn't be able to get over. Then the door swung open. A little old lady climbed on. When I mean old, I mean OLD. Her face was covered with wrinkles. And her hands were shaky. She was covered in blankets from head to toe to try to keep warm. She had the biggest smile on her face, showing only about four teeth. She sat down next to me and grinned, her eyes were black and twinkled with time. We rode for about five minutes when the lady wanted the driver to stop. She got up, patted me on the cheek, and got off the bus and walked away into the snowstorm. The driver had a half a bottle of mountain dew and he gave it to me for over the last pass. The snow cleared. And we were finally THERE!"

"Oh, Sophia," I said. "I am so glad you are here with us now." I wanted to laugh and I wanted to cry, but I pulled her into a hug and smooshed her face into my chest. Bella glanced up from where she was nonchalantly pretending to read and patted her sister's back. I tentatively reached over and placed my hand in Adam's.

After the girls were tucked into bed, Adam and I went up to the rooftop to talk. I expected an explosion: anger, fury, ripping us apart, tearing the fabric of my contentment into shreds. There had been none so far. I had detonated a bomb in the heart of our family, in the middle of our dream trip, and he came to me with forgiveness. I was relieved, grateful. Now, we were alone, and I was ready for the other shoe to drop. I steeled myself and vowed to hear him out.

We gazed out over the hills bathed in moonlight.

"So," he began "I thought about what I would want to do, if I could choose anything in the world."

"You did?" I said, wondering what it would be. Stay here in India? Get his PhD in Buddhist studies at the White Gompa in Boudha? Travel on to China while I took the girls home so Bella could start high school? I was full with the loss of him but ready, ready to be true to my words and support him in whatever it was.

"Yes, I did."

"And?"

"Well, if I could do absolutely anything I choose, it would be this. I would go back to Chico to show you what a loving husband I can be, and finish raising up these girls."

My mouth opened and closed, and nothing came out.

The central plaza in Leh had a bookstore filled with English-language books. Adam and Sophia had visited the store while Bella and I were in Alchi. We wandered in after dinner the following night and Adam handed me a book, *The Prophet*, by Kahlil Gibran. I held it open while he flipped through the pages and found the poem, "On Children." The first two stanzas were familiar. Sweet Honey on the Rock turned them into a song which Bella and I had sung together over the years:

> *Your children are not your children.*
> *They are the sons and daughters of Life's longing for itself.*
> *They come through you but not from you,*
> *And though they are with you yet they belong not to you.*
> *For life goes not backward nor tarries with yesterday.*
>
> *You may give them your love but not your thoughts,*
> *For they have their own thoughts.*
> *You may house their bodies but not their souls,*
> *For their souls dwell in the house of tomorrow,*
> *which you cannot visit, not even in your dreams.*
> *You may strive to be like them,*
> *but seek not to make them like you.*

Adam drew my attention to the final stanza, which I had never seen before, because it is not in the song.

> *You are the bows from which your children*
> *as living arrows are sent forth.*
> *The archer sees the mark upon the path of the infinite,*
> *and He bends you with His might*
> *that His arrows may go swift and far.*

Let your bending in the archer's hand be for gladness;
For even as He loves the arrow that flies,
so He loves also the bow that is stable.

Adam read the last lines aloud. "*Let our bending in the archer's hand be for gladness. For even as He loves the arrow that flies, so He loves also the bow that is stable.*"

"It's a beautiful image," I said.

Adam said, "I had already made my choice, to do whatever it takes to stay and see our family through. When I opened this book randomly and read those words, my decision was confirmed."

A drawing beside the poem depicted a stone statue of an archer, aiming his bow toward the sky. Rock solid, like my Adam.

The Dalai Lama arrived for the week of teaching and ceremonies. The first event took place at a monastery an hour out of town. Leh was stretched to capacity by the numbers of people gathering to see him. The bus to the monastery was so full we could not even get in the door. We availed ourselves of the only transport option, a quintessential Indian experience. One at a time, Bella, Sophia, Adam, and I climbed the metal ladder on the back of the bus to the luggage rack on top. There, we joined maroon-robed monks and Ladhaki youth among boxes and sacks of rice. The bus engine coughed to life and my nerves jumped.

"Sophia! Are you secure? Do you have something to hold onto?"

"Yes, Mom."

"Bella?"

"Yes, Mom."

I grasped the metal bar that rimmed the rack as the bus swerved out of the station. Sitting facing front was too intense, with the sharp wind blowing into our faces. But turned around, wind to our backs, the combined energy of speed, open air, and view was exhilarating. Everything that had gotten us here unfurled behind me, breathtaking in its beauty and precariousness, like a winding Himalayan road.

"How about here?" Adam said, stopping and looking around. We stood on a shaded patch of sidewalk along Leh's town center. The street hummed with the bustle of thousands of extra Indian tourists, Tibetans, and Ladakhis, gathered for the Kalachakra.

Sophia nodded in agreement, "I think this could work."

It was Sophia's idea that our family band should play music at least once, while in India. For years, our family had performed our original folk songs at summer music festivals as the Moes Family Band. Our line-up included guitar, ukulele, and violin, vocals in three-part harmony. Bella had gone off with a group of American high school students volunteering at the Kalachakra grounds, and Sophia decided this made it a perfect time to perform. Adam and Sophia had worked up songs together while on the road. Sophia was ready to be the front and center vocalist, a position her older sister usually held.

As soon as Adam pulled his ukulele out of his backpack, people stopped to look. I grabbed my shaker, and said "Sophia, what should we sing first?"

"How about 'Bird Song,'" Sophia said. "We always start with that one."

I wrote "Bird Song" sitting alone on a beach in Malibu years before I met Adam and had kids. I had been lonely and heartbroken, and longed to know what lay ahead for me. I never imagined it would be my future family band's anthem, and that it would be sung at Burning Man, music festivals, and now here at the Kalachakra on the roof of the world.

"Are you ready?" I asked.

"I'm nervous." She paused and looked around. "But ready."

"You'll have to sing really loud since there's no mic. Just give it everything you've got."

Normally I played rhythm guitar but now we just had Adam's uke. I watched him finish tuning.

"Want me to count us in?" I asked. He nodded.

"Okay, one . . . two . . . three . . . four!"

Adam strummed a lilting rhythm and Sophia stepped in front of us and let her high, clear voice ring out.

"I wanna rush into the waves and disappear at sea.
I wanna sprout wings and fly, gliding gracefully!
I want the moon to pull my tide out with the sea.
I know you won't believe me, but the wind is my destiny!"

I joined her, and we sang in harmony,

"So, let me disappear today.
Don't worry while I am away,
It's impossible for me to stay—
Cuz I am for the birds today!"

A few people stopped to listen, then people stopped to see why people had stopped, and within a couple minutes we had a U-shaped crowd of perhaps sixty or seventy people around us, listening and taking video with their phones. When we finished our song, people clapped and then tossed rupees into Adam's backpack. After "Bird Song," Sophia pulled a recorder out of her purse and she and Adam sang "Country Roads, Take Me Home," punctuated by Sophia's recorder solos. By the time we finished our thirty minute set, the pack was full of coins and rupee notes, and we had sung for cadres of monks and nuns, big Indian families, and Ladakhi youth. We had been immortalized on countless cell phones and South Asian Facebook accounts. We went to dinner in Leh's upscale Chinese restaurant overlooking the city plaza and paid for the meal with our backpack of change.

On a hill above Leh, the Japanese erected a white stupa, called Shanti Stupa, in 1991. From its base, one can view astounding Himalayan panoramas. Adam led our family on the hike up for sunset. We panted and heaved our way up, winded by the strain of the elevation. I wondered if I was having a heart attack and sat on a rock near the top.

"Come on," Adam called to me. "You can do it."

"I know, I know," I said.

At the summit, we looked down at Leh, the Indus valley, the mountains beyond mountains crowned by clouds, spread out before us like a buffet for the eyes. Adam held me close as the colors faded into evening. The girls scurried off to take pictures and I softened into the moment. I realized that I had a laundry list of reasons for wanting to divorce Adam but not loving him was never one of them. Love. I don't even know what that word means anymore, I thought.

Throughout our trip, Indian people had asked us, "Is yours a *love* marriage?" And they were fascinated to hear that it was. Indian tradition does not leave the foundation of family life to the whims and hormones of youth. It is up to parents to select a proper life partner for their children. We in the West balk at arranged marriages, but now I was beginning to see the other side. Falling in love is no guarantee of long-term happiness; it is a game of chance rather than a calculated guess. How can you know in your twenties, pulled by hormones and chemistry, what you will need in a partner at forty, or fifty?

I had fallen in love with Adam when I was twenty-six, under a tree at a Rainbow Gathering. Over the years we had stumbled along, trying our best to grow our love into something deeper than "in love." We always loved each other, but at times we hadn't been very good at it. I was sorry I had torn a hole in our trip, but not sorry that our life would be different on account of it. In that tear, toxic patterns were also cut away. My hike down from Kheerganga alone, sick, in the storm, with the girls, and my finding our way safely to Ladakh, had broken the cycle of my "needing" Adam when things got rough. Now and forever, I knew I did not "need" Adam. Instead, I chose him, knowing that some things about our partnership were great, and some were challenging. That is what our marriage, and our love, would be based on from now on. Choosing it. And that was enough.

CHAPTER 23

DELHI TO THAILAND TO CHICO

I sat on my sister's bed with the wall AC blowing right on us. The monsoon rains were late to Delhi and the city was sizzling like a samosa. Ananya sat on the floor working a wooden puzzle, staring up at me with enormous brown eyes. I had just given Amy the CliffsNotes version of what happened. She gave me her analysis.

"You know, Dena, I think that this was really important for you. You needed time to just be you and figure some things out. I mean, look. You had a serious boyfriend at fifteen. Then, you pretty much always had a boyfriend after that, except occasionally here and there, until you got married. You have always had a man with you, and I think you needed to feel what you can do on your own. Also, I know there were some issues about how you guys ran your home. I mean, I saw it when I visited. You sent a really clear message that you are ready for some changes."

"Yeah. You're right. I still feel bad though. As usual, I could have handled it better. But you can't go back and re-write how you did things, can you?"

"Nope. You can't. And I still say, I know it was hard on Adam, but ultimately it was good for both of you!"

"Thanks, Amy."

I went back into our room where Adam and the girls were sorting through our suitcases. We gave our mountain of school supplies to Amy, to be shared by Ananya and Vandana's sons. We packed up the books and souvenirs that throughout our journey we had mailed to Amy's apartment. Now, we prepared to take them home.

Sophia was reading a graphic novel version of the Hindu epic, the Ramanaya. She sighed. "I am going to miss this place. The little cups of chai and rickshaws and monkeys and shrines under the trees . . ."

"And waking up to get off the train," Bella jumped in. "And wandering out of the railway station to see where we are. And it always being somewhere incredible."

"Yeah, but soon you will get to see our doggie and your room and your friends," I said, "and have a burrito!"

Bella sounded uncertain. "Oh yeah. My friends. Them."

"You'll see. As soon as you see them, it will be as if you never left."

Bella looked at me strangely. "But I don't want it to be like that."

We stopped in Thailand on the way home. Staying a week in the backpacker neighborhood of Bangkok, we indulged in a food orgy. Every two hours one of us would say "I think it is time to eat," and we would troop outside to buy the cheap and delicious food sold in carts and stands along the street—steaming pad thai for $1, grilled skewers of shrimp and squid, bowls of soup fragrant with coconut milk and lemongrass, tall cups of sweet Thai iced coffee. Everything and anything was for sale. At night along the main road the bars and clubs hummed with bands and street artists and drunken college kids from around the world. We walked the brilliantly lit streets dazed by the first night life we had seen in months.

In Koh Phangan we stayed in beach cottages beside the placid turquoise sea, swimming and snorkeling away the last days of summer. We rented scooters to ride around the island, visiting a zipline park, elephants, and temples. It all seemed calm and tame and tourist-ready. We put the girls in their own cottage, and finally had nighttime to ourselves. Under the mosquito-net, damp with tropical heat and longing, Adam and I remembered how to love each other, how vital physical connection is to a marriage. During long, lazy mornings, I sat on the cottage porch gazing at the sea in suspended animation, letting the rush and chaos of India sift out of my bones.

We waited for our connecting flight in the Hong Kong airport. This was it—soon we would board the Long Hauler that would take us all the way to California. Sophia and I sat with our carry-on bags while Adam and Bella wandered.

Bella came over.

"I saw Dad walking with a Tibetan monk who I think is Chokyi Nyima Rinpoche."

"Nah, impossible," I said. "Looks like him, maybe."

Adam came over and told us that, indeed, Chokyi Nyima was in the airport and would be on *our flight*. He was on his way to his annual teaching retreat in California.

I said, "Now I know for sure that we are going to make it home." I couldn't believe the auspicious coincidence—our lama from Boudha would be riding in the plane with us! How is this even possible? I felt a surge of triumph. We did it. We traveled in India for eight months, and we were going to *live*.

We didn't see Rinpoche on the plane because his students set him up in first class, but knowing he was there helped me relax. After the twelve-hour flight we bumped into him at the baggage carousel. He was so happy to see us, he pulled us into a tight embrace. He held us close, his body warm even through the swaths of burgundy robes, like Amma, like a father. We collected our bags and walked beside him into the airport lobby. A group of San Francisco Buddhists stood, waiting to greet their lama, white satin kataks in their hands. The first thing I noticed about them was how clean they were. Even the children wore fresh clean clothes, sparkling new-looking shoes, and had perfectly-combed hair. Everything they wore seemed *new*.

In my sleep-deprived stupor I felt their eyes on me and sensed them wondering who we were. I looked down at my ratty khakis, worn almost daily for eight months, and glanced at my children in their threadbare salwars, worn-to-pieces shoes, and wild, long hair. I looked at Adam, thin and tall and elegantly disheveled. The backpacks we wore, I suddenly noticed, were absolutely filthy from months of shoving them under seats on buses and trains. We were strong and tan and carried our loads with ease. We had ridden elephants and rickshaws and canoes and on top of the bus, and climbed mountains and studied the Dharma, and met Amma and the Dalai Lama, and had changed in ways we didn't even know yet. In the end we had laid bare our own inner chaos while deep in the bosom of Mother India, and yes, we were dirty, but yes, we did it all and found our way home again.

We did it—we backpacked through India and Nepal for eight months and found our way home again. Photo from Udaipur, Rajasthan, India, courtesy of a kind stranger.

POSTSCRIPT

CHICO CALIFORNIA
AUGUST 2014

The reverse culture shock, I did not expect. Of course, I would be overjoyed to come home—my own kitchen, hot baths, Trader Joe's, swimming in our creek. In our minds Chico had taken on mythic qualities of abundance, cleanliness, and space. Our car. Air conditioning. Hot water out of the sink, the list went on and on. The first night home I sat on my porch eating a burrito in the heat, in an uncanny realm of numb familiarity. How I had missed burritos! Yet I could barely swallow it, the bites of beans and rice tasted so bland and heavy in my mouth.

I climbed on my bike and pedaled downtown. With each block I traveled, my heart sank deeper. *What is wrong with this place?* The streets looked abandoned; wide asphalt blacktop lined with big silent houses, empty cars parked out front. During the mile ride I passed only one person, a transient man with a shopping cart of bottles, talking to himself. The eerie emptiness shocked me, and the phrase that popped into my head to describe this summer afternoon was "nuclear apocalypse." This is what a neighborhood will be like after the bomb goes off, I thought.

Where were the people? The throng of children playing cricket in the street, the women squatting at the corner water pump doing their laundry or filling copper pots? The old men in lungis, leaning against the trees? Where were the altars, the sadhus and babas who sit under trees with their flowers and incense? Where were the pots of vermillion powders? The shoe shiners? The chai maker? The man who is outside with his sewing machine, ready to repair anything? The fruit seller, the knife sharpener, the milkman with his cow? Where was the flock of dear little goats walking by, the goatherder cradling a newborn kid in his arm? Where were the cows with their soulful eyes, the chattering monkeys, the rickshaws and carts of fried snacks rolling by? The absence of life was stunning. My eyes filled with tears.

India! Where life in town hums with smells and sounds. Hindi pop music, honking horns, the sounds of prayers and chanting from corner temples and mosques, the smells of curry and piss. Colors of flowers and saris and paint. I felt lost and lonely in this deserted landscape that used to be my home and wondered briefly if we could hop back on a plane. I called my sister when I got home and told her about my distress. "Yup," she agreed with me. "When I visit US cities now, they seem desolate and dull for the first few days."

The following morning, I walked into a grocery store to buy salad dressing. I found the salad dressing aisle but there must have been a hundred and twenty varieties to choose from. I stared at my options for several minutes, baffled. *Who needs 120 salad dressings to choose from? How do you even pick?* I recognized a bottle from my childhood, Bernstein's Italian, and dove for it. I thought wistfully of the stalls that line the roads in India—everything in walking distance, everything human-scaled. This focus on *things*, on commodity choice, on vast parking lots and super-sized stores would take time to get used to again.

CHICO CALIFORNIA
2015-2016

Adam stir-fried the vegetables and tofu while I set the table. Mo-mos sizzled in a pan.

"I can't believe he is coming here, to dinner!" I said. I wiped the table and tossed a handful of crumbs into the sink, as if they were the discarded illusions of here and there, then and now.

Twenty minutes later the doorbell rang. "Girls!" I yelled upstairs. "Come and welcome Rinpoche!" I opened the door for Chamtrul Rinpoche, our teacher from McLeod Ganj, India. Bella and Sophia popped up behind me, hands pressed together in front of their hearts. Rinpoche swept into the room, graceful in his maroon robes. He smiled, showing his dimples below prominent cheekbones and almond eyes. "Tashi delek, Lama-la," I mumbled, bashful.

I gave a friend at the local Dharma center his contact info. She invited him to Chico, and a year after our return, Rinpoche came while on a United States teaching tour. He gave teachings at the center over the weekend and spent an evening in our home. He wanted to be shown around our house, curious to see how Americans lived. As we took him through our house, his presence left a trail of blessings down the hallway. When I showed him my midwifery office, he stood in front of my bulletin board of pictures for several minutes. He silently studied the photographs of beaming mothers and just-born babies. "This is interesting. In Tibet, we don't take pictures like this at the birth," he finally said.

I tried to see these pictures from his perspective. Where he was from, childbirth was often a matter of survival, not something to relish and celebrate. Pregnant women did not prepare for a powerful, sensual birth experience, they prayed to live through it. These disparities in maternal/child health had inspired me to research global health certificate programs. In a few years, I intended to return to India and Nepal, this time with a job in maternal/child health. A friend who worked for the World Health Organization told me that my master's degree in nursing would qualify me, all I needed was extra coursework in public health.

When we sat down to dinner, Rinpoche blessed the meal. As he chanted in Tibetan, even the walls seemed to lean in, listening. Adam placed a platter of mo-mos before him, Tibetan comfort food. As we ate, we chatted and laughed as though we always had a holy *tulku* at the dinner table.

After dinner, I got called to a birth. Rinpoche seemed excited, almost flustered that I was off to deliver a baby. I dawdled, loading my gear into the car slowly.

"Go to the birth, you better go!" he said, nervous that I would miss it on his behalf, then flashing his dimples one more time.

I arrived at Lisa's house and set up my gear. Her toddler watched Sponge Bob in the den with his aunt while Lisa labored in the bedroom. Pizza was delivered around midnight. Lisa got more uncomfortable lying on the bed, switching from side to side restlessly. I suggested she stand up and lean on the bed. She stood and I put pressure on her low back, squeezing her hips to relieve some of the pain. The full moon lit up the room through the sliding glass doors and she said she felt the need to push. Lisa birthed her baby standing up like Queen Mayadevi giving birth to the Buddha. I squatted to catch the baby, and then unwrapped the umbilical cord which was loosely looped twice around the baby's neck. The baby cried and cleared his lungs, and I helped Lisa to lay down on the bed and receive her son.

The Board of Nursing took it's time to resolve my case. In the spring of 2015, my lawyer brokered a deal with them: an $11,000 fine and three years of my nursing license on probation, after which my license would be fully restored and my record wiped clean. The community held a benefit concert for me. They raised the money to pay both my lawyer and the fine with an afternoon of music, a silent auction, and an organic taco bar. Several hundred people came out and donated, which was a show of how much Chico valued home birth midwifery. Despite the outpouring of support, it was a stressful time. I felt like a poster-girl for failure, the shutdown of my beloved baby-business imminent. After signing the agreement with the board, I didn't hear from them again for another year. I attended births for one more year, relishing each one, sensing it would be my last. In the spring of 2016, my license probation began and my home birth service closed. I would have to work under closer supervision for the three-year probation period.

I wasn't sure who would hire a nurse-midwife on probation but thankfully a non-profit reproductive health center snatched me up to work as a clinician. My former home-birth moms could come see me there for gynecologic exams, IUD insertions, and mammogram referrals. Then, children I had ushered into the world began to trickle in to see me for birth control, their first STI screenings, and counseling about adolescent health. Talk about coming full-circle.

Bella and Sophia were sixteen and thirteen years old now. I adored this new stage except for the times when I felt entirely unqualified to handle teenagers and wished some meta-parent could step in and show me how it's done. But the girls were finally providing the help I had longed for, cleaning the kitchen after I cooked, doing their own laundry, and caring for our pets. Bella got her driver's license and could even run errands and pick up Sophia for me. Those lady housemates I had fantasized about, I had them in my own daughters, at least on good days.

Adam kept his promises. He surprised everyone, even himself, to discover that he *can* cook. He cooked up big batches of *dal fry* and invited our friends over for dinner. He cleaned out and organized his things, limited his internet use and suggested we do house work *together*. He held space for me while I grieved the closing of my midwifery service, staying positive while I flailed through cycles of depression and anxiety. He doubled down to make his business thrive, which included taking on two apprentices who worked under him and teaching meditation classes a couple nights a week. With the closure of my home birth service he stepped into the role of provider for the family, something I had never asked of him before.

While unemployed, I was given the chance to go to the Western Highlands of Guatemala for a month to work with indigenous midwives. Adam sent me off on that solo adventure with blessings.

A friend told me that her husband was recently diagnosed with adult ADD. Curious, I read an article online called *Living with a Partner who has Adult ADD*. As I researched, I learned that human brains can be wired in a variety of ways. *At times I have thought Adam uncaring or irresponsible, when it may be a matter of his brain working differently than mine. He is more wired for creative genius and deep thinking than organizing, planning dinners, or remembering pick-up times.* I talked to his birth mother, a wildly creative artist, who told me she has had traits similar to Adam's her whole life. For me, framing the issue as a "brain-wiring difference" rather than a "fault," released my last doubts about our love.

Bella and Adam grew close again, after taking time to listen to and understand each other. "Dad is really awesome these days," she told me. "I feel like I can talk to him about anything. Although I wish he wouldn't dress like such a hippie."

"Let me remind you, your friends like it here because we are hippies," I replied.

"It's true. My friends do think you guys are cool."

As for Sophia, she would remember hitchhiking to Ladakh with her father as the greatest adventure of her life.

The following summer was our twenty-year wedding anniversary. Adam and I decided to renew our wedding vows, on the very spot where we met at the Rainbow Gathering twenty years before. We planned a camp-out weekend, and forty of our friends joined us. Adam located the creekside glen in a remote corner of Mendocino National forest, and even recognized the tree he was sitting under when I first laid eyes on him. The friend who brought me to that gathering in 1996, whom I hadn't seen in eighteen years, surprised me by showing up with her twin toddler daughters.

On a sun-soaked Saturday afternoon, encircled by our daughters and our closest friends, we chanted our wedding vows together and kissed our promise to stay together for twenty more years. The ceremony healed the last of the damage that had been done. For me, this wedding ceremony was more meaningful than our first one because I actually knew what I was getting into. My husband would never be my personal chef and the house would not be featured in *Sunset* magazine. But we would have intimate dinner table conversations about everything imaginable, summer camping expeditions and future travel dreams, music, and Rinpoches from India dropping in for dinner. We would continue to have moments of laughter and transcendence, and at other times everything would tumble into hassle and mess. I was at peace with all of it. Because although we weren't perfect, we were committed to working on our problems. We loved each other, we were a *family*. I remembered what Rama, the wandering Baba in Lapuna, said:

It is good you take your children to
the sacred pilgrimage sites.
But the holiest pilgrimage site of all is
Home, when you are loving to each other.

Om Mani Padme Hum.

The End

PERMISSIONS AND REFERENCES

ACKNOWLEDGMENTS

A deep bow of gratitude.

To my parents Betty and Marvin Kazmin, whose generous love has been a constant source of support. Thank You does not suffice to express the gratitude I have for you. I love you!

To Amy Kazmin, the best sister in the world. You may live on the other side of the planet, but when we see each other time and space collapse into nothing. You have been an incredible investigative journalist for twenty-five years yet have kept yourself out of the public eye. Thank you for allowing me to share details of your life in these pages.

To Adam, Clarabel, and Sophia, for all the crazy beauty of being my family. The story told here belongs to four separate people, and the three of you have graciously deferred to my telling. Adam's version will be coming soon, in a book he will title "What Really Happened." Consider it a companion volume.

To Brian, Nancy and Mark, Ma Rachel, the Raskoff clan, June Moes, Alisa and Derek, for the support and extended family love.

To Healther Altfeld and Neesa Sonoquie for their careful edits and critique.

To Brooke Warner, the Binders, and the team at She Writes Press, for helping me to Greenlight my publishing dream.

To my tribe of beloved friends: Joc and Kelly, Serra, Karen, Amber, Cynthia, Judy Ann, Sarah Shealy, Samantha, the folk of Happy Corner and Chico who enrich my life and make me whole.

To my writer friends: Melina Watts, Joan Dempsey, Lisa Kusel, Annabel Monaghan, Catherine Newman, Kim Dinan, Ariel Gore, Amy Anton, Susan Woolridge for your patience with my zillion questions and asks.

To Laura Yorke at Carol Mann Agency, the first "book-biz" person to love my book and believe in it.

To my home birth mamas and families, deep reverence.

To the folks at the California Nurse-Midwives Association for their assistance and support while navigating my harrowing BRN problems, especially Kim Dau CNM, Kavita Noble CNM, and Yelena Kolodgi CNM

To my teachers Lama Zangpo, Lama Tsering, Lama Lena, Lobsang Samten, Chokyi Nyima, and Chamtrul Rinpoche. To Amma and H.H. the Dalai Lama and H.H the Karmapa, I pray for your long lives!

To the women at Women's Health Specialists who got me back on my feet.

To the wonderful, kind people we met on our journey,

And to you, readers, who give me the chance to share my heart-offering.

In memoriam to the dear ones who passed on during this book's creation: Howard Moes, Molly Amick, Penny Paulus, Liberty Rain, and Baby Solomon Hawk.

Thank you all and Namaste.

ABOUT THE AUTHOR

Dena Moes is a Hollywood-born, Yale-educated midwife with a BA in literature and an MS in Nursing. Dena and her family live in Chico, California, but leave town each summer to attend Rainbow Gatherings, Burning Man, and tour the West Coast festival circuit as the Moes Family Band. They always come home in time for school to start—except in 2014, when they set off for India and Nepal. Dena grew up Reform Jewish, discovered Tibetan Buddhism in her twenties, and joined the heartfelt tradition of the American Jubu.

Dena is a songwriter, storyteller, and essayist whose work has been published in *Midwifery Today, Shasta Parent, Minerva Rising,* and the *Demeter Press* anthology *Travellin' Mama. The Buddha Sat Right Here* is Dena's first book.

Author photo © Sharon Demeyer

SELECTED TITLES FROM SHE WRITES PRESS

She Writes Press is an independent publishing company founded to serve women writers everywhere. Visit us at www.shewritespress.com.

Peanut Butter and Naan: Stories of an American Mother in The Far East by Jennifer Magnuson. $16.95, 978-1-63152-911-5. The hilarious tale of what happened when Jennifer Magnuson moved her family of seven from Nashville to India in an effort to shake things up—and got more than she bargained for.

Gap Year Girl by Marianne Bohr. $16.95, 978-1-63152-820-0. Thirty-plus years after first backpacking through Europe, Marianne Bohr and her husband leave their lives behind and take off on a yearlong quest for adventure.

This is Mexico: Tales of Culture and Other Complications by Carol M. Merchasin. $16.95, 978-1-63152-962-7. Merchasin chronicles her attempts to understand Mexico, her adopted country, through improbable situations and small moments that keep the reader moving between laughter and tears.

Splitting the Difference: A Heart-Shaped Memoir by Tré Miller-Rodríguez. $19.95, 978-1-938314-20-9. When 34-year-old Tré Miller-Rodríguez's husband dies suddenly from a heart attack, her grief sends her on an unexpected journey that culminates in a reunion with the biological daughter she gave up at 18.

Renewable: One Woman's Search for Simplicity, Faithfulness, and Hope by Eileen Flanagan. $16.95, 978-1-63152-968-9. At age forty-nine, Eileen Flanagan had an aching feeling that she wasn't living up to her youthful ideals or potential, so she started trying to change the world—and in doing so, she found the courage to change her life.

Learning to Eat Along the Way by Margaret Bendet. $16.95, 978-1-63152-997-9. After interviewing an Indian holy man, newspaper reporter Margaret Bendet follows him in pursuit of enlightenment and ends up facing demons that were inside her all along.